NASHVILLE

MARGARET LITTMAN

CONTENTS

Although every effort was made to make sure the information in this book was accurate when going to press, research was impacted by the COVID-19 pandemic and things may have changed since the time of writing. Be sure to confirm specific details, like opening hours, closures, and travel guidelines and restrictions, when making your travel plans. For more detailed information, see p. 272.

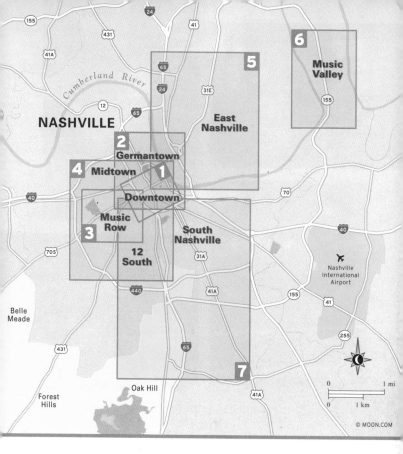

MAPS

DISCOVER
NASHVILLE

When it comes to creative energy, nowhere compares to Music City. People come here with big dreams, big talent, and big ideas. Even before Johnny Cash picked up a guitar or Elvis first stepped foot in RCA Studio B, this was a city that attracted mavericks and iconoclasts. And whether you have a banjo in the overhead bin or you can't tell a harmony from a melody, it doesn't matter. Because Nashville isn't just about the music. People here are willing to try new things and do things differently. You'll get to experience that energy even on a short visit.

6

Creativity of all kinds flows in the veins of folks who call this place home. Nashville is filled with hyphenates like chef-singer-songwriter and artist-fashion-designer-hula-hoop-maker. It fosters an entrepreneurial energy that results in funky music clubs for dancing, quirky boutiques for shopping, and one-of-a-kind roadside eateries for . . . well, eating.

And the "anything can happen" attitude isn't limited just to residents. You don't have to be here more than a day or two to encounter truly talented musicians singing on the sidewalk on Lower Broadway or taste the creative genius emerging from the kitchens of the city's restaurants—both upscale and down home. Whether you're in town for the weekend or for good, take advantage of that optimism, offered with a dash of Southern hospitality. Move to the quirky, and always interesting, Nashville beat.

10 TOP
EXPERIENCES

1 **Listen to Live Music:** Whether it's bluegrass at the **Station Inn** (page 53), country at the **Grand Ole Opry** (page 153), or Western swing at **Robert's Western World** (page 51), you can hear some of the country's best musicians live and in person.

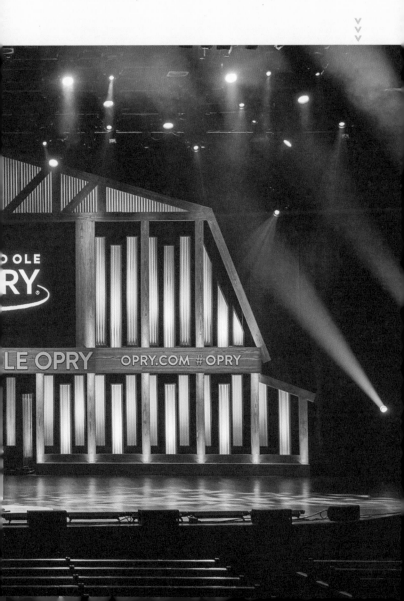

2 **Honor Civil Rights Legacies:** The fight for equality shaped the South physically and psychically. Learn about Nashville's pivotal role with the 1960's sit-ins at the **Civil Rights Room at the Nashville Public Library** (pictured; page 36) then by stop by the **Woolworth Theatre** (page 37).

3 **Shop Local:** From locally themed gifts at Tenn Gallon Hat and Planet Cowboy's colored kicks to signature hats from Daisy May Hat Co, you can leave Nashville with a souvenir that was made by the folks who live here (page 143).

4 **Sip Local Whiskey and Craft Brews:** Nashville likes to toast to good times. Raise a glass at one of the city's distilleries (page 113).

5 **Learn the History of the Enslaved:** Tour the historic **McLemore House** (page 221) in Franklin, hike to the top of **Fort Negley** (pictured; page 161), which was built by Black laborers, and see the cabins of the enslaved people who worked and lived at **The Hermitage** (page 178).

6 **Get Spicy with Hot Chicken:** Nothing says "Nashville" like this daring delicacy. Try it at Hattie B's Hot Chicken, Prince's Hot Chicken Shack, or Bolton's Spicy Chicken & Fish (page 180).

7 Sway to the Roots of African American Music: Gospel, the blues, soul, hip-hop, and more are explained and performed at the **National Museum of African American Music** (pictured; page 41) and at **Fisk University** (page 101), home to the Jubilee Singers since 1981.

∧∧
∧

8 **Get Outside:** The linear **Greenway** (page 189) connects neighborhoods with green space. **Nashville Paddle Co.** (page 195) gets you out on the water, so there's no excuse for not enjoying Nashville's many recreational activities.

9 **Cast a Vote for Women's Suffrage:** Tennessee was the final state needed to ratify the 19th amendment. Learn about the struggle and the victory at **Centennial Park** (page 118), the **Tennessee State Museum** (pictured; page 81), and the **Hermitage Hotel** (page 202).

>>>

10 Make Your Own Print: Letterpress printing is a part of Nashville's aesthetic. Pick up a concert poster or schedule a tour and see behind the scenes at **Hatch Show Print** (page 70).

EXPLORE
NASHVILLE

THE TWO-DAY BEST OF NASHVILLE

Nashville has a 24/7 city-that-never-sleeps vibe, though there are still pockets that are traditionally Southern, with some businesses closed on Sunday. Given how many people work in the music industry, you may find some neighborhoods to be sleepy in the mornings, but raring to go on weekday nights. The following itinerary assumes a Saturday-Sunday stay in Music City, but it can be adjusted for different days of the week (and seasons of the year).

> DAY 1

Arrive in Nashville. Check in early to a swanky hotel, such as the historic **Hermitage Hotel** or the modern, art-filled **Joseph.** Leave your bags so you can make the most of the day unencumbered.

Set out on foot to the **Civil Rights Room at the Nashville Public Library,** where you'll learn about the city's role in the national movement.

From there take in the **Tennessee State Capitol** and then head down the hill for lunch at one of the many restaurants in the

21c Museum Hotel Nashville

MUSIC CITY ON A BUDGET

It's Saturday night. You want to go out and hear some of the sound that makes Nashville groove, but your wallet is empty. Not a problem! They call it Music City for a reason. There's always somewhere to tap your toes without tapping yourself out.

- All the downtown honky-tonks (more than a dozen), including Layla's and Robert's Western World, are cover-charge free, though you are expected to put money in the (actual) hat when the band passes it. The longer you hang out, the more you should contribute.

- Midnite Jamboree is an hour-long, always-free radio show starting at 10pm on Saturday nights at the Ernest Tubb Record Shop. The show doesn't charge for admission, and the caliber of talent that plays is impressive.

- Catch a songwriters' night, an evening where you can hear the people who literally write the music test out their new material and share old favorites. The ones at The Bluebird Cafe are the most famous, but Puckett's Grocery & Restaurant and The Listening Room Café have good options, too. Cover charges and tickets tend to be reasonable. Several hotels, including the Hotel Indigo Nashville and the Aloft West End have listening rooms designed for singer-songwriter nights.

- Record stores in Nashville are more than places to buy a CD (or vinyl). You can do that and also hear free live music played to enthusiastic fans. Grimey's New and Preloved Music and Jack White's Third Man Records are sure bets.

- If making your own music is more your groove, you'll need the right instrument. Gruhn Guitars is considered by some the best vintage guitar shop in the world. You'll likely walk into a jam session when you go to East Nashville's Fanny's House of Music. Like to sing along karaoke-style? Head to Lonnie's Western Room.

Nashville Farmers' Market. Next, take a walk through Bicentennial Capitol Mall State Park, which is between Germantown and downtown. Take the tour of the free Tennessee State Museum. After hearing the carillon bells play "The Tennessee Waltz," check out First Horizon Park, home of baseball's Nashville Sounds, and head back downtown.

Spend the afternoon at the Country Music Hall of Fame and Museum and RCA Studio B. Make a custom Goo Goo Cluster from the interactive Goo Goo Chocolate Co. before heading back to the hotel to clean up for the evening.

Start the night off with drinks and dinner at Pinewood. Walk down the hill to spend the evening strolling, dancing, and drinking at Lower Broadway's honky-tonks. Or check out the show playing at the Ryman Auditorium or the outdoor riverside Ascend Amphitheater. If you're in town between Thanksgiving and New Year's Eve, you'll be able to see the Grand Ole

honky-tonks on Lower Broadway

Opry during its winter run at the Ryman.

>DAY 2

Grab the car and drive through the historic **Fisk University** campus. Stop at both the **Carl Van Vechten Gallery** and the **Aaron Douglas Gallery** on campus.

Make your way to **Arnold's Country Kitchen** for a late breakfast. Standing in line with a crowd of locals and tourists will whet your appetite.

Sated with biscuits, head to bucolic **Centennial Park** and the majestic **Parthenon.** The replica is striking from the outside, but take the time to go inside and see the museum and the shining gold *Athena* sculpture. Grab a snack from one of the many food trucks that gather in Centennial Park.

Fido

Drive through Midtown, looking at the **Vanderbilt University** campus and **Music Row,** where you might see celebs on their way to meetings with their record label executives.

Ryman Auditorium

BACHELORETTE CITY

In recent years Nashville has become the bachelorette party destination, thanks to its easy-to-get-to location and centralized district of restaurants, bars, and live music. Here's how to celebrate the bride-to-be in Music City.

- Get ready: Bach Weekend (www.bachweekend.com) can help you plan the perfect party. East Nashville's Darling Salon and Blowout Bar (1049 W. Eastland Ave., 615/200-7745, www.darlingsalon.com) will do blowouts for your crew to keep you looking sleek in high humidity. Cured Nail Salon (813 Gallatin Ave., 615/953-6284, www.curednails.com) is a chic nail salon. Eastside Nails in the Shoppes on Fatherland is the place for themed nail art.

- Take a tour: See the colorful side of the city with Nashville Mural Tours (11th Ave. S. and Laurel St., 615/285-8429, www.nashvillemuraltours.com). United Street Tours (150 4th Ave. N., 615/447-8107, www.unitedstreettours.com) lets you learn about the history of Nashville. If you want to parake of that famous Tennessee whiskey, let Mint Julep Tours (250 5th Ave. S., 615/436-0187, http://mintjuleptours.com/nashville) do the driving.

- Nab a souvenir: Nashvillian Judith Bright makes customizable rings and bracelets that make for fun bridesmaid gifts. Watch the pieces be made in the small studio in 12 South. Daisy Mat Hat Co is where to find a hat you'll keep for the ages.

- Have a drink: What would a celebration be without a toast? Some local favorite cocktail and wine bars include The Authentique (925 Gallatin Ave.) and By the Bottle, both in East Nashville, and Minerva Avenue in the Buchanan Arts District.

- Stay over: Pick a place that gives you and your friends the ability to hang out together in a communal space. Two lodgings designed for such festivities (with perks like bunk beds and in-room cocktails) are VanDyke Bed and Beverage and BODE Nashville. The Dive Motel & Swim Club has a disco ball in every room. A portion of the rates at the brightly colored Gallatin Hotel (2510 Gallatin Ave., 615/861-1634, http://thegallatinhotel.com) help the city's unhoused community find places to stay and shower.

Shoppers will enjoy the boutiques in **Hillsboro Village.**

Grab an afternoon pick-me-up from **Fido** or **Biscuit Love.**

If the sun is shining, spend the afternoon checking out the museum and gardens at **Cheekwood.** If not, take shelter in a big pink bus and enjoy the rollicking humor of the guides at **Nash Trash Tours.**

Cross the bridge into East Nashville for your evening out. Choose to dine early at **Butcher & Bee,** where you can have both drinks and dinner in an open, high-energy environment.

Then head across the river to Music Valley, to catch the **Grand Ole Opry** in all its grand ole glory.

If you were lucky enough to catch the Opry downtown the night before, then you get a more leisurely night of enjoying East Nashville's cocktails and musical delights at spots like **The 5 Spot** or **The Basement East.**

FOODIE WEEKEND

The city's kitchens are making one "best of" list after another. To that end, the following itinerary is a foodie's fantasy weekend.

SATURDAY
BREAKFAST

Start with the well-edited and well-presented continental breakfast at **Barista Parlor.** The coffee is a work of art. You'll want to keep breakfast light considering all the eating you'll be doing for the rest of the day.

LUNCH

Tour the **Country Music Hall of Fame and Museum,** then take the short walk over to **Assembly Food Hall** for lunch, where you can choose whatever food you might be craving, be it soup dumplings, pizza, or tacos. If you need a snack, grab a signature sweet at **Goo Goo Chocolate Co.** You can choose a pre-made classic or design your own.

A midafternoon snack should involve some of Nashville's signature hot chicken, served on white bread, from **Bolton's Spicy Chicken & Fish.**

Goo Goo Chocolate Co.

DINNER

Do whatever it takes (which means making a reservation online 30 days in advance) to nab one of the coveted 32 seats at acclaimed **The Catbird Seat.** Your three-hour meal is a culinary performance as much as dinner. The evening includes drink pairings and dessert. Enjoy the experience.

SUNDAY
BREAKFAST

Try a traditional Southern brunch, with specialties like chicken and waffles, at **Shugga Hi Bakery & Café.**

LUNCH

Visit the **Parthenon** in Centennial Park. Nearby is your midday meal: The city's movers and shakers dine at **Swett's,** an old-school cafeteria with tasty soul food. The gossip dished up here is as good as the food on the plate.

Afterward, pick out a selection of treats at **Pink Door Cookies.** (The floor has real sprinkles in it!) Stroll among the boutiques and people-watch in the vibrant Wedgewood-Houston neighborhood.

DINNER

Chef Sean Brock's homage to fine hotel dining makes eating at **The Continental** a night to remember. Afterward, walk a few blocks to the home of the best bluegrass in the city: **Station Inn.**

TOP SIGHTS IN NASHVILLE

Nashville's location (within a day's drive for much of the U.S. population), its abundance of live music, and its draw for bachelorette parties mean it has become the "it" city for weekend getaways. Nashville's attractions are spread out among the city's various neighborhoods, and exploring them is part of experiencing Music City's charms.

CIVIL RIGHTS ROOM AT THE NASHVILLE PUBLIC LIBRARY

At the **Civil Rights Room at the Nashville Public Library,** you can see how a few people changed the world and contributed to desegregation efforts in the United States (page 36).

COUNTRY MUSIC HALL OF FAME AND MUSEUM

Head directly to the **Country Music Hall of Fame and Museum** to learn about the genre's complex roots and then be ready to explore the city's live music bounty (page 37).

RYMAN AUDITORIUM

The restored **Ryman Auditorium** is revered by performers and audiences alike (page 42).

BICENTENNIAL CAPITOL MALL STATE PARK

Every hour on the hour you can hear "Rocky Top," "The Tennessee Waltz," and other songs played from 95 carillon bells on the

Country Music Hall of Fame and Museum

CELEBRATE BLACK HERITAGE

Music City is home to four historically Black colleges and universities, a number of African American churches, and historical and cultural sites that hark back to the Civil War, the Civil Rights Movement, and other significant moments.

Among the highlights:

- More than 2,700 men, most of them Black, toiled to build Fort Negley, what was then the largest inland masonry fortification and a crucial fort in the Civil War. As many as 800 people died while building the fort, and many more Black soldiers died during the Battle of Nashville. The Union army did not supply weapons to the Black soldiers or enslaved people; they were forced to protect themselves with whatever tools they had.

- Head to the Civil Rights Room on the second floor of Nashville Public Library to learn about the sit-ins that took place in Nashville and the progress they made to help desegregate public services nationwide.

- First Horizon Park, the home of the Nashville Sounds, was built on the site of Sulphur Dell, which in the 1800s was baseball's home in Nashville. In the 1940s, it was where the Nashville Cubs, a Negro League team, played their games.

- The Fisk Jubilee Singers were the first world-touring musical group and, thanks to Queen Victoria, the inspiration for the Music City moniker for Nashville. Today they continue the tradition of singing spirituals for audiences worldwide.

- Founded in 1912, Tennessee State University has had many achievements; among them it has produced more Olympic gold medalists than any other university in the United States. Graduates include Olympic champion Wilma Rudolph and Oprah Winfrey.

- When the National Museum of African American Music opened in 2021, it became the first museum dedicated to recognizing and celebrating the accomplishments of Black musicians. The space features five galleries covering more than 50 genres of music, including blues, hip-hop, and R&B, plus the context that makes them essential.

north end of **Bicentennial Capitol Mall State Park** (page 78).

PARTHENON

Experience Ancient Greek in the United States at this life-size replica of the **Parthenon.** It's a gathering place, a museum, and one of the reasons Nashville is called "The Athens of the South" (page 98).

GRAND OLE OPRY HOUSE

Two hours at the **Grand Ole Opry House** introduces you to the depth and breadth of country music (page 149).

LANE MOTOR MUSEUM

Find all manner of automobiles, from early hybrids and steam engines to car that's so small it can be "reversed" simply by picking it up and putting it down facing the other direction, at **Lane Motor Museum** (page 162).

CHEEKWOOD

With a winding sculpture garden and acres of botanic gems that wow in every season, **Cheekwood** is Nashville's most colorful outdoor oasis (page 176).

BEST BITES

More than a few high-profile chefs—including *Chopped*'s Maneet Chauhan, Julia Jaksic, and world-famous Jonathan Waxman, just to name three—have opened kitchens here, adding serious street cred to serious eats. You can find anything you want to eat. The Catbird Seat has consistently been named one of the nation's best dining experiences. Farm-to-fork concepts and Vietnamese cuisines shine, too.

Of course, this is the South, and Southern food, in all its interpretations, still reigns supreme. It would be a mistake to dine your way through Nashville without indulging in spicy hot chicken, flaky biscuits, and buttery grits. Don't skip a stop at a **meat-and-three,** a Nashville-style cafeteria where you choose one meat dish (often pot roast or fried chicken) and up to three vegetables (macaroni and cheese counts as a vegetable in this context).

THE CONTINENTAL

A dinner at **The Continental** is an opportunity to feel special. From the care the chef puts into the menu and the beverage pairings to the service, you'll get a night you won't forget (page 48).

ASSEMBLY FOOD HALL

In the heart of downtown, the multilevel **Assembly Food Hall** brings the breadth of Nashville cuisine together in one place. It's a great place to try Kurdish eats, Chinese comfort food, and, yes, several kinds of hot chicken (page 50).

Plaza Mariachi

BUTCHERTOWN HALL

Come for the meat-centric menu that has locals clamoring for a seat at **Butchertown Hall.** The street tacos and meat platters don't disappoint (page 83).

SLIM & HUSKY'S

Slim & Husky's is baking up popular signature pies and design-it-yourself options (page 84).

THE CATBIRD SEAT AND BASTION

Both **The Catbird Seat** and **Bastion** are about world-class dining performances, not just what's on the plate (pages 104 and 164).

ELLISTON PLACE SODA SHOP

Since 1939, the **Elliston Place Soda Shop** has been serving burgers, milkshakes, and pie to Nashvillians. It's a timeless experience (page 105).

MARGOT CAFÉ AND BAR

East Nashville's **Margot Café and Bar** cooks from the freshest ingredients daily. The menu changes based on what's at the market, and it is always simple and elegant (page 131).

GAME POINT CAFÉ

Thanks to a library of more than 300 board games, you can entertain your crew and

Elliston Place Soda Shop

eat and drink well at **Game Point Café** (page 134).

PLAZA MARIACHI

You'll feel like you've gone south of the border with the food, music, dancing, and spirit at **Plaza Mariachi** (page 166).

THE LOVELESS CAFE

Lots of places are known for biscuits chock-full of flaky goodness, but since 1951 **The Loveless Cafe** is the best known (page 179).

PRINCE'S HOT CHICKEN SHACK

Die-hards know it is milk, not water, that cools the mouth after a bite of **Prince's Hot Chicken Shack's** Nashville-style pain (page 179).

Nashville Zoo at Grassmere

Sure, Nashville is filled with beer, bourbon, and late-night carousing: That's the honky-tonk way. But there's no shortage of things for kids to do, see, and eat.

Animal lovers will adore the meerkat exhibit at the Nashville Zoo at Grassmere, as well as the zoo's Wild Animal Carousel. There's something new going on at the zoo almost every week.

The Adventure Science Center and its Sudekum Planetarium offer hands-on exhibits, education disguised as entertainment, and a great option for being indoor on rainy days. Clear nights call for a drive to the Dyer Observatory.

Nashville's many parks and open green spaces are perfect for getting kids moving. The Centennial Sportsplex (222 25th Ave. N., 615/862-8490 or 615/862-8480, aquatics center hours 6am-7pm Mon.-Thurs., 6am-6pm Fri., noon-4pm Sat.) offers ice-skating, tennis, and more. Hillsboro Village's Fannie Mae Dees Park (2400 Blakemore Ave., 615/862-8400, 6am-11pm daily) is known as "the dragon park" because of a giant dragon sculpture that kids love to climb. Cumberland Park adds epic rivers and a little ecology education to the play experience. In warm-weather months, Nashville Shores and Wave Country are great cool-off spots. If you book a room at Gaylord Opryland Resort, you can add a package for the mammoth SoundWaves water park, which is a kid's dream, with indoor and outdoor slides, waves, and floats. Depending on the time of year, the hotel also has scavenger hunts and other kid-friendly activities.

Nashville Children's Theatre has been offering stage productions for little ones since 1931.

Hungry after all that play? Berry Hill's The Pfunky Griddle lets kids (and their parents) cook their own pancakes on a table-side grill, filling them with M&Ms, blueberries, or other toppings.

LISTEN, SIP, AND SWAY IN MUSIC CITY

From concerts to theater, Music City earns its nickname with plenty of entertaining diversions. No trip to Nashville is complete without hearing live music.

Music City overflows with musicians and songwriters and opportunities to hear them. So whether you love to two-step or you prefer something with a different kind of beat, be sure to make time for music during your visit. (Honestly, it will be hard to ignore the sounds of music, no matter where you are in Nashville or why you came here.)

ROBERT'S WESTERN WORLD

Much in Nashville has changed, but boot-scooting and toe-tapping are an essential part of the Music City experience. Get your honky-tonk in at **Robert's Western World** (page 51).

STATION INN

For more than four decades good bluegrass has been played at the **Station Inn.** Don't miss it (page 53).

NASHVILLE JAZZ WORKSHOP

Come join the locals for classes, lessons, and lectures at the **Nashville Jazz Workshop**—the musical heartbeat of the city's jazz scene (page 85).

Fisk Jubilee Singers

country artist Brad Paisley performing at The Grand Ole Opry

FISK UNIVERSITY
Since the late 1800s, the **Fisk Jubilee Singers** have been sharing the gospel of Music City with audiences around the globe (page 101).

CORSAIR ARTISAN DISTILLERY
There are lots of places that make Tennessee whiskey in Music City, but **Corsair Artisan Distillery** is one that is lauded by hipsters, bartenders, and other cocktail connoisseurs (page 111).

GRAND OLE OPRY HOUSE
The **Grand Ole Opry House** is still the place both up-and-coming and veteran musicians want to play, and it still sells out many nights (page 149).

THE BLUEBIRD CAFE
Go to **The Bluebird Cafe** if you want to hear the people who write the songs, not just those who sing them (page 183).

PLANNING YOUR TRIP

WHEN TO GO

There's no wrong time to head to Music City; it just depends on your personal preference. **Spring** and **fall** are generally mild, filled with pleasant days and crisp nights. Wildflowers bloom in the greenways, and streets are lined with flowering dogwoods and cherry trees. Weekends are filled with fun events. Nashville has become one of the country's biggest **bachelorette party** destinations; the windups to June and October wedding seasons are particularly popular.

Summer is **high tourist season.** Free and ticketed concerts alike are booked on indoor and outdoor stages most weekends, and Lower Broadway is filled with folks enjoying the honky-tonks, long summer days, and high-energy atmosphere. The downside of summer is that it will be **hot and humid**—even at night. If you are a high-energy, festival-going kind of traveler, come in the summer and pack accordingly. Remember to bring a sweater for overly air-conditioned hotels and restaurants.

Winter in Nashville is mild compared to cities farther north where snow and slush clog the streets. While Music City will get a light dusting of snow, generally winter

Flowers bloom near the Nashville Farmers' Market.

horse-drawn tour of The Hermitage

means grabbing a coat and hat, not a shovel and gloves. Winter days may seem particularly short due to Nashville's proximity to the eastern edge of the time zone. **Christmastime** at **Gaylord Opryland Resort** is magical for travelers with families, featuring thousands of lights, holiday displays, and annual stage performances.

ENTRY REQUIREMENTS

All citizens of a foreign country need a valid passport to enter the United States. Some also require visas. Nationals of 38 countries may be able to use the **Visa Waiver Program,** operated by Customs and Border Protection. For more information about the Visa Waiver Program, contact the **Customs and Border Protection Agency** (www.travel.state.gov). As of May 2023, U.S. citizens will need a REAL ID or passport to travel by plane anywhere in the nation.

TRANSPORTATION

Nashville has an **international airport.** Visitors making a getaway to Music City may be able to get around without a car by walking or using bicycles, scooters, ride-hailing companies, or taxis. To explore beyond the city, **a car is essential.** If it's practical, bring your own. If you're flying in, arrange a **rental car** ahead of time. A good road map or GPS is helpful to have before you set out.

WHAT TO PACK

A cell phone with GPS, Wi-Fi, and a good roaming plan (if you're based outside the United States) should cover your basic needs. Prepare by downloading maps and apps ahead of time, particularly if you are likely to get off the interstate and out of the range of cell phone signals on excursions away from the city. Download a playlist's worth of Nashville-appropriate

27

BIKING MUSIC CITY

Nashville is no Portland; you won't see a bicycle rack at every storefront. But the city has a growing bike culture, and it is easy to pedal your way across the city to see its highlights.

Music City Bikeway

The first step is to bring your own bike, rent one, or borrow one. City residents (with a local ID) can check out a bike from Nashville GreenBikes (www.greenfleetbikes.com). Once you have your two wheels, it is easy to connect to more than 90 miles (145 km) of greenways and 133 miles (214 km) of on-road bike lanes and shared-use bike routes. B-Cycle (http://nashville.bcycle.com) offers 24-hour usage for just $5 plus hourly rental (or membership for more frequent pedalers), with more than 36 stations across town.

The Music City Bikeway (www.nashville.gov/bikeways) offers a 26-mile (42-km) route that covers the city from east to west and includes city streets, greenway paths, and more. It goes by the Nashville Farmers' Market, which has the most creative bike racks in the city, in the shape of bright vegetables. Eight miles (13 km) of the bikeway include streets with designated bike lanes. The bikeway website offers a downloadable route map. Another good set of downloadable maps is available from Walk/Bike Nashville (www.walkbikenashville.org).

tunes: classic country, bluegrass, blues, and Western swing albums to get you in the mood. **Cowboy boots** and an embroidered jacket aren't required, but they're certainly always appropriate. Grab some stylin' sunglasses for all the photos you'll take.

RESERVATIONS

Even before you arrive in the city, you can plan out your nights thanks to the **Nashville Convention & Visitors Corp** (www.visitmusiccity.com). Through a handy feature on their website, you can check out upcoming concerts a month or more in advance. **Now Playing Nashville** (www.nowplayingnashville.com) is a great resource for entertainment listings and discounted tickets.

But don't panic if you can't plan ahead. One of the attractions of Music City is that there is always a show worth seeing somewhere. And because there are so many, there's always something that hasn't sold out.

If you're coming during peak summer season or for an event and want to stay in the heart of downtown, make **hotel reservations 1-2 months** in advance. Some restaurants, including **Bastion** and **The Catbird Seat,** release tables for reservations about **one month** in advance.

GUIDED TOURS

Jason Buchanan refers to himself as the "$2 Elvis." On the **King of the Road Tour** (http://twodollarelvis.com; tour times vary; $125-150 pp), he'll drive you around town in his light blue 1957 Cadillac DeVille, while dressed like Elvis, showing you the city's highlights. The three-hour tour is part comedy routine, part Elvis impersonation, and part informational outing. Buchanan will pick you up and drop you off at your hotel.

Choose between several different canoe or kayak tours down the Cumberland River with **River Queen Voyages** (615/933-9778, http://rqvoyages.com; May-Oct.; $32-80 for 1.5-hour tours, $42-100 for 2-hour tours, $62-140 for 4-hour tours). The 1.5-hour, 3-mile (5-km) tour starts in Shelby Bottoms Greenway, winding under railway bridges and ending downtown with the skyline in sight. The two-hour, 5-mile (8-km) tour is self-guided and starts near Opryland, ending near Shelby Park with a view of the downtown skyline in the distance. A combined four-hour tour includes some of both. All are self-guided. When booking, you'll be provided with a meeting location to board a shuttle upstream to the tour start.

Shannon Largen and a team of journalist guides will show you their favorite places to eat with **Walk Eat Nashville** (615/587-6138, www.walkeatnashville.com; tour times vary; $85). The tours in downtown, Midtown, and East Nashville include the stories behind the dishes while you walk about 1.5 miles (2.4 km) and enjoy tastings at

cowboy boots for sale

local chef talking to guests on a Walk Eat Nashville tour

5-6 restaurants and artisan food shops. The expert guides narrate as you walk and taste, and you get the benefit of their considerable knowledge of the city. You'll leave satisfied but not overly full. Private tours are available.

Learn about Tennessee whiskey from the comfort of a chauffeured, air-conditioned van with **Mint Julep Tours** (615/436-0187, http://mintjuleptours.com/nashville; tour times vary;

$119-159). Most tours start at the Omni Nashville Hotel, taking you to distilleries around and beyond the city.

Check out the city's vibrant side by seeing its outdoor works of art guided by **Nashville Mural Tours** (www.nashvillemuraltours.com). **United Street Tours** (https://unitedstreettours.com) offers walking tours that do a deep dive into the city's history, particularly its oft-overlooked Black history.

St. Jude Rock 'n' Roll Half Marathon in Nashville

Every marathon is part spectacle. But the St. Jude Rock 'n' Roll Marathon Series (www.runrocknroll.com) is as known for the performances as it is for the racing. Spectators and runners alike cite the event's music vibe for keeping them motivated. Some 30 stages are set up along the route to keep arms pumping and legs moving. After the 26.2 miles, all the runners and their families are invited to post-race concerts.

While some folks enter this event to win, it's not unusual to see runners hula-hooping or dancing to the music as they go by. It's all part of the Nashville beat. The marathon is the main event, but there are plenty of runs for participants to choose from, including the Doggie Dash, a half-mile run/walk with your pup; the Kids Rock, which is open to kids grades K-7; the 5K and Half Marathon Races; and the 1 Mile, which goes through Cumberland Park.

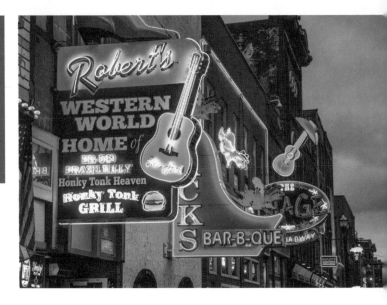

Downtown

Map 1

This is the heart of Music City's beat. It's also Nashville's economic and tourist hub, not to mention the geographic center of the city. **Lower Broad** is lined with **honky-tonks** with Western swing music playing almost every hour of the day. In addition to some of the city's biggest attractions, downtown is home to hotels, restaurants, and great views of the **Cumberland River.** Nearby, **The Gulch** is populated by high-rises filled with **restaurants, bars,** and **shops.**

TOP SIGHTS

- Most Inspiring Place: **Civil Rights Room at the Nashville Public Library** (page 36)
- Learn about the Nashville Sound: **Country Music Hall of Fame and Museum** (page 37)
- Best Place to Experience Black Music History: **National Museum of African American Music** (page 41)
- Most Iconic Music Venue: **Ryman Auditorium** (page 42)

TOP RESTAURANTS

- Most Refined Experience: **The Continental** (page 48)
- Widest Variety of Options: **Assembly Food Hall** (page 50)

TOP NIGHTLIFE

- Best Honky-Tonk: **Robert's Western World** (page 51)
- Best Bluegrass: **Station Inn** (page 53)

TOP ARTS AND CULTURE

- Quintessential Music City Visuals: **Haley Gallery** (page 62)
- Unexpected Place for Art: **21c Museum Hotel Nashville** (page 62)

TOP SHOPS

- Most Iconic Images: **Hatch Show Print** (page 70)
- Best Alternative Record Store: **Third Man Records** (page 72)

GETTING THERE AND AROUND

- Major bus routes: 4, 8, 34, 64, Green Circuit, Blue Circuit, Purple Circuit

SIGHTS

9	The Arcade	48	Ryman Auditorium
28	Civil Rights Room at the Nashville Public Library	59	The Johnny Cash Museum
30	Downtown Presbyterian Church	60	Patsy Cline Museum
38	Frist Art Museum	68	John Seigenthaler Pedestrian Bridge
39	Hume-Fogg	73	Country Music Hall of Fame and Museum
40	Customs House		
46	National Museum of African American Music	96	NashVox

RESTAURANTS

1	Drusie & Darr	62	Johnny Cash's Bar & BBQ
8	Puckett's Grocery & Restaurant	65	The Southern Steak & Oyster
12	Manny's House of Pizza	69	Adele's
21	Gray & Dudley	70	Whiskey Kitchen
24	Chauhan Ale & Masala House	80	Yolan
25	The Mockingbird	86	Biscuit Love
26	Tansuo	89	Arnold's Country Kitchen
27	The Standard	91	Party Fowl
36	The Continental	98	Husk Nashville
44	Assembly Food Hall	100	Pinewood
59	Merchants		

NIGHTLIFE

14	Bobby's Garage	67	Acme Feed & Seed
15	Skull's Rainbow Room	71	Whiskey Kitchen
16	Bourbon Street Blues and Boogie Bar	74	Country Music Hall of Fame and Museum
19	Jane's Hideaway	82	Ascend Amphitheater
20	Lonnie's Western Room	84	Station Inn
34	B.B. King's Blues Club	87	Cannery Ballroom
49	Ryman Auditorium	88	Rudy's Jazz Room
50	Layla's	90	Jackalope Brewing Company
51	Robert's Western World		
52	The Stage on Broadway	93	Tennessee Brew Works
53	AJ's Good Time Bar	94	City Winery
56	Nudie's Honky Tonk	95	The Listening Room Café
63	House of Cards	97	3rd and Lindsley
66	Wildhorse Saloon		

ARTS AND CULTURE

5	Tinney Contemporary	29	Wishing Chair Productions
6	The Rymer Gallery	61	Nashville Symphony
7	Chauvet Arts	75	Haley Gallery
10	The Arcade	99	Nashville Children's Theatre
22	21c Museum Hotel Nashville		

RECREATION

3	iRide Nashville	47	Nashville Predators
4	Nashville Ghost Tours	55	Experience Nashville
31	United Street Tours	72	Nashville Mural Tours
32	Music City Rollin' Jamboree	77	Mint Julep Tours

SHOPS

11	Peanut Shop	58	Boot Country
33	Fire Finch Boutique	64	Goo Goo Chocolate Co.
43	Ariat Nashville	76	Hatch Show Print
45	Tecovas	83	Lucchese Bootmaker
54	Ernest Tubb Record Shop	92	Third Man Records

HOTELS

2	Hermitage Hotel	41	Holston House
13	The Fairlane	42	Renaissance Nashville Hotel
17	Noelle	78	Omni Nashville Hotel
18	Hotel Indigo Nashville	79	The Joseph
23	21c Museum Hotel Nashville	81	BODE Nashville
35	Union Station Hotel	85	Thompson Nashville
37	Holiday Inn Express Nashville-Downtown		

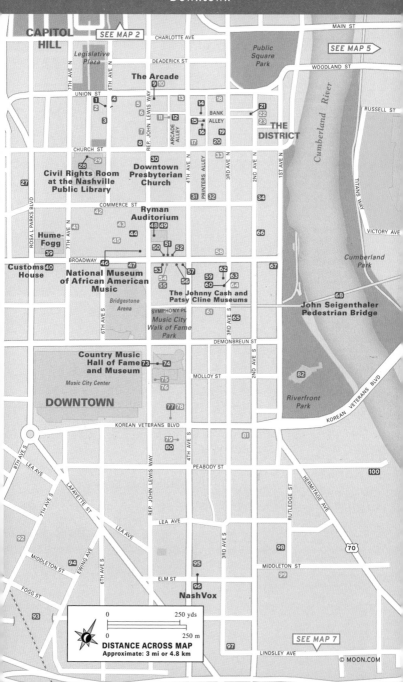

CAPITOL HILL

SEE MAP 2

CHARLOTTE AVE

MAIN ST

SEE MAP 5

Legislative Plaza

DEADERICK ST

Public Square Park

WOODLAND ST

The Arcade

9 10

UNION ST

1

2

4

5

6

3

13

14 18

BANK ALLEY

11 12

15

19

7

16

17

20

21 22 23

RUSSELL ST

THE DISTRICT

CHURCH ST

29

Civil Rights Room at the Nashville Public Library

28

30

Downtown Presbyterian Church

33

27

PRINTERS ALLEY

31 32

34

COMMERCE ST

42

Ryman Auditorium

Hume-Fogg

41

43

44

48 49

45

39

50 51 52

58

BROADWAY

46

47

66

Customs House 40

National Museum of African American Music

53

57

54

56

55

59 62

60 63 64

67

Bridgestone Arena

The Johnny Cash and Patsy Cline Museums

Cumberland Park

68

John Seigenthaler Pedestrian Bridge

SYMPHONY PL

61

65

Music City Walk of Fame Park

DEMONBREUN ST

Country Music Hall of Fame and Museum 73 74

Music City Center

75

76

MOLLOY ST

82

Riverfront Park

DOWNTOWN

77 78

KOREAN VETERANS BLVD

KOREAN VETERANS BLVD

79 80

81

8TH AVE S

LEA AVE

PEABODY ST

100

7TH AVE S

LAFAYETTE ST

6TH AVE S

EWING AVE

LEA AVE

REP. JOHN LEWIS WAY

4TH AVE S

3RD AVE S

LEA AVE

RUTLEDGE ST

HERMITAGE AVE

70

92

MIDDLETON ST

94

95

ELM ST

98

MIDDLETON ST

FOGG ST

96

NashVox

99

93

0   250 yds

0   250 m

DISTANCE ACROSS MAP
Approximate: 3 mi or 4.8 km

97

SEE MAP 7

LINDSLEY AVE

© MOON.COM

Sights

The Arcade

One of Nashville's distinctive downtown structures is the covered arcade that runs parallel to Union Street between 4th Avenue and Rep. John Lewis Way. The two-story arcade with a gabled glass roof was built in 1903 by developer Daniel Buntin, who was inspired by similar arcades he saw in Europe. It has identical Palladian facades at both entrances, on both 4th Avenue and Rep. John Lewis Way.

From the moment it opened, the Arcade was a bustling center for commerce. Famous for its **Peanut Shop** (19 Arcade Alley, 615/256-3394, www.nashvillenut.com), the Arcade has also been the location of photo studios, jewelers, and a post office for many years. Today, restaurants—including **Manny's House of Pizza** (15 Arcade Alley, 615/242-7144)—crowd the lower level, while art galleries, artists' studios, and professional offices line the second floor. Don't miss the bustling activities here during the **First Saturday Art Crawl** (www.nashvilledowntown.com), held on the first Saturday of the month.

MAP 1: 244 Rep. John Lewis Way N.; http://thenashvillearcade.com; hours vary by merchant; free

The Arcade

TOP EXPERIENCE

✪ Civil Rights Room at the Nashville Public Library

The second floor of the main Nashville Public Library houses a powerful freestanding exhibit on the Civil Rights Movement that took place in Nashville in the 1950s and 1960s. Nashville was the first Southern city to desegregate public services, and it did so relatively peacefully, inspiring activists throughout the South. This history is an important part of Nashville's legacy. The library is a fitting location for the exhibit, which includes photographs, videos, and displays, because the block below on Church Street was the epicenter of the Nashville sit-ins during the 1960s.

Nashville Public Library

Inside the Civil Rights Room, large-format photographs show school desegregations, sit-ins, and a march to the courthouse. A circular table at the center of the room is symbolic of the lunch counters where young students from Fisk, Meharry, American Baptist, and Tennessee A&I sat silently and peacefully (even when verbally and physically accosted by segregationists) at sit-ins. The table is engraved with the 10 rules of conduct set out for sit-in participants, including to be polite and courteous at all times, regardless of how you are treated. A timeline of the Civil Rights Movement is presented above the table. Inside a glass-enclosed viewing room you can choose from six different documentary videos, including an hour-long 1960 NBC news documentary about the Nashville sit-ins. Many of the videos are 30 minutes or longer, so plan on spending several hours here if you want to explore the topics in depth.

The centerpiece of the room is a piece of glass inscribed with a quote by Dr. Martin Luther King Jr., who visited the city in 1960 and said, during a speech at Fisk University: "I came to Nashville not to bring inspiration, but to gain inspiration from the great movement that has taken place in this community."

Afterward, walk to **Woolworth Theatre** (221 Rep. John Lewis Way N.) to see the site of one of the lunch counters where the sit-ins took place. The building has been restored to look as it did in the 1960s. (The recreated lunch counter briefly operated as a restaurant, then was reimagined as a theater.) Even if you don't catch a show here, it's worth walking by to look in the windows and read the historical signage. The Walgreens drug store across the street (near the entrance to the Arcade) was also a site of sit-ins, but it does not have any remaining signs of its origins.

MAP 1: 615 Church St., 615/862-5782, http://library.nashville.org; 9am-6pm Mon.-Fri., 9am-5pm Sat., 2pm-5pm Sun.; free

⊙ Country Music Hall of Fame and Museum

The distinctive design of the Country Music Hall of Fame and Museum is the first thing you will notice about this monument to country music. Vertical windows at the front and back of the building resemble piano keys; the sweeping arch on the right side of the building portrays a 1950s Cadillac fin; and from above, the building resembles a bass clef. The hall of fame was established in 1967, and its first inductees were Jimmie Rodgers, Hank Williams, and Fred Rose. Its slogan is "Honor Thy Music."

Country music fans can pay homage to country's greatest stars as well as the lesser-known men and women who influenced the music. Those who aren't fans when they walk in generally leave with an appreciation of the genre's varied roots. Even if you think you aren't interested, rethink your reasons before you skip this museum.

The museum is arranged chronologically, beginning with country's roots and ending with displays on some of the genre's hottest stars of today. In between, exhibits detail themes including the rise of bluegrass, honky-tonk, and the

Country Music Hall of Fame and Museum

world-famous Nashville Sound, which introduced country music to the world. There are half a dozen private listening booths where you can hear studio-quality recordings of seminal performances, as well as a special display of a few of the genre's most famous instruments. Here you can see Bill Monroe's mandolin, Maybelle Carter's Gibson, and Johnny Cash's Martin D-355. The hall of fame itself is set in a rotunda in the museum. Brass plaques honor the inductees, and around the room are the words Will the Circle Be Unbroken, from the hymn made famous by the Carter Family musical group.

The Taylor Swift Education Center is an interactive space upstairs at the museum where kids and parents can think creatively about songwriting and music making and, during scheduled programs, learn to play instruments (check schedules for dates and times for this programming). The museum has several gift shops. The complex also holds the iconic Hatch Show Print poster designers and the Haley Gallery.

The only way to visit Music Row's famous RCA Studio B (1611 Roy Acuff Pl., http://studiob.org), where Elvis once recorded, is to buy your ticket at the museum box office and hop on the hall of fame's guided tour bus. The tour takes about an hour, including the 10-minute drive to Music Row and back. Tours depart every hour between 10:30am and 2:30pm daily. The Studio B tour is an additional fee to your admission but comes as part of a package ($48 adults, $38 children) with admission to the Country Music Hall of Fame. It is worth the time and cost to get this add-on.

In addition to the inspiring Civil Rights Room, the main branch of the Nashville Public Library is also home to the Votes for Women Room (http://library.nashville.org/research/votes-for-women). On the second floor of the library, the room, which opened in 2020, features exhibits that celebrate the centennial anniversary of the ratification of the 19th Amendment to the U.S. Constitution, which gave women the right to vote in 1920. Tennessee was the state that cast the final vote for ratification, and Nashville claims this piece of history with pride.

The room includes a timeline of events leading to the change and an in-depth examination of race and racism in the women's suffrage movement—underscoring the fact that the legislation gave white women the right to vote, but left women of color continuing to fight for the same rights for decades longer. Materials in the room include photos, videos, and reproductions of historic posters and propaganda, as well as books.

MAP 1: 222 Rep. John Lewis Way S., 615/416-2001, http://countrymusichalloffame.org; 9am-5pm Mon.-Thurs., 9am-7pm Fri.-Sat., 9am-6pm Sun.; regular admission $28 adults, $18 children 6-12, children under 6 free

Customs House

The old Nashville Customs House is a historical landmark and architectural beauty. Construction on the Customs House began in 1875, and President Rutherford B. Hayes visited Nashville to lay the cornerstone in 1877. The building is an impressive example of the Victorian Gothic style. Designed by Treasury architect William Appleton Potter, it was completed in 1916. Although it is called a customs house, in truth the building served as the center of federal government operations in the city, with government offices, courts, and treasury offices. The building still houses government offices, so it is open to the public during business hours. But only those who really care about the details of ironwork and woodwork will want to peruse the interior. Otherwise this landmark's ornate design, including its lovely clock tower and Victorian windows, is easily admired from the outside.

MAP 1: 701 Broadway; 9am-5pm Mon.-Fri.; free

Downtown Presbyterian Church

William Strickland, the architect for the Tennessee State Capitol, also designed the Downtown Presbyterian Church, now both a place of worship and the holder of a coveted spot on the National Register of Historic Places. Built in 1848 to replace an earlier church destroyed by fire, the church is in the Egyptian revival style that was popular at the time. It is one of only three surviving churches in the country built in this style. Downtown Presbyterian was used as a Union hospital during the Civil War, and it is where James K. Polk was inaugurated as Tennessee governor in 1839. Book a guided tour in advance by email (info@dpchurch.com). The church's Waffle Shop brunch, held in early December, is a popular local holiday tradition.

MAP 1: 154 Rep. John Lewis Way N., 615/254-7584, http://dpchurch.com; services 11am Sun.; tours weekly

Frist Art Museum

Nashville's foremost visual art space is the Frist Art Museum. The Frist is located in a stately building that once housed the 1930s downtown post office (and there's still a working post office in the basement). High ceilings, art deco finishes, and unique hardwood tiles distinguish the museum. Look carefully in the hallways and you can see the indentations in the walls from folks who leaned here waiting for their turn in line at the post office. The Frist puts on about 12 different major visiting exhibitions annually, many of which have garnered national attention. At any given time, you can see 3-4 different exhibits, many being regional or national premieres. There are typically plenty of ongoing educational activities paired with the exhibitions. The Martin ArtQuest Gallery, a permanent part of the Frist, is an excellent hands-on arts activity room for children and their parents. The **Frist Café** serves better-than-expected salads and sandwiches and has a nice outdoor patio for alfresco dining. There are many free-admission days throughout the year.

MAP 1: 919 Broadway, 615/244-3340, http://fristartmuseum.org; 10am-5:30pm Mon.-Wed. and Sat., 10am-9pm Thurs.-Fri., 1pm-5:30pm Sun.; $15 adults, $10 seniors and students, under 19 free

Hume-Fogg

Located across Broadway from the Customs House is Hume-Fogg Magnet School. It sits on land formerly occupied by Hume School, which was Nashville's first public school. The four-story, stone-clad

Frist Art Museum

1912 building was designed by William Ittner of St. Louis in the Norman Gothic style with Tudor Gothic details. Today, it is a public magnet school with a reputation for high academic standards. Hume-Fogg is not open to the public and can only be viewed from the outside.

MAP 1: 700 Broadway, 615/291-6300, http://schools.mnps.org

The Johnny Cash Museum

Opened in April 2013, this museum has transformed from small storefront with a tiny gift shop to the cornerstone of country music history in downtown Nashville. This private museum holds a wealth of information on all things Johnny Cash. The collection was amassed by one fan-turned-collector and features interactive listening booths, the jumpsuit the Man in Black wore when he flipped the bird in public, and other memorabilia from a varied and lauded career. Locals are crazy for the rebuilt stone wall that was taken from Cash's fire-destroyed suburban home. In just a few years this has become one of the city's most visited attractions. There's an in-house coffee shop, and the Johnny Cash's Bar & BBQ is just next door. The Patsy Cline Museum is upstairs, and the

John Seigenthaler Pedestrian Bridge

Nashville's popularity has caused some prices to skyrocket. But there are many free and low-budget options to explore. If you don't have a lot of jangle in your pockets, check out these sights.

- The Total Access Pass ($99) sold by Visit Music City (800/657-4910, http://visitmusiccity.com/totalaccess) admits you to four out of a list of more than 30 attractions, along with special discounts. The pass is good for 90 days.
- Want to experience Nashville's amazing downtown? Parking is often free in Nissan Stadium's Lot R, which is close to Cumberland Park, a great place to play. Then you can walk across the scenic John Seigenthaler Pedestrian Bridge and explore downtown on foot.
- Many of the city's major attractions, including the Frist Art Museum and Cheekwood, offer free days throughout the year, while the Tennessee State Museum is always free.
- The high-energy Plaza Mariachi complex is home to free salsa dancing classes, mariachi band performances, and other entertainment most nights of the week.
- Fort Negley offers great city views and Civil War history.
- The Civil Rights Room at the Nashville Public Library showcases the city's essential role in the Civil Rights Movement with the 1960s Nashville sit-ins.
- The city is also home to free mega events, including the East Nashville Tomato Art Festival and Independence Day and New Year's Eve celebrations. Some events at the CMA Fest each June are admission-free.

evening magic destination House of Cards is downstairs.

MAP 1: 119 3rd Ave. S., 615/256-1777, www.johnnycashmuseum.com; 9am-7pm daily; $23 adults, $22 seniors and students, $19 youth ages 6-15, children under 6 free

TOP EXPERIENCE

✪ National Museum of African American Music

This museum, honoring the groundbreaking work of musical artists in genres from hip-hop to gospel to jazz, opened in 2021 with a front-and-center location on Broadway and an impressive collection. In the Fifth + Broadway complex, NMAAM features interactive displays, listening rooms, and more. Exhibits cover religious music, the blues, the Civil Rights Movement, and the Harlem Renaissance, putting the music in context of bigger issues of the times. Visitors stop in their tracks when Prince's 2007 Super Bowl performance—singing "Purple Rain" in the rain—comes on the big screen in the hallway.

MAP 1: 510 Broadway, 615/301-8724, http://nmaam.org; 9am-5pm Wed.-Mon.; $25 adults, $19 seniors and students, $13.50 youth ages 7-17, children under 7 free

Patsy Cline Museum

Housed above The Johnny Cash Museum, this small museum chronicling the life of legendary country artist Patsy Cline might seem like an afterthought from the outside. But once you get inside, you'll see it is anything but. Visitors can view Cline's personal belongings and relevant artifacts, many of which were donated by her family, who are delighted to have so many people learn about the vocalist's short but important life. Exhibits include a replica of the soda shop where she worked, her home, and videos about her career. Admission is separate from The Johnny Cash Museum.

MAP 1: 119 3rd Ave. S., 2nd floor, 615/454-4722, www.patsymuseum.com; 9am-7pm daily; $20 adults, $19 seniors and students, $16 youth ages 6-15, children under 6 free

NashVox

When in Nashville . . . you should record a song. You can do it at the Nashville Studio Experience at NashVox. Pick from more than 16,000 options or record your own original tune. A certified sound engineer will work with you and you'll get your track back for same-day delivery. Go solo or book a private session with a group of friends or family. You don't need singing experience or raw talent, but if you have friends who really don't want to participate, you can enlist them to be part of the audience.

MAP 1: 636 4th Ave. S., 615/906-3136, www.nashvox.com; 11am-10:30pm Mon.-Sat., 11am-7:30pm Sun.; $75-425

✪ Ryman Auditorium

The legendary Ryman Auditorium remains one of the best places in the United States to hear live music. Built in 1892 by Thomas Ryman, the Union Gospel Tabernacle (as the Ryman was then called) was designed as a venue for the charismatic preaching of Reverend Samuel P. Jones. During the first half of the 20th century, the Ryman began to showcase music and performances. In 1943, the Ryman began hosting a popular barn dance called the Grand Ole Opry. The legacy of this partnership gave the Ryman its place in history as the Mother Church of Country Music. After the Opry left in 1974, the Ryman fell into disrepair and was virtually condemned until Gaylord Entertainment, the same company that owns the Opry, decided to invest in the grand old tabernacle. Today it is a popular concert venue,

Ryman Auditorium

booking rock, country, and classical acts, plus comedy and more. Performers like to show the building's acoustics off, playing a number or two without a mic. The Opry returns here during the Christmas season, and in the summer there's a weekly bluegrass series.

Seeing a show at the Ryman is by far the best way to experience this venue, but if you can't do that, pay the admission fee to see a short video and explore the auditorium, including museum-style exhibits about the musicians who have performed here through the ages. You can sit for a few minutes on the old wooden pews and even climb on stage to be photographed in front of the classic Opry backdrop. A backstage **guided tour** ($35 adults, $30 children) is available, and isn't just for die-hard fans. It gives lots of insight into how stars behaved when they were behind these famous walls. Plus, you get to walk on the storied stage yourself.

If you need a snack, visit the on-site **Cafe Lula** (www.cafelula.net). MAP 1: 116 Rep. John Lewis Way N., 615/889-3060, www.ryman.com; 9am-4pm daily; self-guided tours $26 adults, $17 children ages 4-11, children under 4 free

John Seigenthaler Pedestrian Bridge

Built in 1909, what was once called the Sparkman Street Bridge (and is still sometimes called the Shelby Street Bridge) was slated for demolition in 1998 after inspectors noted its poor condition. But citing the success of the Walnut Street Bridge in revitalizing downtown Chattanooga, advocates succeeded in saving the bridge. It reopened in 2003 as a pedestrian and bike bridge.

Named after the Civil Rights crusader and journalist, the John Seigenthaler Pedestrian Bridge connects East Nashville neighborhoods with downtown. It was frequently featured on the TV show *Nashville* because of its great views of the city, and many folks have their iconic Music City photos taken here. At the base of the east side of the bridge is **Cumberland Park,** along with the East Bank Landing's kayak, canoe, and paddleboard launches.

MAP 1: Spanning the Cumberland River, one block south of Broadway

Restaurants

PRICE KEY

$	Entrées less than $15
$ $	Entrées $15-25
$ $ $	Entrées more than $25

BARBECUE AND SOUTHERN

Husk Nashville $$$

Nestled in Rutledge Hill, in a former mayoral home, Husk Nashville opened in 2013, and all these years later, it is still one of the city's most coveted tables. Husk relies on Southern ingredients, but not necessarily traditional Southern recipes. The menu changes daily, based on what is available locally and even from the restaurant's own garden. Attention to detail is tantamount at Husk: Order a steak and choose your own handcrafted knife; signage in front lists the source of ingredients. Service is attentive and the ambience welcoming; lunch is a good option for those who don't want to shell out big bucks at dinner.

MAP 1: 37 Rutledge St., 615/256-6565, www.husknashville.com; 5pm-10pm Mon.-Thurs., 5pm-11pm Fri., 10am-2pm and 5pm-11pm Sat., 10am-2pm and 5pm-10pm Sun.

The Southern Steak and Oyster $$$

Locals and visitors alike flock to this sleek downtown bar and restaurant to eat oysters the likes of which are not typically found away from the coasts. In addition to the oysters, The Southern has a fun take on the classic Nashville hot chicken, gumbo, and an impressive cocktail list. Its location makes it a madhouse before the symphony or during conventions, but that buzz is part of its appeal. The affiliated Southernaire Market, around the corner, sells limited grocery items, T-shirts, and other gift items perfect for bringing home to remember your trip.

MAP 1: 150 3rd Ave. S., 615/724-1762, www.thesouthernnashville.com; 5pm-9pm Mon.-Thurs., 10am-3pm and 5pm-10pm Fri.-Sat., 10am-3pm and 5pm-9pm Sun.

The Standard $$$

Located in the historic Smith House, The Standard is a restaurant of ages gone by. The service is to the standards (pun intended) of this Victorian home. You'll feel like a guest on *Downton Abbey* as your every need is attended to. Menu items include wedge salads, crab bisque, and "bacon-wrapped bacon" (that's a pork chop wrapped in bacon). You'll need to forget your diet and bring a credit card, as dining at The Standard is neither healthy nor inexpensive.

MAP 1: 167 Rosa L. Parks Blvd., 615-254-1277, www. smithhousenashville.com; 5pm-9pm Mon.-Thurs., 5pm-10pm Fri.-Sat.

Puckett's Grocery & Restaurant $$

There's no shortage of fried chicken south of the Mason-Dixon. Even so, people often throng to one of Puckett's locations for some of what folks say is among the area's best. The downtown outpost of this regional mainstay has classic Southern food (don't skip the fried green beans) in a casual, often crowded environment. There's live music many nights and a full bar, but the real appeal is stick-to-your-ribs comfort food in a restaurant that will get you in and out in time to see a show at the Ryman. Find other locations in Franklin, Leiper's Fork, and Columbia.

MAP 1: 500 Church St., 615-770-2772, www.puckettsgro.com; 7am-10pm Sun.-Thurs., 7am-11pm Fri.-Sat.

Arnold's Country Kitchen $

You'd be forgiven if you thought Arnold's was just like any other delicious meat-and-three in town. It's in a red cinder-block building on the southern edge of downtown, and to say it is unassuming is an understatement. Certainly, you'll find all the traditional wonders: chocolate pie, congealed salad (that's Jell-O to those who don't know), juicy sliced tomatoes, turnip greens, mashed potatoes, squash casserole, macaroni and cheese—and that's just the "vegetables." But Arnold's also includes some innovative takes on Southern cooking along with the cafeteria-style classics. Choose a vegetable plate, with either three or four vegetables, or a meat-and-three for about a buck more. Meals come with your choice of pillowy yeast rolls or corn bread. The full lunch, plus a drink, will run you under $15. There is usually a line out the door at this popular spot, where you're likely to see everyone from politicians to fellow chefs to tourists to celebrities. The After Dark dinners are a draw for foodies and locals.

MAP 1: 605 8th Ave. S., 615-256-4455, www.arnoldscountrykitchen. com; 10:30am-2:45pm Mon.-Tues., 10:30am-2:45pm and 5pm-10pm Wed.-Thurs., 10:30am-11pm Fri., 11am-11pm Sat.

Biscuit Love $

This biscuit business started as a food truck and now has locations in Hillsboro Village and suburban Franklin, in addition to this spot in The Gulch. The kitchen crew gets creative with its biscuit dough, frying it into doughnuts (aka "bonuts") and using it to make French toast (served with fruit compote). Biscuits also make an appearance in myriad sandwiches, such as the East Nasty, featuring signature Nashville hot chicken and cheddar. There are biscuit-less options to be had, including oatmeal, omelets, and hash, but that's not why those long lines have formed out the door.

MAP 1: 316 11th Ave. S., 615-490-9584, http://biscuitlove.com; 7am-3pm daily

Johnny Cash's Bar & BBQ $

When the owners of Johnny Cash's Bar & BBQ were looking to serve the masses downtown, they asked John Carter Cash about his food memories. He remembered his famous parents taking him out for fried chicken as a child. So the restaurant pays homage to those special memories by serving fried chicken and other classics. Come here for reasonably priced Southern dishes, including the aforementioned chicken, barbecue, meatloaf, and hash brown casserole. There are live music stages (playing Johnny Cash music) on both floors. Upstairs is a bar with a fireplace and stained-glass windows; downstairs is the restaurant. Both spaces are designed to look like Johnny and June's home.

MAP 1: 121 3rd Ave. N., 615/209-9504, www.cashbarandbbq.com; 11am-late Mon.-Wed., 9am-late Thurs.-Sun.

HOT CHICKEN
Party Fowl $$

If you prefer your hot chicken joint to also have live music and a lengthy list of drinks, Party Fowl delivers with spiked slushies, a big beer list, and plenty of craft bourbon cocktails. Warm up for the main event (Nashville hot chicken, of course) with the piggy chips—bacon-fried potato chips with traditional Alabama white barbecue sauce for dipping. There's also a decent selection of salads and non-hot chicken options, including a burger, po' boys, and a whole beer-can chicken. There's another location in suburban Donelson, close to Music Valley and the airport.

MAP 1: 719 8th Ave. S., 615/624-8255, http://partyfowlnashville.com; 11am-10pm Mon.- Fri., 10am-10pm Sat.-Sun.

NEW AMERICAN
Drusie & Darr $$$

Rub elbows with legislators, lobbyists, and other members of the Music City jet set at Drusie & Darr. In 2021, internationally known chef Jean-Georges Vongerichten overhauled this historic kitchen, formerly the Capitol Grille, and renamed it after the children of the Hermitage Hotel's longtime former general manager, Dick Hall. Drusie and Darr Hall lived, played, and grew up in the hotel during the 1950s and '60s. A stone's throw from the Tennessee State Capitol, this is the sort of restaurant where business deals are done and marriages are proposed. The menu is fine dining at its best: choice cuts of meat prepared with exacting care and local ingredients. In fact, the ingredients are grown at the nearby Farm at Glen Leven, and this connection to the land has made the restaurant one of the leaders in the farm-to-fork movement.

Divided from the restaurant by a stylish screen is a modern bar space that's both clubby and intimate. The crafted cocktails are as thoughtfully prepared as the food is. On weekends, the restaurant offers brunch from 11:30am to 1:30pm.

MAP 1: Hermitage Hotel, 231 6th Ave. N., 615/345-7116, www.thehermitagehotel.com; 7am-11am, 11:30am-2pm, and 5pm-10pm daily

Gray & Dudley $$$

Named for the building's former identity as Gray & Dudley Hardware Company, this bar and restaurant is attached to the swanky 21c Museum Hotel. Expect trendy bar snacks, contemporary American entrées, and, for dessert, perhaps the most decadent cream puff you've ever laid eyes on. Also not to be missed: some pretty incredible art, including ceramic sculptures from artist Beth Cavener Stichter. The cozy environment can be either date-night intimate or work-meeting appropriate.

MAP 1: 221 2nd Ave. N., 615/610-6460, www.grayanddudley. com; 7:30am-10:30am Mon.-Tues., 7:30am-10:30am and 5:30pm-10pm Wed., 7:30am-10:30am and 3pm-10pm Thurs.-Fri., 9:30am-10pm Sat., 9:30am-9pm Sun.

Merchants $$$

Since 1892, Merchants has been a fixture in downtown Nashville, first as a hotel and then, beginning in 1988, as a restaurant. In the 1990s it was the go-to place for proms and parents' weekends, and as a result got a little sleepy. The current owners—the folks behind The Catbird Seat, Patterson House, Pinewood, and others—revitalized the joint. Now it is two distinct spaces—one upstairs, one down—that appeal to business diners, visitors, and the special-occasion crowd. The menu is classic: perfectly roasted chicken, Cobb salads, burgers, fried green tomatoes, steaks, chops, and more.

MAP 1: 401 Broadway, 615/254-1892, www.merchantsrestaurant.com; downstairs 11am-11pm daily; upstairs 5pm-10pm daily

Adele's $$

In a former automobile garage in The Gulch, chef Jonathan Waxman offers Music City his signature California-inspired food. The menu utilizes seasonal ingredients, and changes as a result, but not in a heavy-handed way. The JW chicken and JW potatoes are year-round favorites. The open kitchen and sleek design are welcoming but not overly fussy, just like the food. Somehow Adele's, which was named for Waxman's mother, manages to be both a place you can take kids and somewhere to go on a date night. The wine and cocktail lists are impressive.

MAP 1: 1210 McGavock St., 615/988-9700, www.adelesnashville. com; 5pm-9pm Mon.-Thurs., 5pm-10pm Fri., 10:30am-2:30pm and 5pm-10pm Sat., 10:30am-2:30pm and 5pm-9pm Sun.

The Mockingbird $$

This self-professed "modern diner" serves cleverly named, beautifully plated dishes for sharing (or not). Seoul Purpose is *bulgogi*-style flank steak with a potato latke waffle and runny egg. Don't Worry, Brie Happy is a brie-packed grilled cheese with *chimichurri* sauce and jalapeño jam. In Pie We Crust is the classic French dish coq au vin encased in a potpie. Prices are higher than at a traditional diner, but this is anything but traditional. The environment is that of a happening urban cocktail bar, which The Mockingbird also is, so the space is loud. The Mockingbird is in the same building as Tansuo and Chauhan Ale & Masala House.

Pinewood

121A 12th Ave. N., 615/741-9900, www.mockingbirdnashville.com; 4pm-9pm Wed.-Fri., 10:30am-2:30pm and 4pm-9pm Sat.-Sun.

Whiskey Kitchen $$

This restaurant/bar is one of The Gulch's many see-and-be-seen spots. Starting as soon as the office crowd shuts down their laptops, Whiskey Kitchen has a happening bar scene, with both indoor and outdoor space. The outdoor patios are heated so that they can corral the crowds even in cold-weather months. The menu is better than bar food, with good burgers, a variation of Nashville hot chicken, and lots of dishes made with—you guessed it— whiskey. The wine and cocktail list is creative.

MAP 1: 118 12th Ave. S., 615/254-3029, www.mstreetnashville.com/ whiskey-kitchen; 4pm-10pm Tues.-Thurs., 10am-10pm Fri.-Sat.

Pinewood $

Part coffee shop, part restaurant, and part adult playland—there's a little bit of something for everyone at indoor-outdoor Pinewood. It sounds like a disaster—upscale cocktails and bowling and smoked short ribs all together—but it is a delight. Don't miss the fried broccoli or the fried chicken. Cool off with frozen cocktails poolside—yes, there are two small outdoor pools in summer, and also a bocce court, six bowling lanes, and a bar fashioned out of an Airstream trailer. Pinewood anchors a complex of businesses in renovated trolley barns looking at downtown, so the view from the parking lot shouldn't be missed either.

MAP 1: 33 Peabody St., 615/751-8111, www.pinewoodsocial.com; 7am-11pm Mon.-Thurs. and Sat., 7am-1am Fri., 9am-11pm Sun.

✪ The Continental $$$

James Beard Award-winning chef Sean Brock opened this restaurant in the Grand Hyatt at the Nashville Yards as a love letter to hotel restaurants of the past. Diners get all the love here; expect a truly remarkable experience. Special occasion dishes such as pate and prime rib are rolled out on carts as you sit in velvet-bedecked banquettes. Meals are prix fixe, so you don't have to make any decisions. There's a decent selection of zero-proof wines and drinks if you choose not to drink alcohol. If you do, you'll be impressed by the wine selection. Don't skip dessert. The space is as much of a head-turner as the menu, with high ceilings, colorful original art, and tables arranged so that you can have an easy conversation with your dining companions but still feel like you're part of the buzz of the room. Service is impeccable.

MAP 1: 1000 Broadway, 615/622-3225, www.thecontinentalnashville.com; 5:30pm-9:30pm Wed.-Sun.

ASIAN
Tansuo $$$

Owned by celebrity chef Maneet Chauhan, Tansuo is hard to describe. The kitchen is helmed by chef Chris Cheung, who riffs on Chinese cuisine and street fare for lunch, dinner, and Sunday brunch, with a twist of traditional Southern tastes, all inside a beautifully designed restaurant. Variations might include open-faced pork dumplings, wok-crisped fish, and a roast duck that feeds 2-4 diners and requires a 48-hour preorder. The space is open, welcoming, and intimate, and the cocktails are delicious.

MAP 1: 121B 12th Ave. N., 615/782-6786, www.tansuonashville.com; 5pm-9pm Wed.-Thurs. and Sun., 5pm-10pm Fri.-Sat.

INDIAN
Chauhan Ale & Masala House $$

Maneet Chauhan is known for appearing on *Iron Chef America*, *The Next Iron Chef*, and *Chopped* and now as the owner of four restaurants in Nashville, where she lives. Chauhan was drawn to Nashville's entrepreneurial spirit and has helped shaped its culinary renaissance. The eatery that bears her name brought Indian street food and a fusion of dishes and tastes to a city that wasn't known for its Indian cuisine. The vibe is fun and friendly, the cocktails go down easy, and there is even an interpretation of a Nashville hot chicken dish. Validated parking is available in the nearby Whole Foods garage.

MAP 1: 123 12th Ave. N., 615/242-8426, http://chauhannashville.com; 5pm-9pm Mon.-Thurs., 5pm-11pm Fri.-Sat., 11am-2:30pm and 5pm-9pm Sun.

ITALIAN
Manny's House of Pizza $

In the lower level of the downtown Arcade, Manny's House of Pizza serves up thick- and thin-crust varieties (both full pies and by the slice), massive stromboli, mighty lasagna, and huge meatball subs. The restaurant is small; eating in can be a challenge, particularly because Nashvillians flock here for the best slice in town. Note that Manny's is only open to the public on weekdays. (On Saturdays it serves private parties.)

MAP 1: 15 Arcade Alley, 615/242-7144, www.mannyshouseofpizza.com; 11am-4pm Mon.-Fri.

Yolan $$$

The husband-and-wife duo of chef Tony Mantuano and wine expert Cathy Mantuano are in charge at this Italian fine-dining experience inside The Joseph hotel. This is a luxury experience all around, from the museum-quality art collection to the world-class food to the carefully selected wines. Don't miss the cheese cave, a transparent, climate-controlled display case for giant wheels of Parmigiano Reggiano that are the Mantuano's signature fromage. The attentive service will make you feel like a star. If you feel like really indulging, stop at the rooftop's Denim or the first floor's Four Walls, lovely bars where you can grab a drink before or after dinner.

MAP 1: 403 4th Ave. S., 615/231-0405, www.yolannashville.com; 5pm-10pm Wed.-Mon.

FOOD HALLS

✪ Assembly Food Hall $$

This food hall in the mammoth Fifth + Broadway complex is a selection of small eateries that cater to whatever you crave. Many local restaurants, from Steamboys to Thai Esane to multiple hot chicken eateries, have outposts here. This means you have access to Thai, Kurdish, and Mexican food under one roof, with views of Broadway and the Ryman. Assembly Food Hall is a great option for a tasty, affordable meal or drinks before heading out to explore downtown. You'll often find performers playing live music on small stages. Vendors at Assembly Food Hall do not accept cash, but if you don't have a credit or debit card you can get a prepaid gift card (called a Hall Pass) from one of the information desks.

Outside of the second-floor food halls, which have plenty of indoor and outdoor seating, there are other eateries in the Fifth + Broadway complex, including Sixty Vines, Hattie B's, and Slim and Husky's Pizza, which became the first Black-owned restaurant on Broadway when it opened in 2021.

MAP 1: 5055 Broadway, no phone, www.assemblyfoodhall.com; 9am-1am daily, individual eatery hours may vary

Nightlife

HONKY-TONKS

AJ's Good Time Bar

Country megastar Alan Jackson bought one of Lower Broad's long-time honky-tonks, then called The Wheel, and re-opened it as AJ's Good Time Bar in 2016. Since then, the honky-tonk, named after one of Jackson's most popular songs, has focused on country music, an increasingly rare occurrence on Broadway. MAP 1: 421 Broadway, 615/678-4808, www.ajsgoodtimebar.com; 11am-2:30am daily, ages 21 and older after 6pm; no cover, donations to band encouraged

Layla's

A cozy, dark dance hall, Layla's offers that honky-tonk trifecta: cheap beer, a hot dog cart, and no cover. It is often standing room only on Friday and Saturday nights, but that's not the only time to hear good music. Almost any time the lights are on, it's worth stepping inside. Head to the back entrance (which opens onto the alley next to the Ryman) or the upper floor for more space. MAP 1: 418 Broadway, 615/726-2799, www.laylasnashville.com; 4pm-11pm Mon., 7pm-11pm Tues., 3pm-11pm Wed.-Thurs., 11am-11pm Fri.-Sat., noon-11pm Sun., ages 21 and older after 6pm; no cover, donations to band encouraged

Nudie's Honky Tonk

This may be one of the newer honky-tonks on Lower Broad, but it has a serious connection to the past. Owned by the same folks who opened The Johnny Cash Museum and the Patsy Cline Museum, this bar celebrates all things Nudie Cohn. Nudie was the tailor who made suits for Johnny Cash and Elvis, among others. The bar is also a museum, with many of Nudie's famous works behind glass and one of his ostentatious cars, a $400,000 Cadillac El Dorado, hanging from the wall. If you're hungry, food is served here—bar staples like corn dogs, nachos, and hot chicken. MAP 1: 409 Broadway, no phone, www.nudieshonkytonk.com; 10am-3am daily, kitchen closes at 9:30pm; no cover, donations to band encouraged

TOP EXPERIENCE

✪ Robert's Western World

Robert's Western World is often voted the city's best honky-tonk by locals. Originally a store selling boots, cowboy hats, and other country music regalia, Robert's morphed into a bar and nightclub with a good gift shop and even a Sunday morning church service with gospel music. Many of the honky-tonks have similar acts playing similar music, but there's something about the energy of Robert's that makes it feel different from the rest. Hungry? Try the Recession Special, a fried bologna sandwich with chips and a PBR for five bucks. MAP 1: 416 Broadway, 615/244-9552, http://robertswesternworld.com; 11am-3am daily, ages 21 and older after 6pm; no cover, donations to band encouraged

Layla's

It may be known locally as honkytonk, honky tonk, or honky-tonk, and it may be used as a noun (a bar that plays Western swing, where people dance), a verb (dancing to Western swing), or an adjective (a descriptor of the type of music), but one thing is for sure, in Nashville the honky-tonk is what makes Music City sing.

The main strip of these bars is found along Lower Broadway in the heart of downtown. They play a specific strain of country and western swing music, with a live band. Small or large, these venues all have some empty space to cut the rug because dancing is an essential part of Nashville honky-tonk.

The best places to go honky-tonking include Layla's, Robert's Western World, and The Stage on Broadway. Most of these establishments are open to all ages during the day but convert to 21 and up after 6pm. They typically don't have a cover charge, though when the cowboy hat is passed for the band, don't forget to drop a few dollars in.

The Stage on Broadway

The Stage is a honky-tonk that often plays second fiddle to Robert's Western World and Layla's but gets its fair share of movie and TV cameo appearances. It has a large dance floor and music seven nights a week. Those under 21 are welcome before 6pm.

MAP 1: 412 Broadway, 615/726-0504, www.thestageonbroadway.com; 10:30am-2:30am daily, ages 21 and older after 6pm; no cover, donations to band encouraged

LIVE MUSIC
Ascend Amphitheater

This open-air concert venue offers the chance to rock out by the river in Metro Riverfront Park. Between folding seats, box seats, and the lawn, it can hold 6,800 concertgoers, all of whom get a view of the skyline and great sightlines to the stage. Almost immediately after opening in 2015, this became the place to see a big show, with well-known national acts on the schedule as well as the Nashville Symphony. Locals have been known to picnic nearby (or paddleboard or kayak on

Ascend Amphitheater

the river) during shows to hear the music being played.

MAP 1: 301 1st Ave. S., 615/999-9000, www.ascendamphitheater.com; hours vary by event; cost varies by event

COUNTRY AND BLUEGRASS
Country Music Hall of Fame and Museum

The Country Music Hall of Fame and Museum hosts concerts, readings, and musical discussions regularly in an auditorium located inside the hall. These daytime events are often aimed at highlighting a specific type of country music, often in conjunction with a themed exhibit. The hall of fame is well respected, and often you'll find big names playing. Admission to concerts is free with your paid admission to the hall, so it's a good idea to plan your trip on a day when there's a concert scheduled (separate admission to concerts is not available). Check the website for a listing of upcoming events. Museum members get access to small concerts as well.

MAP 1: 222 Rep. John Lewis Way S., 615/416-2001, http://countrymusichalloffame.org; 9am-5pm Mon.-Thurs., 9am-7pm Fri.-Sat., 9am-6pm Sun.; events free with museum admission or museum membership

TOP EXPERIENCE

✪ Station Inn

It doesn't look like much (or anything) from the outside, but inside this cinder-block box is the city's most popular venue for bluegrass and roots music. The Station Inn is perhaps the country's best bluegrass club, and it showcases fine artists every night of the week. This homey and casual club opens nightly two hours before the music begins, typically at 7pm or 9pm. This is a 21-and-up club, unless you come with a parent or guardian. There is no cover for the Sunday-night bluegrass jam, at which almost everyone who is anyone picks up an instrument and plays. Occasionally the beloved **Doyle & Debbie Show** (615/999-9244, www.doyleanddebbie.com; $20) offers its send-up of the music scene through live musical satire. Tickets must be purchased in advance. This cheeky show often sells out.

MAP 1: 402 12th Ave. S., 615/255-3307, http://stationinn.com; 7pm-midnight Mon.-Sat., 3pm-midnight Sun., showtimes vary; $10-20, donations to band encouraged

Station Inn

Wildhorse Saloon

The Wildhorse Saloon is a boot-scootin', beer-drinkin' place to see and be seen, though almost exclusively by tourists. The huge dance floor is often packed with cowboys and cowgirls line dancing to the greatest country hits. Free line dance lessons are offered every day (times vary per season). The Wildhorse books big-name acts many nights of the week, including country music, roots rock, and classic rock stars. The establishment is owned by Gaylord, the same folks who own the Ryman, Opryland, and the Opry, and it often offers deals for hotel guests. There is a shuttle (with a charge) back to the Opryland Resort for folks staying there.

MAP 1: 120 2nd Ave. N., 615/902-8200, http://wildhorsesaloon.com; doors open at 4pm Thurs.-Fri., noon Sat., hours may vary depending on show; cover varies based on show, typically $6 for ages 21 and older

LISTENING ROOMS
The Listening Room Café

If you want to hear up-and-coming singer-songwriters—you know, actually to be able to listen to what they're saying and singing—then this is the place that lives up to its name. The spot books local bands and the occasional national act. Unlike at other listening rooms, there are no rules against conversation, but the idea is to come to hear the songwriters, not your friends. The Listening Room Café has a full menu and bar, including a popular brunch. Large tables make this venue popular with groups who want to go out together. If you weren't able to get tickets at the **Bluebird Café**, this is a great, family-friendly alternative.

The Listening Room Café

Exit/In

It's true: Nashville is known for its country music. But Jack White relocated here. The Kings of Leon live here. The Black Keys are here. Robert Plant is often seen in 12 South. Ben Folds. Bob Dylan even has his own distillery (called Heaven's Door). The list goes on. There is plenty of music being played, made, and heard in Music City that doesn't have a single note of twang (not that there's anything wrong with that).

If you're looking for jazz, blues, and rock music, you have lots of options. For the best and most innovative in the rock music scene, start at **Third Man Records,** the music store/music venue owned by Jack White. Many of the employees are in bands themselves and can tell you what's going on around town.

Other good noncountry venues include **Exit/In, The Basement East,** Marathon Music Works, and **The 5 Spot.**

MAP 1: 618 4th Ave. S., 615/259-3600, www.listeningroomcafe.com; 4pm-11pm Mon.-Fri., 10am-3pm and 4pm-11pm Sat.; tickets $5-12, $7 food/ drink minimum pp per show when seated

JAZZ AND BLUES
B. B. King's Blues Club

If you need to get that country twang out of your head, a good dose of the Memphis blues will do it. B. B. King's Blues Club is a good place to start for a night of the blues. The club is a satellite of King's original Beale Street club, and it books live

blues every night. The cover charge is usually under $10.

MAP 1: 152 2nd Ave. N., 615/256-2727, http://bbkings.com; 11am-11pm Mon.-Thurs., 11am-1am Fri.-Sat., 11am-10pm Sun.; cover varies, usually $3-10

Bourbon Street Blues and Boogie Bar

Located in the nightlife strip of Printers Alley, the Bourbon Street Blues and Boogie Bar is a club that is nothing fancy, but it is where to go if your taste leans toward New Orleans-style jazz and blues. This is a small live music venue, so you get to be up close with the act on stage. Drink prices are reasonable, and the menu, with fried green tomato BLTs, po' boys, and alligator bites, fits the NOLA vibe.

MAP 1: 220 Printers Alley, 615/242-5837, www. bourbonstreetbluesandboogiebar.com; doors open at 4pm Wed.-Thurs., 11am Fri.-Sun.; no cover, donations to band encouraged

ECLECTIC
Cannery Ballroom

Few music venues truly demonstrate the variety of Nashville's music scene than the trio of Cannery Ballroom and its siblings **Mercy Lounge** and **The High Watt.** Over the years, these venues have reliably booked rock, country, soul, and all sorts of other acts, including the likes of Lizzo, Katy Perry, Todd Snider, and The White Stripes. Each venue has a knack for booking an act just before they hit it big time, meaning you get to see them in a more intimate setting than most. Mercy Lounge hosts 8 off 8th on Monday nights, a no-cover open mic where eight different bands each perform three songs. In May 2022 they moved to a new location.

MAP 1: 1 Cannery Row, 615/251-3020, www.mercylounge.com; hours and cover cost vary based on event

City Winery

Yes, this restaurant/wine bar/live music venue is a chain (it has locations in Chicago and New York, among others). But it's the brainchild of Michael Dorf, who created the iconic Knitting Factory, which means that even in a city like Nashville, the musical lineup is impressive. Tickets typically include seating, so you can eat and drink and not crane your neck to see the act. This isn't a place where people generally get up and dance. Walk or take a taxi or a Lyft; parking can be a challenge.

MAP 1: 609 Lafayette St., 615/324-010, www.citywinery.com/nashville; 4pm-10pm Thurs.-Fri., 10:30am-10pm Sat., 10:30am-3pm Sun.; ticket prices vary

House of Cards

House of Cards

Modeled after Los Angeles's Magic Castle, House of Cards is an adults-only (21 and older) magical evening in the making. For the price of dinner, you'll also see a timed magic show in the separate theater, many smaller tableside acts from mind readers (though they prefer the term "mentalist"), and card tricks. You are not allowed to take photos in the venue (lest you document the floating table or ghost playing the piano), so this is a good opportunity to be present and enjoy. Don't miss the amazing collection of antique playing cards hanging on the walls. It might sound hokey, but it's a fun night out. There's a basic dress code—jacket required for men (ties are optional), no flip-flops or tank tops—so pack accordingly. Reservations are recommended. House of Cards is "hidden" underneath The Johnny Cash Museum.

MAP 1: 119 3rd Ave. S., 615/730-8326, www.hocnashville.com; doors open at 6pm Wed.-Thurs., 5pm Fri.-Sat., 10am-3pm and 5pm Sun., kitchen closes 11pm daily; no cover

Ryman Auditorium

The most famous music venue in Nashville, the historic Ryman Auditorium continues to book some of the best acts in town, from just about every genre you can imagine. The hall also boasts some of the best acoustics around, and musicians love to show that off, often playing a song or two without a mic. It is a pleasure to watch artists' reverence for the space. (The church pew-style seats aren't particularly comfortable, but that's part of the experience.) On-site exhibits chronicle the auditorium's history, including an immersive theater experience called Soul of Nashville. The gift shop near the entrance is worth a stop for souvenirs, but if you are looking for custom Hatch Show Prints for the show you're seeing, head to the merch booth on the second floor. Cafe Lula is the on-site restaurant.

MAP 1: 116 Rep. John Lewis Way N., 615/889-3060, www.ryman.com; box office 9am-4pm daily; showtimes and ticket prices vary

3rd and Lindsley

The neighborhood bar and grill 3rd and Lindsley showcases rock, alternative, progressive, Americana, soul, and R&B music. Over the years, they have developed a reputation for solid bookings, though if you were just driving down the street you wouldn't think a place that rocks could reside inside. Monday nights feature The Time Jumpers, a world-class Western swing jam band. The 3rd and Lindsley grill serves a full lunch and dinner menu, the bar is well stocked, and the club offers good sound quality and an adequate dance floor and seating. The atmosphere isn't particularly quirky or welcoming, but you came here for music, not decor.

MAP 1: 816 3rd Ave. S., 615/259-9891, www.3rdandlindsley.com; hours and cover cost vary based on event

BREWERIES, DISTILLERIES, AND TASTING ROOMS

Jackalope Brewing Company

Nashville's third-oldest brewery, Jackalope offers tastings of its craft brews and tours of its small taproom. The beer selection changes monthly, so there's always an excuse to go back and try another. Jackalope's beers include Rompo Red Rye Ale, Thunder Ann American Pale Ale, and Bearwalker Maple Brown Ale. Growlers are available for purchase as well. They offer 45-minute **tours** (Fri.-Sat.; $7, book online), which include a tasting and a souvenir pint glass.

MAP 1: 701 8th Ave. S., 615/873-4313, http://jackalopebrew.com; 2pm-10pm Wed.-Thurs., noon-10pm Fri.-Sat., noon-6pm Sun.

Tennessee Brew Works

At this taproom, you can taste the latest brews in pints, pitchers, and five-sample flights, plus order from

What's next after you become a big country music artist? Open your own bar and music venue on Broadway, of course. Here's a quick overview of which bars might result in a megastar sighting.

- Alan Jackson bought former honky-tonk The Wheel and turned it into AJ's Good Time Bar (421 Broadway, 615/678-4808, www. ajsgoodtimebar.com).

- Country megastar and Nashville local Dierks Bentley opened Whiskey Row (400 Broadway, 629/203-7822, http://dierkswhiskeyrow.com) in late 2017.

Casa Rosa

- *The Voice* judge and country music hottie Blake Shelton teamed up with Ryman Hospitality to open Ole Red (300 Broadway, 615/780-0900, www.olered. com) in 2018.

- The initials at FGL House (120 3rd Ave. S., 615/961-5460, http://fglhouse.com) stand for Florida Georgia Line, the band that owns this multi-level bar.

- Singer Gavin DeGraw and his brother are behind Nashville Underground (105 Broadway, 615/964-3000, www.nashunderground.com).

- There's no cover at Jason Aldean's Kitchen + Rooftop Bar (307 Broadway, www.jasonaldeansnashville.com), but if you're headed just for the view, note that the rooftop has different hours than the rest of the bar.

- Luke Bryan's Luke's 32 Bridge (301 Broadway, www.lukes32bridge.com) has three floors of music, an outdoor patio, and a sushi menu behind a historical building facade.

- Casa Rosa (308 Broadway, https://casarosanashville.com) is the first bar on Broadway with the backing of a female country star: Miranda Lambert. Explore three floors of music, Tex-Mex eats, and fun.

a menu of elevated bar food, such as a pork belly BLT, an artisanal cheese board, and Nashville hot frog legs. There's live music nightly from Wednesday through Saturday, while Sunday is vinyl record day (BYO favorite to play). Tours (3pm, 4pm, and 5pm Sat., $10) include a 16-ounce pint of your choice.
MAP 1: 809 Ewing Ave., 615/436-0050, www.tnbrew.com; 11am-10pm Mon.-Sat., 11am-8pm Sun.

BARS
Acme Feed & Seed

In the center of the city, where Broadway meets the Cumberland River, this historical building has been brought back to life. The multilevel bar, restaurant, and event space always has something going on in its 22,000 square feet of space, from trivia nights hosted by Geeks Who Drink to Americana music showcases to rooftop yoga and soul brunch. While the location screams "tourist," the combination of good views, cocktails, and events attracts plenty of locals, too.

MAP 1: 101 Broadway, 615/915-0888, http://theacmenashville.com; 4:30pm-11pm Mon.-Thurs., 11am-1am Fri.-Sat., 11am-11pm Sun., closing times can vary

Lonnie's Western Room

If you think your karaoke skills can keep up with all the Music City pros, head to Lonnie's Western Room. For 27 years this was the staple of Printers Alley. Development in the area forced Lonnie's to move just around the corner, but it is still the city's number one spot for singing your heart out to prerecorded tracks. It is standing room only on the weekends; weeknights you can slip in and get a seat. Despite the name, folks do sing along to more than country and western music here.

MAP 1: 308 Church St., 615/613-7500, http://lonnieswesternroom.com; 6pm-3am daily; two-drink minimum

Rudy's Jazz Room

New Orleans jazz is the vibe of Rudy's, with its late-night crowd, Cajun cooking, and high-energy music from the Crescent City. But lots of touches are distinctively Music City, too. The Steinway Model B piano was funded through a Kickstarter campaign: Nashvillians expect quality equipment on their stages. The 50-seat venue is designed so that there are no muffled sounds or blocked sightlines. Some shows don't have a cover (although you ought to tip the band), so check the website for a bargain.

MAP 1: 809 Gleaves St., 615/988-2458, www.rudysjazzroom.com; 5pm-midnight Wed.-Mon., kitchen closes at 10:30pm; cover varies by show

Skull's Rainbow Room

This historical venue originally opened in 1948 and has been restored to its earlier-era night-out vibe. A classic cocktail from the dark wood-paneled bar is a must-have if you're on a sipping tour of downtown. Owned by Bill Miller (the brains behind Nudie's Honky Tonk and the Johnny Cash and Patsy Cline Museums), Skull's hosts live jazz seven days a week and burlesque shows Thursday, Friday, and Saturday. The burlesque is the draw: Make a reservation to get a good table. The dinner menu served here is chock-full of hearty dishes, such as rack of lamb, pork chops, and prime rib, plus shrimp cocktail and wedge salads.

MAP 1: 222 Printers Alley, 615/810-9621, http://skullsrainbowroom.com; 5pm-2am daily, kitchen closes at 11pm; no cover for jazz; $20 for burlesque

Jane's Hideaway

While much of Printers Alley is about being louder than the place next door, Jane's Hideaway is a little more chill. This is the ideal place if you want to be in the action, with live music and good food and drinks. The music is more likely to be bluegrass and Americana, and you'll be able to hear what your companions are saying. (Of course, don't interrupt the musicians with your conversation.) The menu includes items like *ropa vieja* (Cuban braised beef), roasted beets, risotto, and scallops.

DRINKS WITH A VIEW

If you want evidence of Nashville's growth, look up. Music City's newest batch of hotels and high-rises brought with it a new rooftop bar scene. Want to take in the view while you sip and socialize? Try these favorites.

The Stage on Broadway

- Swanky L27 (807 Clark Pl., 629/800-5070, http://l27nashville.com), atop the Westin, has an outdoor pool and two levels of city views, with food and drink. For the VIP experience, rent a cabana.

- The hip L.A. Jackson (401 11th Ave. S., 615/262-6007, www.lajacksonbar.com) at the Thompson hotel features DJ action from Third Man Records.

- The country-themed UP (901 Division St., 615/690-1722, http://uprooftoplounge.com) in The Gulch's Fairfield Inn & Suites serves spiked punch and a Music City Sour (with apricot liqueur, lemon juice, and fresh rosemary) to sip while you take in the scene.

- One of the four levels at Lower Broad's The Valentine (312 Broadway, 629/202-6979, http://thevalentinenashville.com) is a stunning rooftop space.

- While Nudie's Honky Tonk (409 Broadway, www.nudieshonkytonk.com) boasts about its mega-long indoor bar, its rooftop deck is also a scene-stealer.

- Once you've checked out the three stages for live music, six bars, and two patios at Crazy Town (308 Broadway, 615/254-5460, http://crazytownnashville.com), be sure to experience the rooftop deck.

- Open-air imbibing and dancing are on the menu at The Stage on Broadway (412 Broadway, 615/726-0504, www.thestageonbroadway.com).

- Live music, yoga classes, private parties, and more take place on the top of Acme Feed & Seed (101 Broadway, 615/915-0888, http://theacmenashville.com), which has some of the best river views in the city.

- The tallest rooftop bar in the city, the Bourbon Sky JW Marriott Rooftop Bar (201 8th Ave. S., 615/291-8600, www.jwnashvillehotel.com) comes with high prices, but they are worth it for these views. There's even a skyscape view from the women's restroom.

- Be sure to look down as well as up when you're at Denim (401 Korean Veterans Blvd., 629/231-3186, www.thejosephnashville.com), the rooftop bar at The Joseph hotel. A few art installations are designed to be seen from above.

- The Pool Club atop Virgin Nashville (1 Music Sq. W., 615/667-8000, https://virginhotels.com/nashville) offers its namesake swimming pool, plus a rare vantage point above Music Row.

MAP 1: 209 3rd Ave. N.,
615/942-7809, www.janeshideaway.
com; 5pm-midnight Wed.-Fri.,
10:30am-midnight Sat.-Sun.

Bobby's Garage

Found on the lower level of the
Bobby Hotel, with an entrance
from Printers Alley, Bobby's Garage
is an edgy bar, decorated with art
made by a Los Angeles street artist.
Come here for a PBR, loud music,
and close conversation before
heading out to explore the rest of
Printers Alley. The space has been
designed to look and feel like a garage: The small stage that hosts occasional live music is lit with car
headlights.

MAP 1: 230 4th Ave. N., 615/782-7100,
http://bobbyhotel.com/
bobbysgaragebar; 5pm-1am daily

Whiskey Kitchen

Sip your choice of bourbon, scotch,
or whiskey neat or in cocktails at
this hip hangout. The food menu
features funky pub grub (think jalapeño fried pickles, yam fries, and
calamari with smoked tomato dipping sauce), salads, sandwiches,
burgers, and brick-oven pizza.
Tuesdays, order two-for-one cocktails 2pm-10pm.

MAP 1: 118 12th Ave. S., 615/254-3029,
www.mstreetnashville.com/
whiskey-kitchen; 4pm-10pm
Tues.-Thurs., 10am-10pm Fri.-Sat.

Arts and Culture

GALLERIES

The Arcade

If the second floor of the Arcade
looks locked up, it's because small
galleries and artists have studio spaces here, and their public
hours are erratic at best. During
the monthly First Saturday Art
Crawl (www.nashvilledowntown.
com, free), however, all the doors
are open and the lights are on. This
is one of the best places and times
to see innovative and affordable art
in the city, when the energy is high
and the wine flows. Galleries feature
artwork in media like sculpture,
photography, painting, and print-
making. If you see something you
like, buy it. Many of these galleries
are essentially pop-up shops, and it

may be hard to find the works again
next month.

MAP 1: 244 Rep. John Lewis Way N.;
hours vary by gallery, 6pm-9pm first
Sat. of the month; free

Chauvet Arts

One of downtown's most accessible
and eclectic galleries, Chauvet Arts
offers exhibits of the works of local
and national artists, with contemporary works ranging from the avant-
garde to the everyday, all chosen to
encourage viewers to think about
what they're seeing. The works are
shown in a gallery space in an invit-
ing historical building.

MAP 1: 215 Rep. John Lewis Way N.,
615/278-9086, https://chauvetarts.com;
10am-5pm Tues.-Sat.; free

✪ Haley Gallery

A small gallery inside the mammoth Country Music Hall of Fame complex, Haley offers historical restrikes of original posters from the Hatch Show Print collection, as well as monoprints from Hatch master printer Jim Sherraden. The contemporary works are interpretations of the Hatch Show Print style of classic prints—usually works on paper, but sometimes jewelry and decorative objects, too. If you're looking for a fine art souvenir of your time in Nashville, this is the quintessential stop.

MAP 1: 224 Rep. John Lewis Way S., 615/577-7711, http://hatchshowprint. com/haley-gallery; 9:30am-6pm daily; free

The Rymer Gallery

Perhaps the most cosmopolitan of all Nashville's galleries, The Rymer Gallery installs thought-provoking exhibits with works from artists of national renown. With 3,000 square feet of exhibition space, this is often the center of activity for art crawls and other art community events, and the work shown is typically high caliber. The Rymer also has a satellite space on 3rd Avenue, just a few blocks away.

MAP 1: 233 Rep. John Lewis Way N., 615/752-6030, http://therymergallery. com; 11am-5pm Tues.-Sat.; free

Tinney Contemporary

Susan Tinney and Sarah Wilson bring some of the most challenging contemporary works to Nashville's walls. The gallery displays the works of local, regional, national, and international artists. Its welcoming space provides one of the best gathering places to sip wine and debate art during the monthly art crawls. Tinney also curates exhibits at the nearby Bobby Hotel.

MAP 1: 237 Rep. John Lewis Way N., 615/255-7816, http:// tinneycontemporary.com; 11am-5pm Tues.-Sat.; free

MUSEUMS

✪ 21c Museum Hotel Nashville

The 21c Museum Hotel Nashville is, yes, a hotel, but it also houses a 10,500-square-foot contemporary art museum that is free and open to the public and unlike anything else in Nashville. The collection, like all of those in 21c hotels, is focused on art of the 21st century (hence the name) and tends to be provocative work, including many interactive pieces. Exhibits change about once a year and rotate through the hotel chain's locations (which include Louisville and Cincinnati). The public art spaces, which are on the entry, lower level, and third floor, are free and open 24 hours a day. (If the meeting rooms are open, poke your head in there, too.) This is a great place to wander after a night of eating and drinking downtown or after a show at the Ryman.

MAP 1: 221 2nd Ave. N., 615/610-6400, www.21cnashville.com/museum; 24 hours daily; free

CHILDREN'S THEATER

Nashville Children's Theatre

Nashville Children's Theatre is the oldest children's theater company in the United States. During the school year, the company puts on plays for children from preschool to elementary-school age in its colorful, state-of-the-art theater, a space that rivals a theater for grown-ups. In the summer there are drama classes for youngsters, plus lots of activities that include Mom and Dad. Recent years have included original NCT productions as well as nationally recognized plays.

MAP 1: 25 Middleton St., tickets 615/252-4675, office 615/254-9103, http://nashvillechildrenstheatre.org; box office 7:30am-4:30pm Mon.-Fri., 1pm-4pm Sun. Sept.-May; showtimes vary; $23 adults, $17 children ages 2-17

Wishing Chair Productions

Neither adults nor kids should miss the marionette shows at the Nashville Public Library. Using marionettes from the collection of former library puppeteer Tom Tichenor (dating back to the 1940s), plus others acquired from Chicago's Peekaboo Puppet Productions, the library's children's room staff put on excellent one-of-a-kind family entertainment. The group also partners with the Nashville Symphony and the Nashville Jazz Workshop, among other local institutions. Schoolchildren sometimes get to see the Wishing Chair Puppet Truck in their school parking lot.

MAP 1: 615 Church St., 615/862-5800, http://nashvillepubliclibrary.org/ wishingchair; showtimes typically 10:30am and noon Tues.-Wed. but may vary; free

CLASSICAL MUSIC
Nashville Symphony

The Nashville Symphony is housed in the remarkable Schermerhorn Symphony Center next to the Country Music Hall of Fame, one of the downtown buildings that were renovated as a result of 2010

Schermerhorn Symphony Center

flood damage. Nominated for 20 Grammies and selling more recordings than any other American orchestra, the symphony is a source of pride for Music City. Costa Rican conductor Giancarlo Guerrero is the symphony's seventh music director. The symphony puts on more than 200 performances each year, including classical, pops, and children's concerts. Its season spans September-May. Buying tickets online is a breeze, especially since you can easily choose where you want to sit. Discounted parking for symphony-goers is in the Pinnacle at Symphony Place, across the street from the Schermerhorn. During the summer, the symphony plays its Community Concerts series at locations across the city.

In late August or early September the Schermerhorn building is a roosting spot for purple martins heading south for the winter. Come at sunrise or sunset to witness a free show from Mother Nature.

MAP 1: Schermerhorn Symphony Center, 1 Symphony Pl., 615/687-6400, www.nashvillesymphony.org; showtimes and ticket prices vary

Festivals and Events

WINTER
New Year's Eve
Also known as the Bash on Broadway, New Year's Eve near downtown Nashville includes—what else?—a music note drop. This huge celebration was moved from the riverfront to Bicentennial Mall to accommodate even bigger crowds. It offers lots of free outdoor fun and, of course, lots of live music. Musicians like Kings of Leon and Keith Urban play free concerts while the Music City Bowl game attracts football fans.
Downtown: Broadway, www. visitmusiccity.com; Dec. 31, free

Antiques and Garden Show of Nashville
More than 150 dealers set up in the Nashville Convention Center for the upscale Antiques and Garden Show of Nashville in February. One of the largest such shows that combines both indoor furniture and outdoor, garden antiques, the event includes workshops, demonstrations, and vintage finds to meet most budgets and tastes. Proceeds from the show benefit the Cheekwood Botanical Garden and Museum of Art.
Downtown: Music City Center, 201 Rep. John Lewis Way S., 615/352-1282, http:// antiquesandgardenshow.com; Feb.; $25

SPRING
Fisk Jubilee Singers Spring Sing
In 1871 the Fisk Jubilee Singers were formed to travel the world, singing spirituals, gospel music, and other traditional songs, in an effort to raise funds for the university. Every year a new crop of Fisk students auditions to join this prestigious and talented group. They travel and perform throughout the school year. Spring Sing is often

held at the Ryman Auditorium, resulting in a rare opportunity to hear some of the most beautiful voices in music in one of the best venues in the world.

Downtown: Ryman Auditorium, http://fiskjubileesingers.org; Mar., $39-75

St. Jude Rock 'n' Roll Marathon

Part of the Rock 'n' Roll Marathon circuit, the St. Jude Rock 'n' Roll Nashville Marathon is good fun for both participants and spectators. In addition to the course's hard-core 26.2 miles, there are a half marathon, wheelchair marathons and half marathons, and a kids' event. Plenty of live music (more than 28 stages) is performed along the course, which winds its way through the city. High school cheerleading squads root for the runners.

Downtown: www.runrocknroll.com; late Apr., free for spectators, $35-89 for runner registration

SUMMER

Bluegrass Nights at the Ryman

In 1945 Earl Scruggs brought his banjo to the stage of the Ryman Auditorium—and with that, bluegrass became a vital part of the Grand Ole Opry. This summer series, which takes place on Thursday nights, honors that legacy. Bluegrass features some of the best pickers in the country. Starting in June and ending in July, this Ryman Auditorium series is always popular. Season passes are available, and many locals take advantage of that because they don't want to miss even one of these shows.

Downtown: 116 Rep. John Lewis Way N., 615/889-3060, http://ryman.com/bluegrass; 7:30pm Thurs. June-July; $45

National Museum of African American Music Celebration of Legends

This one-day event honors those who have had significant impact on both the sound and the business of African American music. The event is a fundraiser for the educational programs produced by the National Museum of African American Music. Held in the museum's various performance spaces, the day includes history lessons, context, and, of course, live music.

Downtown: 510 Broadway, 615/301-8724, http://nmaam.org; June

CMA Music Fest

CMA Music Fest is a four-day mega-music show in downtown Nashville. Once called Fan Fair (and some locals still use that term), it is the event where country music stars thank their fans. Stages are set up throughout downtown by day: Expect to hear some of top names in country music, with as many as 400 performers. The focus is on top-40 contemporary country, not bluegrass or Western swing. At night the hordes move to Nissan Stadium to hear a different multi-act show every night. Four-day passes, which range $235-1,435 per person, include the stadium shows, but much of the smaller acts, including access to the exhibit hall, where you can get autographs and meet up-and-coming country music artists, are free. This is one of Nashville's biggest events of the year (more than 85,000 fans), so you are wise to book your hotel early. Plan to stay downtown so that you don't need a car; parking and traffic can be tricky and ridesharing apps have may have surge pricing.

Downtown: www.cmaworld.com; June, from $235 for four-day pass

Craft Beer Festival

Hosted by the Nashville Predators and benefiting the Nashville Predators Foundation, the 21-and-up Craft Beer Festival features food, entertainment, and of course, an abundance of craft beer. The festival takes place in late June at the Bridgestone Arena, which is where the hockey team regularly plays.

Downtown: Bridgestone Arena, www.nhl.com; late June; $49-149

Nashville Pride Festival

Late June sees Nashville's gay, lesbian, bisexual, and transgender community show its rainbow colors at the Nashville Pride Festival, a two-day event at Public Square Park. This is not just an average parade. There's an artists' village, where local artisans show off their wares, plus live music, a drag stage, and much more.

Downtown: www.nashvillepride.org; late June, free

Independence Day: Let Freedom Sing!

Yes, most cities, towns, and even neighborhood groups in America shoot off fireworks for the Fourth of July. But this is a big bang in Nashville. In 2019 more than 349,000 people headed downtown for Independence Day: Let Freedom Sing! In true Nashville fashion, there are riverfront concerts broadcast live on television, from country to classical. Expect some big-name country stars, but the signature is when the Nashville Symphony plays in unison with the pyrotechnics. Related

festivities include kids' games and food and drink vendors; depending on the year, sometimes there's a soccer game or other sporting event. Arrive downtown early to enjoy these festivities because you'll need extra time to navigate the crowds, and you'll want to stroll and listen before the fireworks begin. To make room for all the fun, many downtown streets will be closed. Street closures are posted online, but walking, taking the bus, and using a ride-hailing app to drop you close by are all better options than driving. Many of the city's hotels with rooftop bars offer packages for watching the fireworks.

Downtown: www.visitmusiccity.com; July 4; free

Music City Brewer's Festival

The Music City Brewer's Festival is a one-day 21-and-up event held in late July at the Music City Walk of Fame downtown. Come to taste local brews, learn about making your own beer, and enjoy good food and live music. It typically has about 50 different brewers and 100 different beers, plus live music and other entertainment. Tickets are required; the event benefits local charities and typically sells out.

Downtown: Music City Walk of Fame, 4th Ave. S., www.musiccitybrewersfest.com; late July; $20-75

FALL
Southern Festival of Books

Nashville's literary traditions run deep, and the three-day Southern Festival of Books allows locals and visitors alike to indulge in all things written word. Held during the second full weekend of October on Legislative Plaza in downtown Nashville, the weekend features book readings, autograph sessions with well-known and regional authors, and discussions. The festival, organized by Humanities Tennessee, is a must for book lovers.

Downtown: Legislative Park, www. humanitiestennessee.org; Oct.; free

Americana Music Festival

A multivenue conference/music showcase, the Americana Music Festival in September has become one of the city's most popular events. Professionals (musicians, songwriters, producers, and more) come for the connections and the workshops during the day. Locals join them at night for concerts—more than 230 at nearly 40 different venues—that show off the genre. There's an award show and an end-of-week big-budget concert at Ascend Amphitheater.

Downtown: http://americanamusic. org; Sept., $249-499 for conference registration, $175-199 for festival wristbands

Recreation

SPECTATOR SPORTS
ICE HOCKEY
Nashville Predators

The NHL's Predators play in the 17,000-seat Bridgestone Arena, on Broadway in the heart of downtown. In 2017, the whole country saw what a hockey town Nashville has become, when the Predators went to the Stanley Cup playoffs, the city closed off major streets for viewing parties, and game tickets were in extremely high demand. Even when the team isn't in the playoffs, getting tickets requires advance planning. The regular season begins in October and ends in early April. Tickets for games against the archrival Chicago Blackhawks are particularly sought after. Home games include live country music performances between quarters and other activities for the fans.

MAP 1: 501 Broadway, 615/770-7800, www.nhl.com/predators; game times vary Oct.-Apr.; tickets $20-350

TOURS
Nashville Mural Tours

Many of Nashville's building walls and alleys have become canvases. It can be hard to navigate on your own to see them all, so if you're a mural fan, invest a couple hours to see the city's best murals from the comfort of a van. Your guide will take you to some of the most well-known and oft-photographed images, as well as some secret installations. Not only will you see the works, you'll learn about the artists and why they painted what they did where they did.

MAP 1: 11th Ave. S. and Laurel St., 615/285-8429, www. nashvillemuraltours.com; 10am and 1pm Fri.-Sun.; $35

Experience Nashville

What makes Music City Music City? Songwriter Kaysie Young will take you on her Famous Footsteps tour of downtown, which hits some of the

Nashville Predators

area's music hot spots and historic sites. The two-hour tour only covers about six blocks, so you won't burn a lot of calories, but you will learn a lot about Patsy Cline, Dolly Parton, Keith Urban, and others who made the city what it is. Tours depart from the Ernest Tubb Record Shop on Lower Broad.

MAP 1: 417 Broadway, 615/788-6384, www.experiencenashvilletours.com; tour days and times vary; $30 adults, $20 seniors, $15 children under 13

iRide Nashville

Explore Music City atop a different two-wheeled vehicle on a 1.5-hour sanctioned Segway tour. You'll cover about 10 miles (16 km), navigating past pedestrians and tourists stuck in car traffic and passing by many of the big tourist sites, including the Country Music Hall of Fame and Museum and the Bridgestone Arena. Riders must be older than 12. Helmets and other gear are provided, as is Segway training, which is included in the 2.5-hour tour time.

MAP 1: 217 6th Ave. N., 615/244-0555, http://iridenashville.com; 8:30am-2:30pm daily; $49-75 pp

Music City Rollin' Jamboree

There's a joke—funny because it is true—that nothing in Nashville takes place without live music. Music City Rollin' Jamboree is a tour that proves the point. Your guides are professional musicians, and you'll at least get singled out for some audience participation or perhaps be asked to sing along. For 90 minutes you'll roll through the city, hearing stories, catching a bit of a comedy routine, and learning about what makes Nashville sing. You must be 21 and older to see this show on wheels. You are permitted to bring your own beverages, including alcohol (no glass, please), on the bus.

MAP 1: 330 Commerce St., 615/430-3109, http://musiccityrollinjamboree.com; tour times vary; $38 pp

Nashville Ghost Tours

If you're interested in learning about spirits and want to see Nashville's spooky side, Amerighost offers three different Haunted Nashville options, all of which take place after the sun sets, seven nights a week. A hearse tour leaves from Union Station Hotel and visits the city's oldest cemetery; a haunted pub crawl visits the spirits hanging out in the taverns (drink prices are not included), and the main downtown tour discusses ghosts in the Ryman Auditorium and other local legends. Tours require some walking, generally less than half a mile. The main tour begins across the street from the Hermitage Hotel. Tavern goers will be given a meeting spot when they register for the tour.

MAP 1: 6th Ave. N. and Union St., http://amerighost.com; 8pm daily; $20 adults, $15 children 7-12, children under 7 free

United Street Tours

Nashville's Black history is complex and powerful, including events that changed the course of American history. United Street Tours offers 90 minutes of insight into significant places in the city, like Fisk University and the Civil Rights Room at the Nashville Public Library. A shorter tour highlighting Black-owned businesses in the city is also available.

MAP 1: 150 4th Ave. N., 615/447-8107, www.unitedstreettours.com; tour times vary; $29-67

Mint Julep Tours

Tennessee whiskey is one of the area's most distinctive products. One of the best ways to learn about the local spirit is on a van that someone else drives. From air-conditioned comfort and with a designated driver, you can check out several local distilleries on public or custom tours. Routes and length (and prices) vary, with more than nine different distillery options, as well as a stop at the Donut Distillery in East Nashville. Most tours start at the Omni Nashville Hotel. A tour of Nashville murals is always offered.

MAP 1: 250 Rep. John Lewis Way S., 615/436-0187, http://mintjuleptours.com/Nashville; tour times vary; $79-199

Shops

GIFTS

Fire Finch Boutique

Country music sweetheart Taylor Swift has been known to shop here when in town, but it is a favorite of mere mortal locals, too. Fire Finch is the go-to shop for trendy jewelry, handbags, and accessories. Look here for candles, books, scarves, and more. There are a few sweet home decor items, too.

MAP 1: 305 Church St., 615/385-5090, www.welovefirefinch.com; 11am-5pm daily

GOURMET AND SPECIALTY FOODS

Peanut Shop

Walking into the Peanut Shop is a trip back in time. The floorboards creak; nuts are roasting, boiling, or getting candied; and everything is still measured on the original over/under scale. This was the first home of Planters Peanuts and the original destination of generations of Nashvillians on coffee break (as it still is today). Though they specialize in nuts, there's also a generous assortment of candies and, in the summer, soft-serve ice cream.

MAP 1: 19 Arcade Alley, 615/256-3394, http://nashvillenut.com; 9:30am-5pm Mon.-Fri. and during most Art Crawls on the first Sat. of the month

Goo Goo Chocolate Co.

Nashville's legendary candy company has been selling sweets for more than a century. In this flagship interactive shop it serves its full array of treats, plus some varieties

Goo Goo Chocolate Co.

made in the open kitchen and only available on-site. Sign up for a make-your-own chocolate class that would make Willy Wonka's mouth water or use the kiosk to make a custom Goo Goo Cluster on the fly. Pick up a batch of Goo Goo Clusters, King Leo Peppermints, and other treats for folks at home. Goo Goo-branded hats and T-shirts, Hatch Show Print posters, and other goodies are also for sale.

MAP 1: 116 3rd Ave. S., 615/490-6685, http://googoo.com; 10am-7pm daily, hours may vary seasonally

HOME DECOR

TOP EXPERIENCE

✪ Hatch Show Print

Part gallery and part historic landmark, Hatch Show Print is one of the country's best-known places to buy and see printed art. Hatch has been making colorful posters for more than a century, and they design and print handouts, posters, and T-shirts

Everything old is new again, particularly in Nashville, where vintage goods are the height of onstage fashion.

- Folks rummaged their way through yard sales and flea markets long before there was a History Channel show that told them how. But even more people love the hunt for that long-forgotten gem thanks to *American Pickers*, which has been on the air for more than 20 seasons. The show's host, Mike Wolfe, has two Antique Archaeology stores in the country, and one of them is in Nashville (1300 Clinton St., 615/810-9906, http://antiquearchaeology.com). See some of the show's favorite "picks," plus branded merchandise and the occasional real find.

- Other favorite retailers who know how to salvage goods include East Nashville's Old Made Good (3701B Gallatin Pike, 615/432-2882, http:// oldmadegoodnashville.com) and Hip Zipper (1008 Forrest Ave., 615/228-1942, http://hipzipper.com).

- High Class Hillbilly (4604 Gallatin Pike, 615/840-7328, www.highclasshillbilly. com) stocks well-merchandised jewelry, clothing, and boots, some modernized or updated.

- Backslide Vintage (4606 Gallatin Pike, 615/649-8562) is owned by Zack Smith and Caitlin Doyle-Smith, the voices of Smooth Hound Smith. Check out the 1970s and '80s aesthetic in their shop, which is chock-full of period finds.

- Star Struck Vintage Nashville (604 Gallatin Pike, 615/679-9675, www. starstruckvintage.com) is in a funky strip mall. Inside you will find 3,000 square feet of goods packed onto shelves and racks.

- Gaslamp Antique and Decorating Mall (100 Powell Pl., Ste. 200, 615/297-2224, http://gaslampantiques.com) and East Nashville's Wonders on Woodland (1110 Woodland St., 615/226-5300) are known for their furniture and home decor.

- If you'd rather sift through the parts and pieces yourself, Nashville has no shortage of flea markets and thrift stores. For more than 50 years the best bet for furniture, art, and other funky finds has been the Nashville Flea Market (500 Wedgewood Ave., 615/862-5016, www.thefairgrounds.com), held on the fourth weekend of every month at The Fairgrounds Nashville. (In December, the Flea Market is held on the third weekend, due to Christmas.)

in their iconic letterpress style for local and national customers. Visitors to the shop, which is connected to the Country Music Hall of Fame and Museum, can gaze at the cavernous warehouse operation through windows and buy small or large samples of their work, including reproductions of classic country music concert posters. This is a great place to find a special souvenir of your trip to Nashville. Hatch posters are up all over town. If you catch a show at the Ryman, you may have the chance to buy the show's Hatch poster while you're there. If you want to see behind the scenes, book a **tour** ($20 adults, $15 children); they take place several times a day throughout the week. MAP 1: 224 Rep. John Lewis Way S., 615/577-7710, http://hatchshowprint. com; 9:30am-5:30pm Mon.-Thurs., 9:30am-7:30pm Fri.-Sat., 9:30am-6:30pm Sun.

MUSIC
Ernest Tubb Record Shop

The Texas Troubadour, aka Ernest Tubb, founded his famous record store on Broadway in 1947. It remains a solid source of classic and modern country music recordings, as well as DVDs, books, clothing, and souvenirs. At the back of the shop you can see the stage where Ernest Tubb's Midnite Jamboree was recorded and aired after the Grand Ole Opry on Saturday nights. The Jamboree is the second-longest running show on the air and in 2021 returned to this location on Broadway, airing at 10pm every Saturday night. If you're looking for old-fashioned country in an area of town that's gone full-on pop-country, this is a must-stop.

MAP 1: 417 Broadway, 615/255-7503, http://ernesttubb.com; open from 10am Tues.-Sun.

✪ Third Man Records

It may look like a fairly small building, but it houses big ideas. Third Man is a record label, recording studio, and record store all in one. The idea behind the label is simple: All the music in the building has owner (and musician/producer) Jack White's stamp on it in some way. That's not a bad thing. Seven-inch vinyl Blue Series records are recorded by bands traveling through town and recording one or two songs. Green Series records comprise nonmusical ideas: spoken word, poetry, or instructional discussions. There are bands on the label too, with full-length LPs, as well as reissues of unusual and beautiful things. Even those who are not fans of White's own music appreciate the noncountry street cred he gave the city before it was popular. The modern painted exterior makes the shop easy to find. Inside, there's a recording booth where you can opt to make a Music City souvenir of your own stylings.

MAP 1: 623 7th Ave. S., 615/891-4393, http://thirdmanrecords.com; 11am-6pm daily

WESTERN WEAR

Ariat Nashville

You can't leave Nashville without a pair of boots. If you want a stylish, durable, affordable pair, check out this boot shop in the Fifth + Broadway complex. Ariat is a well-known, woman-owned brand available at other shops around town. But they've gone all out in this standalone shop. The dressing room wall is a bright red art element, made of leather and hand stitched—just like their boots. The life-size horse sculpture made of vinyl records, instruments, guitar strings, and belt buckles simply has to be seen in person. Ariat sells a wide selection of styles, including lightweight boots with a flexible, rubber sole, and boots with elastic to accommodate wider calves.

MAP 1: 5034 Broadway Pl., 615/701-6445, www.ariat.com/ariatnashville; 10am-7pm Mon.-Thurs., 10am-9pm Fri.-Sat., 11am-6pm Sun.

Boot Country

It's all about the boots. Boot Country stocks a huge variety and organizes them by size. If you want boots, this is the place to go. If, in fact, you want three pairs of boots, this is the place to go, as they are always "buy one get two free." If you can't fit three pairs of boots in your luggage, organize a couple of friends and you can each get a pair. Buying a single pair is somewhat pricey, and these aren't necessarily custom, high-end boots, but they'll let the folks at home know where you've been on vacation.

MAP 1: 304 Broadway, 615/259-1691, www.twofreeboots.com; 10am-10pm Mon.-Thurs., 10am-11pm Fri.-Sat., 11am-7:30pm Sun.

Lucchese Bootmaker

A boot is not just a boot—at least not in Nashville, where boots are a status symbol as much as footwear. And in a town that loves boots, people really love Lucchese (pronounced "loo-KAY-see"). This luxury brand has been around since 1883, but only since 2012 has it had its own retail shop in The Gulch. The boots (and belts and clothes) are made in the United States, and custom orders are taken.

MAP 1: 503 12th Ave. S., 615/242-1161, http://lucchese.com; 10am-7pm Mon.-Sat., noon-6pm Sun.

Tecovas

Tecovas is a Texas brand, but its classic styles fit right in here. The Fifth + Broadway store is not just a place to try on and buy boots: There's also a free boot shine station, so you can get cleaned up, regardless of what boots you're wearing when you walk in. Enjoy a beer or Topo Chico while you browse. An in-store debosser will imprint your initials on the boots or belts you buy.

MAP 1: 5011 Broadway, 615/787-8027, www.tecovas.com; 10am-8pm Mon.-Sat., 11am-7pm Sun.

Germantown and Capitol View

Map 2

Historic **Germantown** is chock-full of **chef-driven restaurants, bars** locals love to frequent, and leafy streets dotted with historic homes and former factories. The adjacent **Buchanan Arts District** is in a burgeoning neighborhood of restaurants and **artists' studios** and **galleries.** North of downtown, **Capitol View** is home to the **Tennessee State Capitol.**

TOP SIGHTS

- Where to Hear the Bells Ring: **Bicentennial Capitol Mall State Park** (page 78)
- Best Place to Learn about Local History: **Tennessee State Museum** (page 81)

TOP RESTAURANTS

- Best Brisket Tacos: **Butchertown Hall** (page 83)
- Best Reason to Stand in Line for Pizza: **Slim & Husky's** (page 84)

TOP NIGHTLIFE

- Best Place to Hear Non-Country Music: **Nashville Jazz Workshop** (page 85)

TOP RECREATION

- Best-Named Baseball Team: **Nashville Sounds** (page 88)

TOP SHOPS

- Best Place to Buy a Skateboard (Made by a Kid): **Maple Built** (page 90)

GETTING THERE AND AROUND

- Major bus routes: 9, 29, 42

JONES-BUENA VISTA

SALEMTOWN

BUENA VISTA

Tennessee State Museum

CAPITOL VIEW

Frankie Pierce Park

SEE MAP 4

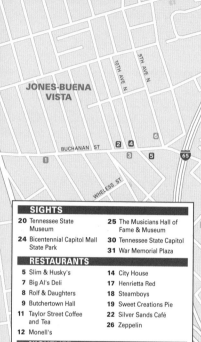

SIGHTS
- **20** Tennessee State Museum
- **24** Bicentennial Capitol Mall State Park
- **25** The Musicians Hall of Fame & Museum
- **30** Tennessee State Capitol
- **31** War Memorial Plaza

RESTAURANTS
- **5** Slim & Husky's
- **7** Big Al's Deli
- **8** Rolf & Daughters
- **9** Butchertown Hall
- **11** Taylor Street Coffee and Tea
- **12** Monell's
- **14** City House
- **17** Henrietta Red
- **18** Steamboys
- **19** Sweet Creations Pie
- **22** Silver Sands Café
- **26** Zeppelin

NIGHTLIFE
- **2** Nashville Jazz Workshop
- **4** Minerva Avenue
- **10** Bearded Iris Brewing
- **28** M.L.Rose Craft Beer and Burgers

ARTS AND CULTURE
- **1** Elephant Gallery
- **32** War Memorial Auditorium
- **33** Nashville Ballet
- **34** Nashville Opera Association
- **35** Nashville Repertory Theatre
- **36** Live on the Green

RECREATION
- **21** Nashville Sounds
- **23** Nash Trash Tours
- **29** Frankie Pierce Park

SHOPS
- **3** Maple Built
- **6** Nisolo
- **15** Wilder
- **16** Abednego

HOTELS
- **13** The Germantown Inn
- **27** TownePlace Suites Nashville Downtown

```
0          400 yds
0          400 m
```
DISTANCE ACROSS MAP
Approximate: 3 mi or 4.8 km

© MOON.COM

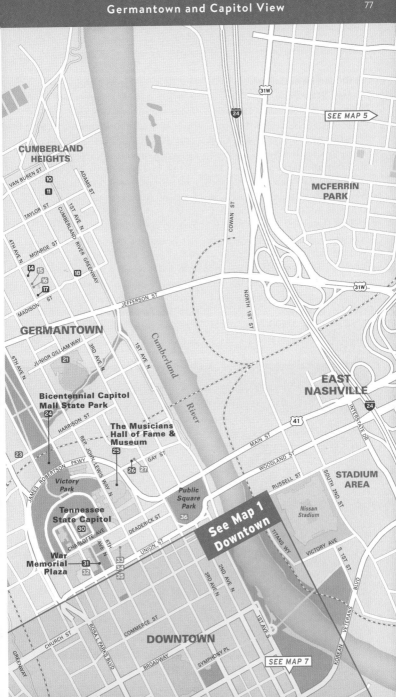

CUMBERLAND HEIGHTS

VAN BUREN ST
10
11
TAYLOR ST
ADAMS ST
1ST AVE N
CUMBERLAND RIVER GREENWAY
MONROE ST
4TH AVE N
14
15
16
18
17
MADISON ST

JEFFERSON ST

31W

SEE MAP 5

MCFERRIN PARK

COWAN ST

NORTH 1ST ST

31W

GERMANTOWN

6TH AVE N
JUNIOR GILLIAM WAY
3RD AVE N
21

1ST AVE N

Cumberland River

EAST NASHVILLE

INTERSTATE DR

Bicentennial Capitol Mall State Park
24

HARRISON ST

23

REP. JOHN LEWIS WAY N

The Musicians Hall of Fame & Museum
25

GAY ST
26 27

41

MAIN ST

US 24

WOODLAND ST

RUSSELL ST

STADIUM AREA

JAMES ROBERTSON PKWY

Victory Park

Public Square Park
36

See Map 1 Downtown

Nissan Stadium

SOUTH 2ND ST

Tennessee State Capitol
30

DEADERICK ST

UNION ST

TITANS WY

VICTORY AVE

1ST ST S

War Memorial Plaza
31
32

CHARLOTTE AVE
6TH AVE N
33
34
35

2ND AVE N

3RD AVE N

1ST AVE S

KOREAN VETERANS BLVD

CHURCH ST

ROSA L PARKS BLVD

COMMERCE ST

DOWNTOWN

GREENWAY

BROADWAY

SYMPHONY PL

SEE MAP 7

Sights

✪ Bicentennial Capitol Mall State Park

Tennessee celebrated its 100th anniversary in 1896 with the construction of the beloved Centennial Park, so it made sense to celebrate its 200th anniversary in much the same way. The Bicentennial Capitol Mall State Park occupies 19 acres on the north side of the capitol building and offers excellent views of the capitol, which towers over it. The mall and the capitol are separated by a steep hill and more than 200 steps, which may look daunting but are worth the climb for the views and access to downtown.

Bicentennial Mall has dozens of features that celebrate Tennessee and Tennesseans, including a 200-foot (61-meter) granite map of Tennessee embedded in concrete; a River Wall with 31 fountains, each representing one of Tennessee's rivers; and a timeline with Tennessee events, inscriptions, and notable quotes from 1796 to 1996. A mile-long path that circles the mall's perimeter is popular with walkers and joggers, and a 2,000-seat amphitheater is used for special events. The park may be a civics lesson incarnate, but it is also a pleasant place to pass the time. Ninety-five carillon bells (for the state's 95 counties) play "The Tennessee Waltz," "Rocky Top," and other Tennessee-themed songs every hour on the hour.

carillon bells at the Bicentennial Capitol Mall State Park

Bicentennial Capitol Mall State Park

Park rangers offer programs and tours year-round, including full moon and firefly walks kid-centric educational programs, and history lectures. Most programs are free but require advance registration. Check the website for specific times.

To the west of the mall is the vibrant Nashville Farmers' Market (900 Rosa L. Parks Blvd., 615/880-2001, http://nashvillefarmersmarket.org), where you can buy fresh produce, flowers, gourmet breakfasts and lunches, and locally made crafts. Locals often picnic in the mall after buying goodies from the market. There's ample free parking here, except when there's a Nashville Sounds baseball game at nearby First Horizon Park. Watch your speed when driving here. Because this is a state park, tickets come from the state police, and they're pricier than Metro Nashville tickets.

MAP 2: 600 James Robertson Pkwy., 615/741-5280, http://tnstateparks.com; sunrise-sunset daily; free

The Musicians Hall of Fame & Museum

Not to be confused with the Country Music Hall of Fame, The Musicians Hall of Fame & Museum (MHOF) honors the people who pick and strum—not necessarily the stars and not the songwriters, but the guitar players, drummers, and others who, regardless of genre or instrument, make a song something to which we want to tap our toes. The MHOF was displaced when the city built the mammoth Music City Center. Located inside Municipal Auditorium, the MHOF has memorabilia and instruments from the unsung heroes of the industry. Inductees are nominated by current members of the American Federation of Musicians and others. The 8,500-square-foot (790-square-meter) Grammy Museum Gallery explores the creative process behind making music, from songwriting to recording.

Nashville Farmers' Market

MAP 2: 401 Gay St., 615/244-3263, www.musicianshalloffame.com; 10am-5pm Mon. and Thurs.-Sat.; $25 adults, $22 seniors and students, $15 youth

Tennessee State Capitol

Set on the top of a hill and built with the formality and grace of classic Greek architecture, the capitol building of Tennessee strikes a commanding pose overlooking downtown Nashville. Construction of the capitol began in 1845; it took 14 years to finish the building. The capitol is made of limestone, much of it from a quarry located near present-day Charlotte and 13th Avenues. The interior marble came from Rogersville and Knoxville, and the gasoliers were ordered from Philadelphia. The capitol was designed by architect William Strickland, who considered it his crowning achievement and is buried in a courtyard on its north end. At the information desk is a printed guide that identifies each of the rooms and many of the portraits and sculptures both inside and outside the building.

If the legislature is not in session, you can go inside both the House and Senate chambers, which look much as they did back in the 19th century. In the second-floor lobby, you can see two bronze reliefs depicting the 14th and 19th amendments to the U.S. Constitution, both of which were ratified by the state of Tennessee in votes held at the capitol. **Self-guided tours** (9am-4pm

Tennessee State Capitol

Mon.-Fri.) are available to groups with eight or fewer people. Ask at the information desk inside for details.

MAP 2: Charlotte Ave. between 6th Ave. and 7th Ave., 615/741-0830, http://capitol.tn.gov; 8am-4pm Mon.-Fri.; free

TOP EXPERIENCE

✪ Tennessee State Museum

The Tennessee State Museum is chock-full of interactive displays that show the breadth and depth of the Volunteer State. The children's area, designed by artist Lucie Rice, is a bright, colorful space where you literally walk into maps of the state. There's a detailed overview of Tennessee history, from Native Americans to the New South era of the 1880s. Exhibits detail the state's political development, explore the Revolutionary and Civil Wars, and profile famous Tennesseans. They also cast a spotlight on the lifestyles and diversions of Tennesseans of various eras, from early frontierspeople to a free African American family before Emancipation. Special artifacts include a musket that belonged to Daniel Boone and the jawbone of a mastodon that called Tennessee home some 10,000 years ago. Check the calendar for free programming, including artist talks. The massive, open building affords great views of Bicentennial Mall and easy access to the Nashville Farmers' Market, which can be a good place for post-museum lunch.

MAP 2: 1000 Rosa L. Parks Blvd., 615/741-2692, www.tnmuseum.org; 10am-5pm Tues.-Sat., 1pm-5pm Sun.; free

Tennessee State Museum

War Memorial Plaza

This stone plaza on the south side of the capitol is an open space surrounded by Doric columns and tablets inscribed with the names of more than 3,000 Tennesseans who died in World War I. It's a lovely place to people-watch. The famous War Memorial Auditorium is also here.

MAP 2: Charlotte Ave. at 7th Ave. N.; dawn-dusk daily

Restaurants

PRICE KEY

$	Entrées less than $15
$$	Entrées $15-25
$$$	Entrées more than $25

ASIAN

Steamboys $

This casual spot was dreamt up by five friends with a common love of Chinese comfort food. Learn the difference between dumplings and *bao,* drink a bubble tea, and savor noodle soup in this affordable, laid-back eatery. Steamboys has several locations, including an outpost in the Assembly Food Hall in the Fifth + Broadway complex.

MAP 2: 1200 2nd Ave. N., 615/678-6336, www.steamboys.com; 11:30am-8:30pm Sun.-Thurs., 11:30am-9:30pm Fri.-Sat.

BARBECUE AND SOUTHERN

Monell's $$

Family-style dining is not for everyone. But if your party wants to share heaping platters of fried chicken and country ham, then you ought to consider a visit to Monell's. Located in a brick house in Germantown, Monell's is the local's go-to for a family brunch or celebratory Southern dinner. Everything is all-you-can-eat, and the menu changes based on the day of the week. Contributing to its family-friendly appeal: Kids under 3 eat free, and children 4-12 dine at a reduced price. There are two other locations across the city.

MAP 2: 1235 6th Ave. N., 615/248-4747, http://monellstn.com; 8am-3pm Mon., 8am-3pm and 5pm-8:30pm Tues.-Sat., 8am-4pm Sun.

Big Al's Deli $

More of a meat-and-three-style cafeteria than a deli, Big Al's serves up homemade Southern specialties from a modest house in Salemtown, just north of Germantown. The menu changes daily, but expect classics like pork chops and jerk chicken served with sweet tea. Whatever you do, don't skip the smashed potatoes. Al will likely come out from behind the kitchen to chat; it's fun listening to his stories.

MAP 2: 1827 4th Ave. N., 615/242-8118, www.bigalsdeliandcatering.com; 7am-2pm Tues.-Fri., 9am-1pm Sat.

Silver Sands Café $

Sophia Vaughn runs her family's meat-and-three restaurant, serving steamed oxtails, pork chops, and other soul food prepared using time-honored recipes passed down through the generations. When the restaurant was damaged by a tornado in 2020, other high-profile chefs in town helped Vaughn reopen. You might see some of them dining while you're here—they'll be waiting in line just like everyone else.

MAP 2: 937 Locklayer St., 615/780-9900, www. silversandsnashville.com; 6am-2:30pm Tues.-Fri., 11am-3pm Sun.

COFFEE SHOPS
Taylor Street Coffee and Tea $

Tucked inside The Space at 100 Taylor (a co-working and event space), this friendly, family-run coffee shop sells coffee, tea, baked goods, and other morning essentials. Sip your coffee while you browse the studios and small retail shops in the building. Taylor Street Coffee also sells cut flowers, so if you need a bouquet for a hostess gift or a hot date, swing by for a farm-fresh option.

MAP 2: 100 Taylor St., 615/707-7582, https://taylorstcoffee.com; 8:30am-4:30pm Mon.-Fri., 8:30am-1:30pm Sat.

NEW AMERICAN
✪ Butchertown Hall $$

Honoring the neighborhood's historic butcher shops, Butchertown Hall has a meat-centric menu that has fans clamoring for a seat. The menu is ample, but most locals opt for either the street-style brisket tacos or platters of meat. The interior is a buzzy, exciting space surrounded in subway tile and sleek, modern fixtures. As a result, the rooms inside can be loud; Butchertown isn't the place for an

intimate conversation. Outside patio dining is a different decibel level.

MAP 2: 1416 4th Ave. N., 615/454-3634; 3pm-9pm Mon.-Thurs., 3pm-10pm Fri.,10am-10pm Sat., 10am-9pm Sun.

Henrietta Red $$

From the team behind Pinewood and Bastion, along with Nashville native and chef Julia Sullivan, Henrietta Red is a seafood-friendly barroom, with an emphasis on seasonal contemporary cooking. The room is sleek and well-designed, and buzzing with activity, making for a space that's loud, but not overbearing. The marble-topped oyster bar is popular with locals from the surrounding Germantown neighborhood, in part because of the quality of oysters, and in part because of the service and experience of dining here. Henrietta Red is one of the more coveted dining spots in town; make a reservation to ensure you get a seat.

MAP 2: 1200 4th Ave. N., 615/490-8042, www.henriettared.com; 5pm-10pm Tues.-Fri., 10am-2pm and 5pm-10pm Sat., 10am-2pm and 5pm-9pm Sun.

Rolf & Daughters $$

While it is one of several farm-to-fork-focused restaurants in Germantown, Rolf & Daughters stands out from the rest. The pasta-centric, rustic, contemporary restaurant has a killer cocktail list. The tables are communal, so you'll get to meet your neighbors as you sample from a menu that changes with the seasons. In addition to the pasta, the chicken liver and crostini is a local favorite. The restaurant is in the century-old Werthan Factory building, which was once a textile factory. Chef Philip Krajeck also owns upscale pizza eatery **Folk** (823 Meridian St.) in East Nashville. MAP 2: 700 Taylor St., 615/866-9897, www.rolfanddaughters.com; 5:30pm-10pm Wed.-Sun.

Zeppelin $$

Located atop the TownePlace Suites hotel, Zeppelin is a rooftop bar and restaurant that feels like a pink cloud floating above the city. Come for snacks and drinks before hitting the town or for a full dinner of oysters, salad, and steak. The open-air brunch is popular with locals as well as hotel guests.

MAP 2: 505 3rd Ave. N., 629/236-0035, www.zeppelinnashville.com; 4pm-10pm Sun.-Thurs., 4pm-11pm Fri.-Sat.

ITALIAN

City House $$$

One of Nashville's most acclaimed restaurants, City House is nestled in a brick building on an unassuming block of Germantown. Chef Tandy Wilson has received many of the nation's important culinary accolades, including being named one of the best chefs in the South by the James Beard Foundation. The menu is modern Italian, often heavy on the pork, with inventive pizzas and cocktails. Service can be slow, particularly if you come with a large group, and the space is loud, so don't expect an intimate conversation. It is always an option to eat at the bar, which is a fun choice if you want to chat with locals. Don't skip the desserts, which are crafted by pastry chef Rebekah Turshen.

MAP 2: 1222 4th Ave. N., 615/736-5838, http://cityhousenashville.com; 5pm-9pm Sun.-Mon., 5pm-10pm Wed.-Sat.

PIZZA

✪ Slim & Husky's $

Perhaps the cornerstone of the burgeoning Buchanan Street district, this North Nashville pizzeria (named for the respective builds of its owners) bakes up über-popular signature pies and design-it-yourself options, plus local beer. Pizzas come in slim (10-inch) and husky (14-inch) sizes. Novel options include a pizza with three kinds of pepperoni and a vegan option with dairy-free cheese. Expect long lines if you come at peak times, particularly on Tuesday evenings. The team also owns **The Rollout** (1006 Buchanan St.), a takeout cinnamon roll joint across the street. There are several other locations of Slim & Husky's, including in Antioch and in the Fifth + Broadway complex, where the shop became the first Black-owned business on Broadway when it in opened in 2021.

MAP 2: 911 Buchanan St., 615/647-7017, www.slimandhuskys.com; 11am-9pm daily

SWEETS

Sweet Creations Pie $

If being in the South makes you think you ought to eat pie, Sweet Creations is where you should do it. Barbara Toms is a native North Nashvillian and bakes up a selection of pies based on her own mother's recipes. You'll find pecan, chocolate chip pecan, sweet potato, and others. If the idea of consuming an entire nine-inch pie on vacation seems too much, don't despair; the three-inch minis are great for a snack.

MAP 2: 942 Jefferson St., 615/255-5519, www.sweetcreationsllc.net; 9am-5pm Thurs.-Sat.

Nightlife

LIVE MUSIC
JAZZ AND BLUES
✪ Nashville Jazz Workshop
The Nashville Jazz Workshop is more than a venue—it is the musical heartbeat of the city's jazz scene. Locals come here for classes, lessons, and lectures. But if you just want to listen, no worries. This is a great venue for jazz in all its definitions, from New Orleans sound to contemporary, performed by big names and serious students. It's not unusual to see a Grammy winner onstage. The Jazz AM series is a free option geared at getting young kids excited about the genre.
MAP 2: 1012 Buchanan St., 615/242-5299, www.nashvillejazz.org; hours and cover cost vary based on show

BARS
Minerva Avenue
Don't get confused: This largely outdoor cocktail bar is named after the street where the owner was raised, not its actual address in the growing Buchanan Arts District. Come here for crafted cocktails and music from the 1970s to present day. Dress the part to match the drinks: There's a standard dress code (no tank tops, gym shoes, or baggy clothing).

MAP 2: 1002 Buchanan St., 615/499-4369, www.minervaavenue. com; 5pm-midnight Sun. and Tues.-Thurs., 5pm-2am Fri.-Sat.

Bearded Iris Brewing
Lots of craft beer taprooms look the same: industrial and casual. Not Bearded Iris! It's reminiscent of a speakeasy, complete with billiards tables, velvet booths, and original art on the walls. Bearded Iris brews IPAs, DIPAs, and seasonal beers from this location, which is easy to access from the Cumberland River Greenway. There's a second, smaller location in the Sylvan Supply building on the city's west side.
MAP 2: 101 Van Buren St., 615/928-7988, https:// beardedirisbrewing.com; noon-10pm Mon.-Thurs., noon-11pm Fri.-Sat., noon-8pm Sun.

M.L.Rose Craft Beer and Burgers
Locals love M.L.Rose, which has expanded from a small craft beer bar with good burgers to a regional chain. The Capitol View outpost has a lovely patio and a central location so you can browse the nearby shops before or after your visit here. The vibe in this neighborhood hangout

is relatively chill in comparison with the rowdier spots downtown. Weekend brunches, with the requisite bloody Marys, are popular, but the focus is the long list of craft beers, with an emphasis on local and regional labels. The beers on tap change often based on season and availability.

MAP 2: 431 11th Ave., 615/729-4445, https://mlrose.com; 11am-midnight Mon.-Fri., 10am-midnight Sat.-Sun.

Arts and Culture

CONCERT SERIES
Live on the Green
During Thursday nights in late summer, Public Square Park transforms for Live on the Green. The outdoor concert series tends to attract a lot of indie rock acts, and in recent years the names have gotten bigger, with performances from Alabama Shakes, Sheryl Crow, and Shakey Graves, among others. Live on the Green's audience is young, cool, and socially aware. Food and arts and crafts vendors line the sidewalks under tents.

MAP 2: 1 Public Sq., Public Square Park, 615/242-5600, www.liveonthegreen. com; 5pm Thurs.and select weekends Aug.-early Sept.; free general admission, $75-125 VIP tickets

GALLERIES
Elephant Gallery
Perhaps the most visible building in the Buchanan Arts District in North Nashville, Elephant Gallery is a place that oozes creativity. Sculptor Alex Lockwood welcomes local and regional artists from all genres to exhibit here. Expect thought-provoking work that is a little bit weird. The gallery also offers working studio space to ceramists and others.

MAP 2: 1411 Buchanan St., 917/969-9755, www.elephantgallery. com; noon-6pm Tues.-Sat. and by appointment; free

War Memorial Auditorium

PERFORMANCE VENUES
War Memorial Auditorium
Built in 1925 to honor Tennesseans who died in World War I, the War Memorial Auditorium is one of several live music venues that were once the home of the Grand Ole Opry (in this case 1939-1943). After the floods of 2010, it again hosted the Opry while the Opry House was under renovation. The space has a

crescent-shaped stage and is known for having good acoustics, which attracts a wide variety of acts. Today the venue welcomes regular songwriter nights, live musical acts, comedians, and others, including live public radio tapings.

MAP 2: 301 6th Ave. N., 615/782-4030, http://wmarocks.com; showtimes and ticket prices vary

BALLET
Nashville Ballet

Founded in 1981 as a civic dance company, the Nashville Ballet became a professional dance company in 1986. Entertaining more than 40,000 patrons each year, the ballet performs both classical and contemporary pieces. The 22-person company often performs at Andrew Jackson Hall,

part of the Tennessee Performing Arts Center. Productions have included traditional story ballets such as *Romeo and Juliet, The Nutcracker,* and *Sleeping Beauty* as well as more modern-minded works from choreographers such as George Balanchine and Jiri Kylian.

MAP 2: Andrew Jackson Hall, 505 Deaderick St., 615/297-2966 ext. 710, http://nashvilleballet.com; box office 10am-6pm Mon.-Fri. and 90 minutes prior to any performance; showtimes and ticket prices vary

OPERA
Nashville Opera Association

Middle Tennessee's only opera association, the Nashville Opera Association puts on an average of four mainstage performances per

Elephant Gallery

season (Oct.-Apr.) and does a six-week tour to area schools. The opera performances typically take place at the Andrew Jackson Hall, part of the Tennessee Performing Arts Center. The opera's headquarters in Midtown, the **Noah Liff Opera Center** (3622 Redmon St.), hosts smaller performances and private events.

MAP 2: Andrew Jackson Hall, 505 Deaderick St., 615/832-5242, http:// nashvilleopera.org; box office 9am-5pm Mon.-Fri.; showtimes and ticket prices vary

THEATER
Nashville Repertory Theatre

The Nashville Repertory Theatre is Tennessee's largest professional theater company. It stages big-name shows and off-Broadway productions annually. The Rep performs in the Andrew Johnson Theater, part of the Tennessee Performing Arts Center. Some of their productions have included *Sense and Sensibility*, *Sweeney Todd*, and *Doubt*. The season runs October-May.

MAP 2: Andrew Johnson Theater, 505 Deaderick St., 615/782-4040, https:// nashvillerep.org; box office 10am-5pm Mon.-Fri., showtimes and ticket prices vary

Festivals and Events

Oktoberfest

Held in Germantown north of the Bicentennial Mall, Oktoberfest is a weekend tradition enhanced by its setting in what was historically Nashville's German enclave. The festival events include a walk/run, church services, a Dachshund Derby, a bratwurst-eating contest, and a street fair with German music, food, and other entertainment. Oktoberfest usually takes place in early or mid-October.

Germantown: www. thenashvilleoktoberfest.com; Oct., free

Recreation

SPECTATOR SPORTS
BASEBALL
✪ Nashville Sounds

What an appropriate name for a minor league baseball team in Music City. The Sounds are a AAA affiliate of the Oakland A's, and they play about 40 home games a year April-September. In 2015 the Sounds got a new stadium, now called **First Horizon Park.** The stadium was built on the site of Sulphur Dell, which was Nashville's baseball stadium from 1885 to 1963. In the 1940s, it was also where the Nashville Cubs, a Negro League team, played their games.

Inside the stadium there's a full miniature golf course called The Country Club, which was designed by local artists. You can't miss the **guitar-shaped scoreboard,** complete with a view of the skyline behind it. In right field, **The Band Box** is a delicious place to hang out during the game. You'll find gourmet spins on classic burgers and hot dogs, plus options like a quinoa chopped salad. Alcoholic drinks include fun frozen cocktails and local craft beers. There are also board games and other diversions if the baseball isn't entertaining enough. Note: Junior Gilliam Way was once called Jackson Street, so some GPS maps may still list the stadium at 401 Jackson Street.

MAP 2: 19 Junior Gilliam Way, 615/690-4487, http://nashvillesounds.com; box office 9am-5pm or 8th inning on game days Mon.-Fri., 10am-8th inning on game days Sat.-Sun. Apr.-Sept.; tickets $10-40

Frankie Pierce Park

Named for Juno Frankie Pierce, a Black suffragist who worked for equality in her native Nashville, this is a joyful 2.5-acre urban park. It includes colorful murals honoring Pierce and the suffrage movement, playground equipment, a dog park, and more. If you are looking for something less active you can sit and watch the trains lumber along the tracks that border the park. Bike or walk along the Gulch Greenway to get to the heart of The Gulch neighborhood.

MAP 2: 130 LifeWay Plaza, 6am-11pm daily

First Horizon Park, home to the Nashville Sounds

TOURS
Nash Trash Tours

Nashville's most notorious tour guides are Sheri Lynn and Brenda Kay Jugg, sisters who ferry good-humored tourists around town in a big pink school bus. A Nash Trash Tour is a raunchy, rollicking, rib-tickling tour of city attractions, some of which you won't even find in this guidebook. Be prepared to be the butt of some of the jokes yourself—their "I Got Trashed" T-shirts have a double meaning. You'll snack on canned cheese, and there's even a pit stop to buy beer.

These tours are not appropriate for children or adults who aren't comfortable laughing at themselves and others. As Sheri Lynn says: "If we haven't offended you, just give us some time." Nash Trash Tours sell out early and often. If you think you want this perspective on the city, make your reservation now. Tours depart from the Nashville Farmers' Market (900 Rosa Parks Blvd.).

MAP 2: Meeting point: 900 Rosa Parks Blvd., 615/226-7300, www.nashtrash. com; generally 11am and 2pm daily; $35-40

Shops

CLOTHING AND ACCESSORIES
Abednego

One of Germantown's sleek boutiques, Abednego carries clothes and accessories made in the United States—some is even crafted by Nashville designers. Owned by a local musician, Abednego stocks goods for men and women in a minimalist loftlike environment. The emphasis is on fashion-forward, yet affordable, togs you can't find elsewhere.

MAP 2: 1210 4th Ave. N., 615/712-6028, www.abednegoboutique.com; 11am-5pm Tues.-Fri., 11am-6pm Sat., 11am-4pm Sun.

Nisolo

Feel guilty about shopping for shoes? Enter Nisolo. The company offers classic men's and women's leather shoes and accessories—all made without extra bells or whistles—by Peruvian craftspeople. The people who make the goods are paid more than a fair wage and have access to job training. The production processes are also light on the carbon footprint. The shop is in the maker-friendly Buchanan Arts District and a good stop for a stroll in the area.

MAP 2: 1803 9th Ave. N., 615/953-1087, http://nisolo.com; 10am-5:30pm Mon.-Fri., 11am-5pm Sat., 1pm-5pm Sun.

GIFTS
✪ Maple Built

Perhaps Nashville's best-loved social enterprise, Maple Built teaches youths from low-income communities to make high-end wood skateboards by hand. The craftsmanship is clear in every piece. Come check out their workshop in the Buchanan Arts District (complete with a skate park) and peruse the handmade goods, T-shirts, hats, and other apparel.

MAP 2: 1003 Buchanan St., no phone, www.maplebuilt.com; 1:30pm-5:30pm Mon.-Fri.

HOME DECOR

Wilder

New York transplants Ivy and Josh brought their interior design eyes to the South. The duo opened a Germantown atelier to show off the kinds of wares with which they can transform a home. Come browse the furnishings, textiles, lighting, mirrors, and more, all with a modern sensibility and many not found elsewhere in the area.

MAP 2: 1212 4th Ave. N., 615/679-0008, www.wilderlife.com; 10am-5pm Mon-Fri.

Music Row, Midtown and 12 South

Maps 3 & 4

Midtown is where the work gets done: It's home to Music Row, where record deals are signed. The 12 South neighborhood is abuzz with activity: It boasts thoughtful **boutique shopping,** compelling restaurants, and an **active nightlife,** from **live music venues** to **comedy clubs.** The area lends itself to leisurely strolls down neighborhood streets. The **Belmont** and **Vanderbilt University** campuses bring **youthful energy** to the area.

TOP SIGHTS

- Best Place to Appreciate Greek Architecture: **Parthenon** (page 98)
- Best Spot to Hear the Famed Jubilee Singers: **Fisk University** (page 101)

TOP RESTAURANTS

- Best Culinary Performance: **The Catbird Seat** (page 104)
- Best Old-School Vibe: **Elliston Place Soda Shop** (page 105)

TOP NIGHTLIFE

- Where to Hear Singer-Songwriters: **Bobby's Idle Hour Tavern** (page 108)
- Best Place to Sip Whiskey: **Corsair Artisan Distillery** (page 111)

TOP ARTS AND CULTURE

- World-Class Art Collection: **Carl Van Vechten Gallery** (page 115)
- Where to Meet the Bard: **Nashville Shakespeare** (page 117)

TOP SHOPS

- Best Place to Buy Nashville-Style Kicks: **Planet Cowboy** (page 121)

GETTING THERE AND AROUND

- Major bus routes: 5, 17, 21, 25

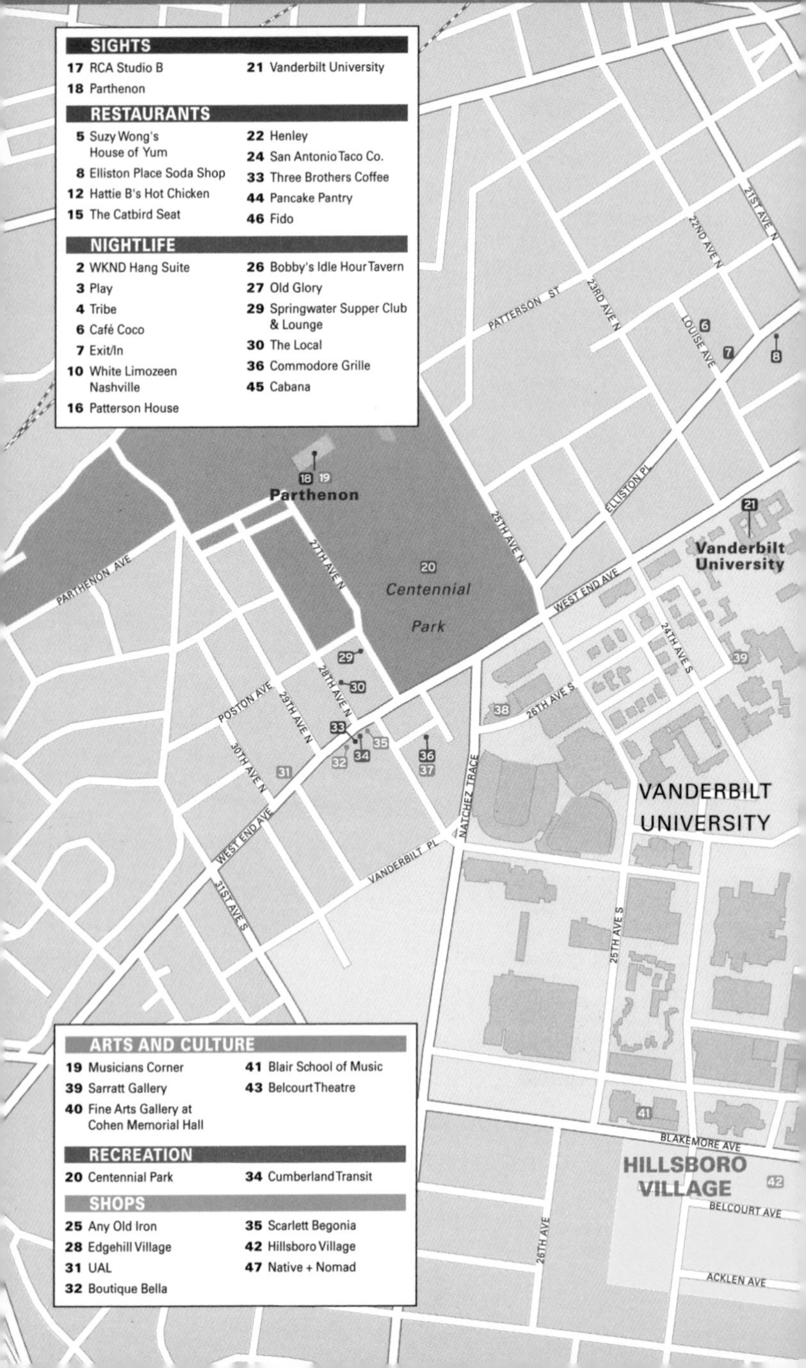

SIGHTS
17 RCA Studio B
18 Parthenon
21 Vanderbilt University
RESTAURANTS
5 Suzy Wong's House of Yum
8 Elliston Place Soda Shop
12 Hattie B's Hot Chicken
15 The Catbird Seat
22 Henley
24 San Antonio Taco Co.
33 Three Brothers Coffee
44 Pancake Pantry
46 Fido
NIGHTLIFE
2 WKND Hang Suite
3 Play
4 Tribe
6 Café Coco
7 Exit/In
10 White Limozeen Nashville
16 Patterson House
26 Bobby's Idle Hour Tavern
27 Old Glory
29 Springwater Supper Club & Lounge
30 The Local
36 Commodore Grille
45 Cabana
ARTS AND CULTURE
19 Musicians Corner
39 Sarratt Gallery
40 Fine Arts Gallery at Cohen Memorial Hall
41 Blair School of Music
43 Belcourt Theatre
RECREATION
20 Centennial Park
34 Cumberland Transit
SHOPS
25 Any Old Iron
28 Edgehill Village
31 UAL
32 Boutique Bella
35 Scarlett Begonia
42 Hillsboro Village
47 Native + Nomad
21ST AVE N
22ND AVE N
23RD AVE N
PATTERSON ST
LOUISE AVE
ELLISTON PL
25TH AVE N
Parthenon
Vanderbilt University
PARTHENON AVE
27TH AVE N
Centennial Park
WEST END AVE
24TH AVE S
28TH AVE N
POSTON AVE
29TH AVE N
26TH AVE S
30TH AVE N
NATCHEZ TRACE
VANDERBILT UNIVERSITY
VANDERBILT PL
31ST AVE S
25TH AVE S
BLAKEMORE AVE
HILLSBORO VILLAGE
BELCOURT AVE
26TH AVE
ACKLEN AVE

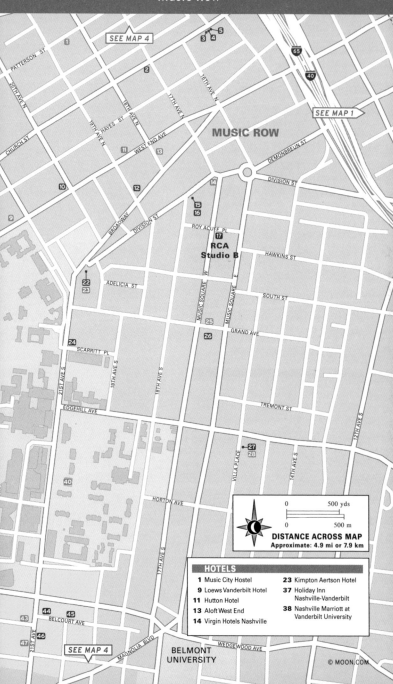

MUSIC ROW

RCA
Studio B

HOTELS

1 Music City Hostel
9 Loews Vanderbilt Hotel
11 Hutton Hotel
13 Aloft West End
14 Virgin Hotels Nashville

23 Kimpton Aertson Hotel
37 Holiday Inn
    Nashville-Vanderbilt
38 Nashville Marriott at
    Vanderbilt University

0   500 yds
0   500 m
DISTANCE ACROSS MAP
Approximate: 4.9 mi or 7.9 km

SEE MAP 4

BELMONT
UNIVERSITY

© MOON.COM

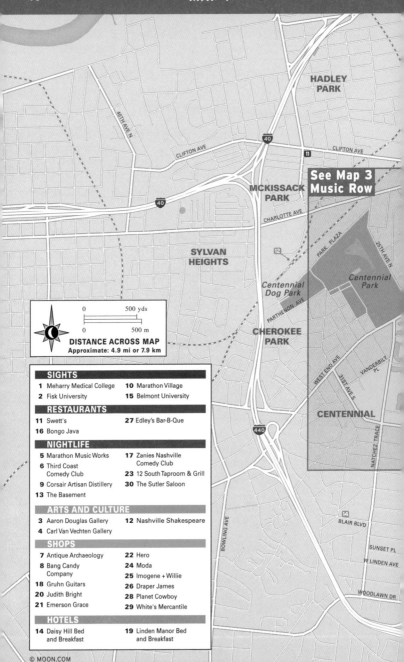

HADLEY
PARK

MCKISSACK
PARK

See Map 3
Music Row

SYLVAN
HEIGHTS

Centennial
Dog Park

Centennial
Park

CHEROKEE
PARK

CENTENNIAL

0   500 yds
0   500 m

DISTANCE ACROSS MAP
Approximate: 4.9 mi or 7.9 km

SIGHTS	
1 Meharry Medical College	**10** Marathon Village
2 Fisk University	**15** Belmont University

RESTAURANTS	
11 Swett's	**27** Edley's Bar-B-Que
16 Bongo Java	

NIGHTLIFE	
5 Marathon Music Works	**17** Zanies Nashville
6 Third Coast	Comedy Club
Comedy Club	**23** 12 South Taproom & Grill
9 Corsair Artisan Distillery	**30** The Sutler Saloon
13 The Basement	

ARTS AND CULTURE	
3 Aaron Douglas Gallery	**12** Nashville Shakespeare
4 Carl Van Vechten Gallery	

SHOPS	
7 Antique Archaeology	**22** Hero
8 Bang Candy	**24** Moda
Company	**25** Imogene + Willie
18 Gruhn Guitars	**26** Draper James
20 Judith Bright	**28** Planet Cowboy
21 Emerson Grace	**29** White's Mercantile

HOTELS	
14 Daisy Hill Bed	**19** Linden Manor Bed
and Breakfast	and Breakfast

© MOON.COM

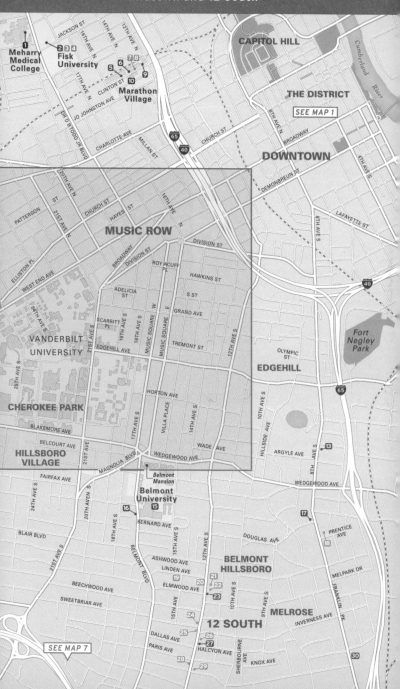

CAPITOL HILL

Cumberland River

JACKSON ST

18TH AVE N

17TH AVE N

14TH AVE N

12TH AVE N

1 Meharry Medical College

2 3 4 Fisk University

5 6 7 8

10 9

Marathon Village

CLINTON ST

JO JOHNSTON AVE

DR D B TODD JR BLVD

CHARLOTTE AVE

MILLAN ST

65

40

CHURCH ST

THE DISTRICT

SEE MAP 1

8TH AVE N

Broadway

4TH AVE S

DEMONBREUN ST

DOWNTOWN

LAFAYETTE ST

8TH AVE S

40

PATTERSON

21ST AVE N

20TH AVE N

CHURCH ST

HAYES ST

16TH AVE N

MUSIC ROW

DIVISION ST

ELLISTON PL

WEST END AVE

Broadway

DIVISION ST

ROY ACUFF PL

HAWKINS ST

S ST

ADELICIA ST

GRAND AVE

24TH AVE N

21ST AVE S

VANDERBILT UNIVERSITY

SCARRITT PL

19TH AVE S

18TH AVE S

MUSIC SQUARE W

MUSIC SQUARE E

TREMONT ST

EDGEHILL AVE

12TH AVE S

OLYMPIC ST

EDGEHILL

Fort Negley Park

65

25TH AVE N

CHEROKEE PARK

HORTON AVE

VILLA PLACE

14TH AVE S

BLAKEMORE AVE

17TH AVE S

10TH AVE S

HILLSIDE AVE

8TH AVE S

13

BELCOURT AVE

HILLSBORO VILLAGE

21ST AVE S

MAGNOLIA BLVD

WADE AVE

WEDGEWOOD AVE

ARGYLE AVE

FAIRFAX AVE

Belmont Mansion

Belmont University

WEDGEWOOD AVE

24TH AVE S

20TH AVE S

16

15

BELMONT BLVD

15TH AVE S

12TH AVE S

BERNARD AVE

DOUGLAS AVE

17

PRENTICE AVE

18

BLAIR BLVD

ASHWOOD AVE

LINDEN AVE

BELMONT HILLSBORO

MELPARK DR

21ST AVE S

BEECHWOOD AVE

19

ELMWOOD AVE

20

21

22

23

10TH AVE S

8TH AVE S

FRANKLIN PK

SWEETBRIAR AVE

15TH AVE S

24

MELROSE

INVERNESS AVE

SEE MAP 7

DALLAS AVE

25

26

12 SOUTH

PARIS AVE

27

HALCYON AVE

SHERBOURNE AVE

KNOX AVE

28

29

30

Sights

MUSIC ROW

✪ Parthenon

No, your eyes are not deceiving you. That is, in fact, a life-size replica of the Greek Parthenon in Centennial Park. In 1893, funds began to be raised for a major exposition that would celebrate the 1896 centennial of the state of Tennessee. Though the exposition would start a year late, in 1897, it exceeded all expectations. The old West Side Race Track was converted to a little city with exhibit halls dedicated to transportation, agriculture, machinery, minerals, forestry, and African American history and culture, among other themes. It had Chinese, Cuban, and Egyptian villages; a midway; and an auditorium. The exposition attracted 1.7 million people over its six-month run.

When the exposition closed in the fall of 1897, all the exhibit halls were torn down except for the replica of the Parthenon, which had housed an art exhibit during the centennial. The exposition grounds were made into a public park, aptly named Centennial Park, and Nashvillians continued to admire their Parthenon. The replica had been built out of wood and plaster, and it was designed only to last through the centennial. Remarkably, it survived well beyond that. But by the 1920s, the Parthenon was crumbling. City officials, responding to public outcry to save the Parthenon, had it rebuilt in tinted concrete. Today the Parthenon remains one of Nashville's most iconic landmarks.

It is a monument to the creativity and energy of the New South and to Nashville's distinction as the Athens of the South.

statue of Athena in the Parthenon

You can see the Parthenon by visiting Centennial Park. Pathways, both pedestrian and vehicular, show off the structure from all sides. You are encouraged to climb its steps and walk onto it. It is, in many respects, most beautiful from the outside, particularly at night: An automatic lighting system slowly comes on at dusk and replicates the way it would have been lit in ancient Greece.

As breathtaking as it is from the exterior, it is worth paying to go inside the Parthenon, where there are three gallery spaces; the largest is used to display works from its permanent collection of 63 pieces of American art. The other two galleries host interesting changing exhibits. Upstairs is the remarkable

Vanderbilt University

42-foot statue of the goddess Athena by local sculptor Alan LeQuire. *Athena* is designed to replicate what the statue would have looked like in its original form. In ancient Greece, the statue would have been seen from a distance. Luckily, in Nashville, Athena's gilded features are front and center.

MAP 3: 2500 West End Ave., 615/862-8431, http://nashville.gov/parthenon; 9am-7pm Mon.-Thurs., 9am-4:30pm Fri.-Sat., 12:30pm-4:30pm Sun.; $10 adults, $8 seniors and children

RCA Studio B

As a rule, the music labels in Music Row are open for business, not tours. The lone exception is RCA Studio B. The RCA studio was the second recording studio in Nashville and the place where artists including the Everly Brothers, Roy Orbison, Dolly Parton, Elvis Presley, and Hank Snow recorded hits. Also called the RCA Victor Studio, this nondescript studio operated from 1957 to 1977. Visitors on the one-hour tour, which departs from the Country Music Hall of Fame downtown, hear anecdotes about recording sessions at the studio and see rare footage of a 1960s Dottie West recording session. Tours can only be purchased in conjunction with admission to the Country Music Hall of Fame.

MAP 3: 1611 Roy Acuff Pl., 615/416-2001, http://studiob.org; tours hourly 10:30am-4:30pm daily; $46 adults, $36 youth

RCA Studio B

Vanderbilt University

Named for philanthropist and robber baron Commodore Cornelius Vanderbilt, who donated $1 million in 1873 to found a university that would "contribute to strengthening the ties which should exist between all sections of our common country," Vanderbilt University is now one of the region's most respected institutions of higher education. A private research university, Vanderbilt has an enrollment of 6,800 undergraduates and 5,900 graduate students. The university comprises 10 schools, a medical center, public policy center, and The Freedom Forum First Amendment Center. Vanderbilt's campus life is vibrant and includes a daily roll call of lectures, recitals, exhibits, and other special events for students, locals, and visitors alike. Check http://calendar.vanderbilt.edu for an up-to-date listing of all campus events. Vanderbilt offers a self-guided tour of the campus's trees, which form the Vanderbilt Arboretum. Most trees on the tour are native trees common to Nashville and Middle Tennessee. Download a podcast, print a copy of the tour from the website (http://vanderbilt.edu/trees/tours), or contact the university for more information.

Designated visitor parking is in several lots on the Vanderbilt campus. Look on the eastern edge of the sports facilities parking lot off Natchez Trace, in the Wesley Place parking lot off Scarritt Place, or in the Terrace Place parking lot between 20th and 21st Avenues north of Broadway. Pay attention to the signs, as the university parking monitors do ticket those who park in prohibited areas.

MAP 3: 2201 West End Ave., 615/322-7311, http://vanderbilt.edu; 24 hours daily; free

MIDTOWN AND 12 SOUTH

Belmont University

Founded as a school for girls in 1890, in 1991 it became Belmont University, a higher-education institution with links to the Tennessee Baptist Convention. Today Belmont is a fast-growing university with highly respected music and music business programs. In 2011 the school opened the first new law school in the state in the last century and in 2021 broke ground on a new medical school. Belmont, which has hosted two presidential debates, has about 6,400 students. Campus tours are available twice a day on weekdays.

Several Belmont facilities are worth visiting, including the **Curb Event Center** (2002 Belmont Blvd., 615/460-8500), which hosts sporting events, concerts, and lectures. The campus is also home to **Belmont Mansion** (1900 Belmont Blvd., 615/460-5459, www.belmontmansion.com; 9:45am-3:30pm Mon.-Sat., 10:45am-3:30pm Sun.; $16 adults, $15 seniors, $7 youth ages 13-18, $5 children ages 6-12), an 1853 restored Victorian mansion with an art collection and manicured gardens. Though the Belmont campus has increased its scholarship about the enslaved people who built the school's structures, visiting these sites (the mansion in particular) may not be of interest to all travelers.

MCKISSACK AND MCKISSACK, ARCHITECTS

The oldest African American architectural firm in Tennessee can trace its roots to Moses McKissack (1790-1865), a member of the West African Ashanti tribe. Sold into slavery to William McKissack of North Carolina and then Middle Tennessee, Moses became a master builder. He passed his knowledge on to his son, Gabriel Moses McKissack, born in 1840. Gabriel Moses passed his knowledge of the building trade to his own son, Moses McKissack III, born in 1879.

Moses McKissack III was born in Pulaski, where he received a basic education in the town's segregated schools. In 1890 he was hired by a local white architect. Until 1905, McKissack designed and built homes throughout the area, including many in Mount Pleasant in Maury County. He developed a reputation as an excellent architect and tradesman.

In 1905 McKissack moved to Nashville, where he started his own construction company. Within a few years, he was working on major projects. He built a home for the dean of architecture and engineering at Vanderbilt University and the Carnegie Library at Fisk University. In 1922, Moses's brother, Calvin, joined him, and they opened McKissack and McKissack, Tennessee's first African American architectural firm.

The McKissacks have continued to distinguish themselves in the building industry, and they have also kept the business in the family. Since 1990 the company has been led by Deryl McKissack, a fifth-generation McKissack. The firm employs more than 170 people and has offices across the country.

To see some of their work around town, check out MLK Magnet School (613 17th Ave. N.) and the Morris Memorial Building (330 Charlotte Ave.).

MAP 4: 1900 Belmont Blvd., 615/460-6000, www.belmont.edu; 24 hours daily; free

Jubilee Hall, Fisk University

TOP EXPERIENCE

✪ Fisk University

Founded in 1866 to educate formerly enslaved people, Fisk University has a long and proud history as one of the United States' foremost Black colleges. W. E. B. Du Bois attended Fisk, graduating in 1888, and Booker T. Washington married a Fisk alumna and sent his own children to Fisk. In more modern times, Knoxville native and poet Nikki Giovanni attended Fisk. Fisk sits at the corner of Jefferson Street and Dr. D. B. Todd Jr. Boulevard, about 10 blocks west of downtown Nashville. The campus is a collection of elegant red-brick buildings set on wide green lawns, though a few more modern buildings, including the library, break up the classical feel. The oldest Fisk building is **Jubilee Hall,** on the north end of the campus, which was the first permanent building constructed for the education of African Americans in the country. It was built with money raised by the Fisk Jubilee Singers, who popularized the spiritual during a world

THE JUBILEE SINGERS

In 1871, Fisk University needed money. Buildings at the school established in old Union army barracks in 1866 were decaying, while more and more African Americans came to seek education.

So in what might now be considered a very Nashville-style idea, the school choir withdrew all the money from the university's treasury and left on a world tour. The nine singers were Isaac Dickerson, Maggie Porter, Minnie Tate, Jennie Jackson, Benjamin Holmes, Thomas Rutling, Eliza Walker, Green Evans, and Ella Sheppard. Remembering a biblical reference to the Hebrew "year of the jubilee," Fisk treasurer and choir manager George White gave them their name, the Fisk Jubilee Singers.

The choir struggled at first, but before long audiences were singing their praises. They toured first the American South, then the North, and in 1873 sailed to England for a successful British tour. Their audiences included William Lloyd Garrison, Wendell Phillips, Ulysses S. Grant, William Gladstone, Mark Twain, Johann Strauss, and Queen Victoria. Songs like "Swing Low, Sweet Chariot" and "Nobody Knows the Trouble I've Seen" moved audiences to tears. The singers introduced the spiritual to mainstream audiences and erased negative misconceptions about African Americans and African American education.

In 1874 the singers returned to Nashville. They had raised enough money to pay off Fisk's debts and build the university's first permanent structure, an imposing Victorian Gothic six-story building now called Jubilee Hall. It was the first permanent structure solely for the education of African Americans in the United States.

Every October 6, the day in 1871 that the singers first departed Fisk, the university recalls their struggle and their triumph with a convocation featuring the modern-day Jubilee Singers. It's free and open to the public.

The singers—an always-impressive group of students—still perform regularly. If you have an opportunity to hear them, don't miss it.

---

tour 1871-1874. Another notable building is the Little Theatre, a white clapboard building that once served as a Union hospital during the Civil War.

The campus is beautiful from many approaches but is particularly striking if you enter on 17th Avenue North from the south, where you will be greeted by the big iron Fisk University gate. There is some metered and free street parking on the side streets in the neighborhood, and campus lots are well marked for visitors.

MAP 4: 1000 17th Ave. N., 615/329-8500, www.fisk.edu; 24 hours daily; free

Marathon Village

This neighborhood dates back to 1881. A former auto factory, Marathon Village now houses sleek urban condos, restaurants, a tasting room for Corsair Artisan Distillery, Bang Candy Company, and shops like Antique Archaeology, owned by Mike Wolfe of TV's *American Pickers* fame. Live music venue Marathon Music Works brings out the locals, and architecture and history buffs love the buildings' bones.

MAP 4: Bordered by 12th Ave., Jo Johnston Ave., 16th Ave., and Clinton St., www.marathonvillage.com

Meharry Medical College

Just across Dr. D. B. Todd Jr. Boulevard from Fisk University is

Marathon Village

Meharry Medical College, the largest private, comprehensive, historically Black institution educating medical professionals. It was founded in 1876 as the Medical Department of the Central Tennessee College of Nashville, under the auspices of the Freeman's Aid Society of the Methodist Episcopal Church. At one time in its history, Meharry was responsible for graduating more than half of all African American doctors and nurses in the United States. Today it has an enrollment of almost 800 students.

MAP 4: 1005 Dr. D. B. Todd Jr. Blvd., 615/327-6000, http://home.mmc.edu; 24 hours daily; free

Restaurants

PRICE KEY

$	Entrées less than $15
$ $	Entrées $15-25
$ $ $	Entrées more than $25

MUSIC ROW

HOT CHICKEN
Hattie B's Hot Chicken $

For some people, Nashville-style hot chicken, that spicy local delicacy, is only legitimate if it is served pan fried in a shack without air-conditioning or adequate seating. If that's your criteria, then this is not the spot for you. But for many people Hattie B's is the answer to their hot chicken prayers. The recipes are delicious, with options for everyone, ranging from mild to Shut the Cluck Up, with all the amenities of a traditional restaurant, including beer and some vegetarian-friendly side dishes. Hattie B's has several locations, including ones in

West Nashville and Melrose, that often have shorter lines. The restaurant has expanded to Memphis, Birmingham, Las Vegas, and Atlanta.

MAP 3: 112 19th Ave. S., 615/678-4794, http://hattieb.com; 11am-10pm Mon.-Thurs., 11am-midnight Fri.-Sat., 11am-4pm Sun.

NEW AMERICAN
☼ The Catbird Seat $$$

To describe The Catbird Seat as a restaurant is a bit of a misnomer. It is a culinary performance that happens to include dinner. There are just 22 seats in this U-shaped space. Once you get a coveted reservation (available online only), you'll be treated to three hours of wines paired with a seasonal meal made before your eyes. Some of the ingredients sound odd, but most of them will blow your mind. Catbird works something like a chef incubator, with new chefs coming in every year or so. Chefs who have worked their magic here include Josh Habiger, Trevor Moran, Liz Johnson, and Brian Baxter. Reservations are opened 30 days in advance. The 9- to 11-course tasting menu is $145 without drinks. The nonalcoholic pairings are as inventive as the wines.

MAP 3: 1711 Division St., 615/810-8200, www.thecatbirdseatrestaurant.com; 5:30pm-9pm Wed.-Sat.

Henley $$$

This sleek American brasserie inside the shiny Kimpton Aertson Hotel feels like a Southern mansion tucked inside a stream-lined new building. Headed by Kristin Beringson, a past winner of the TV show *Chopped,* Henley is a full-service hotel restaurant, so expect breakfast, brunch, lunch, and dinner, plus an impressive lineup of signature cocktails. The cuisine is seasonal, and dishes are meant for sharing, which is easy to do from a comfy back-room leather bench or up front at the gleaming popular bar. Happy hour is particularly affordable and features signature whiskey cocktails.

MAP 3: 2023 Broadway, 615/340-6378, www.henleynashville.com; 7am-10am and 5pm-10pm Mon.-Fri., 7am-2pm and 5pm-10pm Sat., 7am-2pm and 5pm-9pm Sun.

ASIAN
Suzy Wong's House of Yum $$

The name of this restaurant reveals that it is not your average Chinese food joint. Owned by *Top Chef* alumnus Arnold Myint, Suzy Wong's has a menu of shared plates with an Asian fusion spirit, combined with an inventive cocktail menu and a high-energy soundtrack. This is a great place to go and paint the town red with friends. The food is fun—think Asian nachos—and there are plenty of vegetarian and gluten-free options on the menu, too. While it might be less than ideal for those who don't want to speak over a din, Suzy Wong's aims to welcome all. On the weekend, come by for the family-friendly Drag'n Brunch (10am-3pm Sat.-Sun.), complete with drag performances.

MAP 3: 1515 Church St., 615/329-2913, www.suzywongsnashville.com; 5pm-10pm Tues.-Thurs., 5pm-11pm Fri., 10am-3pm and 5pm-11pm Sat., 10am-3pm and 5pm-10pm Sun.

Elliston Place Soda Shop

DINERS AND COFFEE SHOPS

✪ Elliston Place Soda Shop $

In today's retro-happy world, it isn't too hard to find an old-fashioned soda shop. But how many of them are the real thing? Elliston Place Soda Shop, near Centennial Park and Vanderbilt, is an interesting holdover from the past. Since 1939 this soda fountain has served milk shakes and pie from a small storefront. In 2021 the restaurant moved next door, with new owners who are committed to preserving the shop's past. The menu features meat-and-three, burgers, and those same pie recipes, as well as the same decor, in an updated space.

MAP 3: 2105 Elliston Pl., 615/327-1090, www.ellistonplacesodashop. com; 6:30am-8:30pm Mon.-Thurs., 6:30am-9pm Fri.-Sat.

Fido $

Fido is more than a coffee shop. It is a place to get work done, watch deals being made, and see and be seen. It's where you'll see music producers, songwriters, Vanderbilt and Belmont students, medical workers, families, and tourists all sharing tables. Take a seat along the front plate-glass windows to watch people as they stroll by the upscale boutiques of Hillsboro Village. Don't let the laid-back vibe fool you; you can get a real meal here, from big salads and sandwiches to pasta dishes, not to mention the daily specials. In addition to Bongo Java coffee, the menu also offers tempting baked goods.

MAP 3: 1812 21st Ave. S., 615/777-3436, www.bongojava.com; 7am-2pm Mon.-Wed., 7am-8pm Thurs.-Sat., 7am-noon Sun.

Pancake Pantry $

There's a lot of hype surrounding Nashville's favorite breakfast restaurant, the Pancake Pantry. Founded in 1961, the Pantry serves some of the most popular pancakes in the city. The menu offers more

105

than 23 varieties, and that doesn't include the waffles. Try the fluffy buckwheat cakes, savory cornmeal cakes, sweet blintzes, or the old standby buttermilk pancakes. The Pantry offers egg-white omelets for the health-conscious, and it's very kid-friendly as well, except for the fact that on weekend mornings, and many weekdays, the line for a seat goes out the door.

MAP 3: 1796 21st Ave. S., 615/383-9333, www.thepancakepantry.com; 6am-3pm Mon.-Fri., 6am-4pm Sat.-Sun.

Pancake Pantry

Three Brothers Coffee $

Vanderbilt students and Centennial Park-goers visit this coffee shop for a boost of caffeine before they go about their day. The shop serves up a cup of joe made from beans that come from a variety of microroasters. You can get a basic cup of drip coffee or an espresso. Specialty drinks change with the seasons. Photographers like the small alleyway next to the front door, an immersive space covered in black-and-white "hieroglitches"—interpretations of Egyptian hieroglyphics created by artist Adrien Saporiti.

MAP 3: 2813 West End Ave., 615/835-2166, www.threebrothers. coffee; 7am-6pm Mon.-Fri., 8am-5pm Sat.

MEXICAN
San Antonio Taco Co. $

This Tex-Mex joint has an obsessive fan base among Vanderbilt students and alumni, who spend hours here downing tacos, soda, and oddly addictive *queso* (cheese) dip served with light, crunchy chips. The soundtrack has literally not changed in 35 years, nor has the decor. But the real appeal of SATCO, as locals call it, is the deck, which is perfect for people-watching while drinking cold beers.

MAP 3: 416 21st Ave. S., 615/327-4322, www.thesatco.com; 11am-11pm Sun.-Thurs., 11am-midnight Fri.-Sat.

MIDTOWN AND 12 SOUTH
BARBECUE AND SOUTHERN
Swett's $$

One of Nashville's most beloved meat-and-threes is Swett's, family owned and operated since 1954. People come from all over the city to eat at this Nashville institution, which combines soul food, barbecue, and Southern cooking with great results. The food is homemade and traditional, down to the real mashed potatoes, the vinegary greens, and the yeast rolls. Swett's is set up cafeteria-style. Start by grabbing dessert—the pies are excellent—and then move on to the good stuff: Country-fried steak, pork chops, meat loaf, fried catfish, and ham are a few of the usual suspects. A standard plate comes with one meat, two sides, and a serving

San Antonio Taco Co.

of either yeast roll or corn bread, but you can add more sides if you like. Draw your own iced tea—sweet or unsweet—at the end of the line, and then find a seat. Swett's also has a location at the Nashville airport.

MAP 4: 2725 Clifton Ave., 615/329-4418, www.swettsrestaurant. com; 11am-8pm daily

Edley's Bar-B-Que $

Edley's is one of the places that changed people's perception of Nashville as a town with legitimate barbecue. Since opening in 2011, they've become an essential smoker on the scene—in part because they offer something for every taste, be it pork, brisket or vegetarian options, plus pork-free sides. In addition to this 12 South outpost, they also have locations in East Nashville and West Nashville.

MAP 4: 2706 12th Ave. S., 615/953-2951, www.edleysbbq.com; 11am-9pm Sun.-Thurs., 11am-10pm Fri.-Sat.

DINERS AND COFFEE SHOPS
Bongo Java $

Nashville's original coffee shop, Bongo Java is popular and community-minded. Located near Belmont University, Bongo Java is regularly full of students chatting, texting, and studying, thanks to free Wi-Fi. Set in an old house with a huge front porch, Bongo feels homey, welcoming, and perhaps a bit more on the laid-back side than other Nashville coffee shops. Breakfast, including Bongo French toast, is served all day. There are several other Bongo Java locations, including Bongo East/Game Point Café in East Nashville, and many restaurants in town serve Bongo coffee.

MAP 4: 2007 Belmont Blvd., 615/385-5282, www.bongojava.com; 7am-8pm daily

Nightlife

MUSIC ROW
LIVE MUSIC
✪ Bobby's Idle Hour Tavern

Over its many years of existence, Bobby's has been Music Row's steadfast purveyor of intimate singer-songwriter nights and cold beer—even through ownership changes and other upheaval. Its location practically guarantees an audience of regulars who know their way around the music biz. Expect an evening of acoustic guitars and good stories told through song. You won't necessarily be shushed during a show here, but you do want to be respectful of the musicians and keep conversation to a minimum.

Remember to tip the musicians when the hat is passed.
MAP 3: 9 Music Sq. W., 615/649-8530, www.bobbysidlehour.com; noon-1am daily; no cover, donations to band encouraged

Commodore Grille

Commodore Grille is nestled inside the Holiday Inn near the Vanderbilt campus. Nothing about that makes it sound like a local hangout. But this has become a favorite listening room for Nashville singer-songwriters who want to perform in a quiet place with a good vibe. Their fans and friends appreciate the low-key nature and relatively

Bobby's Idle Hour Tavern

easy parking. Call ahead to get info on songwriters' nights.

MAP 3: 2613 West End Ave., 615/327-4707; 6am-10am and 5pm-10pm Sun.-Thurs., 7am-11am and 5pm-11pm Fri.-Sat.; no cover

Café Coco

Coffee shop by day, bar and live music venue by night. That describes Elliston Place's Café Coco and, frankly, Nashville as a whole. The space is small, but it offers a wide cross section of live music. Tuesday and Thursday are open-mic nights for songwriters. Metal and rock bands and hip-hop groups play other nights, when the cover is typically $10 or less.

MAP 3: 210 Louise Ave., 615/321-2626, http://cafecoco.com; 8am-9pm Mon.-Thurs., 8am-10pm Fri.-Sun.; cover cost varies by event

Exit/In

Since 1971, the Exit/In has been the city's leading rock music venue, booking alternative acts and even blues and reggae. The club is convenient to the Vanderbilt campus and therefore draws some students, but its history and solid calendar draw a diverse audience of locals. The venue may look a little worn around the edges when the lights are on, but when it is dark and the music is playing, you won't notice. Grab a beer before the show at sibling bar Hurry Back (2212 Elliston Pl., 615/915-0764, www.hurry-back. com).

MAP 3: 2208 Elliston Pl., 615/321-3340, www.exitin.com; hours and cover cost vary by event

BARS
Cabana

In Hillsboro Village, Cabana is a popular place to people-watch and unwind. It is a bar/restaurant/late-night hangout that attracts a youthful and well-dressed crowd from local universities, plus loyal old-timers. Lounge at the bar or in the expansive backyard, or reserve one of the semiprivate cabanas for your party of 2-12. Choose from dozens of beers, wines, and excellent martinis. The happy hour specials are some of the best in town.

MAP 3: 1910 Belcourt Ave., 615/577-2262, www.cabananashville. com; 4pm-10pm Mon.-Fri., 10am-10pm Sat.-Sun.

The Local

Equal parts bar, restaurant, and music venue, The Local draws folks for its 24 beer taps (many local), short but varied food menu (think Korean tacos, a pimento cheese-topped burger, and a daily offering of pie), and live music most every night of the week. Given its location near the Vanderbilt campus, it can be popular with students.

MAP 3: 110 28th Ave. N., 615/320-4339, www.localnash.com; 4pm-2am Mon.-Thurs., 11am-2am Fri.-Sun.

Old Glory

A variety of things bring Nashvillians to this Edgehill Village bar, whether it be the airy, industrial interior (it was a boiler room in the 1920s), the seasonal cocktails, or the DJ sets. You won't find a flashy entrance or even a sign. Get to the entrance (marked by a large gold triangle painted over the brick exterior) in the alley behind nearby restaurant Taco Mamacita. Prepare to be dazzled by the staircase as you descend and by the vision of the two sisters who own the joint.

MAP 3: 1200 Villa Pl. #103, 615/679-0509; 5pm-midnight Sun.-Thurs., 5pm-1am Fri.-Sat.

Patterson House

Cocktails at Patterson House are mixed with care, and as there's no standing room, you're expected to drink them with care, too. You must have a seat in order to be served. This contributes to a civilized cocktail hour but can also mean you'll wait for a spot. This is not a pickup scene, but a place to savor your drink, from its creation to its last drop. Above Patterson House is the acclaimed restaurant The Catbird Seat.

MAP 3: 1711 Division St., no phone, http://thepattersonnashville.com; 5pm-1am Sun.-Thurs., 4pm-2am Fri.-Sat.

Springwater Supper Club & Lounge

There are three things you need to know about Springwater: It's a dive bar. (In fact, it claims to be the oldest dive bar in the state.) The beer is cheap. It's cash only. It's an actual dive bar, not a hip bar trying to be a dive—although somehow it has become hip, either because of this or in spite of it. The musical acts, which perform nightly, are the very definition of eclectic. Though the name says, "supper club," the food here is strictly bar food. Shooting pool at Springwater is a popular pastime.

MAP 3: 115 27th Ave. N., 615/320-0345, http://thespringwater.com; noon-3am daily; cover charge varies, donations to band encouraged

LOUNGES
WKND Hang Suite

The Memphians who opened this welcoming but not casual nightspot describe it as an "anti bar." You'll get great drinks and attentive service with good music as your backdrop. Before 8pm you can wear almost anything (no caps ever). Afterwards, a "no gym shoes, no baggy jeans" dress code applies. Or, in their words, "let's be appropriately dressed for a great night out with like-minded individuals." The bar is 23 and older for women and 25 and older for men. Drink order minimums apply to the booths (called "suites").

MAP 3: 1703 Church St., 615/739-6345, www.wkndhangsuite.com; 5pm-2am Thurs.-Sat., 3pm-8pm Sun.; $10 cover weekends after 10pm

White Limozeen Nashville

Named after a 1989 song and album by Dolly Parton, and with a giant pink chicken-wire sculpture of Dolly, White Limozeen is an explosion of fun on the top level of the Graduate Nashville hotel. Sit in a crushed velvet chair, order a fancy cocktail, take a dip in the rooftop pool, and enjoy life like Dolly does. White Limozeen is 21 and older after 7pm.

MAP 3: 101 20th Ave. N., 615/649-7239, www.graduatehotels.com/ nashville; 3pm-midnight Mon.-Fri., 10am-midnight Sat.-Sun.; no cover

LGBTQ
Play

Play is the city's highest-energy LGBTQ+ club, with drag shows and performances by adult-film stars. Although it is a gay bar, everyone is welcome, as long as they're happy to be here. The drag shows are high quality, but it is the dance floor (right next to the stage) that draws people in. On weekends that dance floor is packed. If you want more room to get your groove on, come on weeknights without drag shows.

MAP 3: 1519 Church St., 615/322-9627, www.playdancebar.com; 6pm-3am Wed.-Sun.; cover cost varies by event

Tribe

The dance floor at this gay club is one of the best in the city, and the atmosphere is hip, fun, and welcoming. You don't have to be LGBTQ to be here; anyone can dance along. Classic cocktails and other specialty drinks are the poison of choice at this Midtown club. It has changed names and owners over the years but has been the go-to gay dance spot for decades.

MAP 3: 1517 Church St., 615/329-2912, www.tribenashville.com; 3pm-1am Wed.-Thurs., 3pm-2am Fri., midnight-2am Sat., midnight-1am Sun.; no cover

MIDTOWN AND 12 SOUTH
LIVE MUSIC
The Basement

The Basement calls itself a cellar full of noise, but it's a good kind of noise. Indie rock is the most common art form here, but they book other acts, too. Admission is 21 and older, unless accompanied by a parent or guardian. The brick walls and subterranean feel give The Basement its cool atmosphere. Its owners are also behind East Nashville's Grimey's New and Preloved Music and The

Basement East. Parking is available behind the club and on side streets.

MAP 4: 1604 8th Ave. S., 615/645-9174, http://thebasementnashville.com; showtimes and cover cost vary; doors open one hour before showtime

Marathon Music Works

Housed in Marathon Village, this venue brings a modern take to an old space. This brick-lined warehouse has two bars, a fun loftlike VIP space, and plenty of room to cut a rug when the acts warrant it. Eclectic acts are booked here; this is definitely not a country-music-only club. There's a parking lot in the back, and sometimes free parking is available on the street. For a preshow drink, stop in William Collier's Room, an adjacent bar that's open before, during, and after shows.

MAP 4: 1402 Clinton St., 615/891-1781, www.marathonmusicworks.com; showtimes and cover cost vary by event; box office noon-6pm Fri. and one hour before showtime

BREWERIES, DISTILLERIES, AND TASTING ROOMS
✪ Corsair Artisan Distillery

This local distillery and brewery (they call it a "brewstillery") makes high-end spirits, including rum, whiskey, moonshine, and vodka, plus high-gravity beers. The team has won industry awards around the globe for its offbeat and limited-edition beverages. You can take a tour of the distillery to see how the whole thing works and then sample up to five of the creations. Afterward, eat some house-made pizza in the taproom. Weekend tours sell out, so book in advance. Corsair's headquarters is in Wedgewood-Houston.

MAP 4: 1200 Clinton St. #110, 615/200-0321, www.corsairdistillery. com; noon-7pm Wed.-Mon.; $14 tour and tasting, $7 tour only, tours free for kids under 12

PUBS
The Sutler Saloon

In the 1970s The Sutler was a dive bar/restaurant owned by country music personality Johnny Potts. In 2014 it was reopened in the same, albeit revitalized, Melrose Theater location. It was immediately embraced by locals who remembered it (as well as those who didn't live in Music City back in the day). The Sutler has an impressive craft cocktail menu, a full food menu, an upstairs saloon, a lower-level cellar called Rambler Cocktail Bar, and a see-and-be-seen vibe.

MAP 4: 2600 8th Ave. S., 615/840-6124, www.thesutler.com; 11am-11pm Tues.-Thurs., 10am-11pm Fri.-Sat., 10am-3pm Sun.

12 South Taproom & Grill

The extensive list of brews on tap has earned 12 South Taproom & Grill a loyal local following. The above-average bar food includes several vegetarian-friendly options, but people come here because of the beer. Expect a crowd—in all likelihood it will be standing room only on weekends. The staff know their stuff and can help direct you to the right brew for your tastes.

MAP 4: 2318 12th Ave. S., 615/463-7552, http://12southtaproom.com; 11am-11pm Sun.-Thurs., 11am-midnight Fri.-Sat.

COMEDY
Zanies Nashville Comedy Club

Zanies books big stand-up comedy acts, like TV stars and stand-up comedians from Aziz Ansari to Maz Jobrani and Chelsea Handler. Go wanting to laugh, and you will likely get what you paid for. There's a two-item minimum of drinks or food, neither of which is particularly remarkable. But you're there for the act, not the menu. No photos or recordings are allowed in the building; when you enter, you'll need to hand over your phone, which will be locked away for the duration of the show.

MAP 4: 2025 8th Ave. S., 615/269-0221, http://nashville.zanies.com; showtimes vary; tickets $15-30, plus a two-item minimum

Third Coast Comedy Club

Located in Marathon Village, Third Coast Comedy Club is Nashville's only brick-and-mortar improv venue, offering about 150 shows a year. Founders Scott Field and Luke Watson created this purpose-built space for Nashville's comedians, who otherwise perform at restaurants or live music venues. The space also hosts sketch, standup, and other types of comedy, and trains aspiring comedians.

MAP 4: 1310 Clinton St., 615/745-1009, www.thirdcoastcomedy.club; tickets generally $10-12

TENNESSEE WHISKEY— AND WHERE TO DRINK IT

When in Rome, do as the Romans do. Ergo, when in Tennessee, drink Tennessee whiskey. Bourbon whiskey made here is considered Tennessee whiskey, and there is no shortage of different whiskeys to sip or places to sip them.

By definition, a Tennessee whiskey must be aged for two years in new oak barrels and made from at least 51 percent corn. It's made with charcoal, a process that mellows the flavor. As its name suggests, it must also be made in Tennessee. The Tennessee Whiskey Trail (www. tennesseewhiskeytrail.com) is an organized itinerary to the state's signature distilleries, which are scattered across the state, like the world-famous Jack Daniel's Distillery (133 Lynchburg Hwy./Hwy. 55, 931/759-6357, www. jackdaniels.com) and George Dickel (1950 Cascade Hollow Rd, 931/408-2410, www.georgedickel.com).

tour group at the Jack Daniel's Distillery

Not up for a day trip? Pick a few distilleries that are in city limits and leave the driving to Mint Julip Tours (712 Dickerson Pike #202, 615/436-0187, www.mintjuleptours.com/nashville). They'll take you to a selection of area distilleries, talk to you about what you're sipping, and let you relax in air-conditioned comfort.

- Tours and tastings are available at the award-winning, small-batch Corsair Artisan Distillery, with locations in both Marathon Village (1200 Clinton St. #110, 615/200-0321, www.corsairdistillery.com) and Wedgewood-Houston (601 Merritt Ave.).

- Nelson's Green Brier Distillery (1414 Clinton St., 615/913-8800, www. greenbrierdistillery.com) brought back a local brand, Belle Meade Bourbon, that was popular in the 1800s.

- While Pennington Distillery (900 44th Ave. N., 615/678-8986, www. penningtondistillingco.com) does distill Tennessee whiskey, their facility in The Nations neighborhood is also known for sipping cream (a whiskey and cream liqueur) and vodka. It's a good alternative when you've sampled enough of the brown spirits.

- For a whiskey cocktail at a bar, belly up to Patterson House (1711 Division St., no phone, http://thepattersonnashville.com).

- For something completely different, head to Donut Distillery (311 Gallatin Ave., 615/319-4535, www.donutdistillery.com) for a whiskey-glazed doughnut.

Arts and Culture

MUSIC ROW

CONCERT SERIES
Musicians Corner

Held in early summer and early fall, Musicians Corner is a concert series in its own location inside Centennial Park. There's some permanent seating in the form of stone benches, but most people bring blankets and camp chairs and hang for the day. Since 2010, more than 1,000 artists of all genres have graced this stage. Food trucks and kids' activities are on-site, but the focus is the music.

MAP 3: 2500 West End Ave., http:// musicianscornernashville.com; Fri.-Sat. May-June, Thurs. Sept.-Oct.; free

GALLERIES
Sarratt Gallery

The Sarratt Gallery is housed in the main student center on the Vanderbilt campus, which has a more contemporary bent than the other on-campus gallery, the Fine Arts Gallery. The Sarratt frequently exhibits the work of alumni and students and kicks off the shows with popular opening receptions. The annual holiday sale is one of the best places to shop for artisan crafts in the city. The tall space is in a well-trafficked lobby of the student center, alongside a small courtyard with a fountain.

MAP 3: Vanderbilt University, 2301 Vanderbilt Pl., 615/343-0491, http:// vanderbilt.edu/sarrattgallery; 9am-9pm Mon.-Fri., 10am-10pm Sat.-Sun. Sept.-mid-May, 8:30am-4:30pm Mon.-Fri. mid-May-Aug.; free

Fine Arts Gallery at Cohen Memorial Hall

In 2009 this university gallery moved into the historical 1928 McKim, Mead and White building on Vanderbilt's pretty Peabody campus. The gallery is home to a permanent collection of more than 6,000 objects of art. Exhibitions can be up for several months at a time and are often tied in with special lectures and other events on campus.

MAP 3: Vanderbilt University, 1220 21st Ave. S., 615/322-0605, http:// as.vanderbilt.edu/gallery; 11am-4pm Mon.-Fri., 1pm-5pm Sat.-Sun. Sept.-early May, noon-4pm Tues.-Fri., 1pm-5pm Sat. early May-Aug.; free

PERFORMANCE VENUES

Blair School of Music

The Blair School of Music presents student, faculty, and visiting artist recitals frequently during the school year. Blair's ensembles include woodwind, string, brass, and big band. As Vanderbilt University's music school, Blair addresses music through academic, pedagogical, and performing activities.

MAP 3: 2400 Blakemore Ave., 615/322-7651, http://blair.vanderbilt. edu; showtimes and ticket cost vary by event

CINEMA

Belcourt Theatre

Once the home of the Grand Ole Opry (as is true of so many buildings in Nashville), the Belcourt Theatre is the city's best venue for independent and art films. Built in

Belcourt Theatre

1925 as a silent movie house, the Belcourt now screens a refreshing variety of independent and unusual films, plus hosts live music concerts and other quirky performances, lectures, and film fests. In the summer the Belcourt screens some films outdoors. A renovation in 2016 expanded and upgraded the space (and the seats, for which regulars are grateful). Parking in the theater's Hillsboro Village lot is free for moviegoers, although it can fill quickly. Ask for a code when you buy your ticket.

MAP 3: 2102 Belcourt Ave., 615/383-9140, www.belcourt.org; showtimes vary; $10.50 adults, $9 children under 12 and students

MIDTOWN AND 12 SOUTH
GALLERIES
Aaron Douglas Gallery

Unassumingly nestled on the third floor of Fisk University's library is the Aaron Douglas Gallery, which houses the school's collection of African, African American, and folk art. It also hosts visiting exhibits and works by Fisk students and faculty. The gallery is named after painter and illustrator Aaron Douglas, who also established Fisk's first formal art department. Nearby Cravath Hall is home to several Aaron Douglas murals that are worth seeing. The murals are only open to the public Monday through Friday, when the administrative offices are open.

MAP 4: Fisk University, 1000 17th Ave. N., 615/329-8685, http://fisk.edu; open during library hours (variable); free

✪ Carl Van Vechten Gallery

The Carl Van Vechten Gallery is named for the art collector who convinced artist Georgia O'Keeffe to donate to Fisk University a large portion of the work and personal collection of her late husband, Alfred Stieglitz. The college retains 50 percent interest in the collection,

115

FISK'S STIEGLITZ COLLECTION

When photographer Alfred Stieglitz died in 1946, his wife, Georgia O'Keeffe, herself one of the most important artists of her generation, was left with the responsibility of giving away his massive art collection. Stieglitz had collected more than 1,000 works by artists including Arthur Dove, Marsden Hartley, O'Keeffe, Charles Demuth, and John Marin. He also owned several African sculptures.

Stieglitz's instructions regarding this art collection were vague. In his will he asked O'Keeffe to select the recipients "under such arrangements as will assure to the public, under reasonable regulations, access thereto to promote the study of art."

O'Keeffe selected several obvious recipients for parts of the collection: the Library of Congress, the National Gallery of Art in Washington, the Metropolitan Museum of Art, the Art Institute of Chicago, and the Philadelphia Museum of Art. Nashville's Fisk University was a surprise, and Carl Van Vechten, a writer, photographer, and friend of Stieglitz and O'Keeffe, is credited with making the suggestion. Van Vechten was keenly interested in African American art and was close friends with Fisk president Charles Johnson.

O'Keeffe and Fisk did not find an easy partnership. According to an account by C. Michael Norton, when she first visited the university, a few days before the Carl Van Vechten Gallery would open on campus, O'Keeffe ordered major changes to the gallery space, eventually flying in a lighting designer from New York on the day before the opening. At the opening ceremony on November 4, 1949, held at the Memorial Chapel at Fisk, O'Keeffe declined President Johnson's invitation to the lectern and spoke from her chair, saying curtly: "Dr. Johnson wrote and asked me to speak and I did not answer. I had and have no intention of speaking. These paintings and sculptures are a gift from Stieglitz. They are for the students. I hope you go back and look at them more than once."

The Stieglitz Collection at Fisk consists of 101 remarkable works of art, including 2 by O'Keeffe, 19 Stieglitz photographs, prints by Cézanne and Renoir, and 5 pieces of African tribal art.

For years, cash-strapped Fisk had sought to sell parts of the collection to raise funds. In 2012, Walmart heiress Alice Walton's Crystal Bridges Museum in Bentonville, Arkansas, acquired a 50 percent share in the collection for $30 million. Now the collection rotates between Crystal Bridges and Fisk's Carl Van Vechten Gallery every two years. While some decry the deal as not following the stipulations in O'Keeffe's will, others see it as the only option to keep the collection in the public eye and to keep Fisk solvent. The influx of cash has helped maintain the collection and provided for new resources, such as a printed catalog of the impressive works. When the collection is in Arkansas, the gallery exhibits other worthy works.

having sold the other half to Crystal Bridges Museum of American Art, in Arkansas, to raise funds for the cash-strapped private school. The collection rotates between Crystal Bridges and the Van Vechten every two years. Other exhibits are on display when the Stieglitz collection is in Arkansas. The collection includes works by Stieglitz and O'Keeffe, as well as acclaimed European and American artists including Pablo Picasso, Paul Cézanne, Pierre-Auguste Renoir, Diego Rivera, Arthur Dove, Gino Severini, and Charles Demuth. It is truly a remarkable collection and one worth seeing, but call ahead to confirm hours, particularly when school is not in session. Ring the bell to the right of the door to be let in.

MAP 4: Fisk University, 1000 17th Ave. N., 615/329-8720, http://fisk.edu; 10am-4pm Mon.-Fri.; $10 adults, $6 seniors, $5 students, free for children

Carl Van Vechten Gallery

THEATER

✪ Nashville Shakespeare

The city's Shakespeare troupe brings the Bard to Music City audiences all year long. The winter performances take place at Belmont University's Troutt Theater (2100 Belmont Blvd.) and Tucker Theatre, on the campus of Middle Tennessee State University in Murfreesboro. But it is the summer show, held outside at The Yard at OneC1TY (8 City Blvd.), that really grabs headlines and welcomes big audiences. Since its founding in 1988, Nashville Shakespeare has worked to get the Bard's words to audiences who might not otherwise be exposed to these classics. Many of its performances are designed to be inexpensive or free and are often mounted in parks and schools. Also fun are the monthly Shakespeare Allowed! readings at the main public library. Everyday folks, not actors, gather to read the works as they were meant to be heard—aloud.

MAP 4: The Yard at OneC1TY, 8 City Blvd., 615/255-2273, www. nashvilleshakes.org; showtimes vary by performance; free, donations accepted

Festivals and Events

Tennessee Craft Fair

At the Tennessee Craft Fair in Centennial Park, more than 200 artists are juried and selected for their quality works. You'll find jewelry, painting, ceramics, and many other media on display, as well as food and activities to keep the kids busy. This is not a place to expect a bargain, but you may find a work of art you'll keep for years. The fair occurs in spring and fall each year.

Music Row: Centennial Park, http:// tennesseecraft.org; early May and Oct.; free

Celebrate Nashville Cultural Festival

International organizations set up in Centennial Park and offer food, dance, music, crafts, and other pieces of different cultures from around the world during the Celebrate Nashville Cultural Festival each October. There are separate activity areas for teens and younger children.

Music Row: Centennial Park, www. celebratenashville.org; Oct., free

Jubilee Day

Every October 6, the day in 1871 that the first Fisk Jubilee Singers departed Fisk University for a worldwide tour, the school remembers their efforts with a convocation, a concert, a walk to the cemetery to lay wreaths made from campus magnolia trees, and more. Jubilee Day is a moving day with remarkable live music performances.

Midtown and 12 South: Fisk University, 1000 17th Ave. N., www.fisk.edu; Oct., free

Recreation

MUSIC ROW
PARKS

TOP EXPERIENCE

Centennial Park

Nashville's best city park, Centennial is most known as home of the Parthenon, the center of activity in this 132-acre gem. One of the park's highlights is its celebration of women's suffrage in the form of a sculpture by local artist Alan LeQuire. In the center of the park, the Tennessee Woman Suffrage Monument features five women, four of whom were Tennesseans, who all fought for the right of women to vote. The park is also a pleasant place to relax. A small lake

Centennial Park

surrounded by vibrant flower gardens provides a habitat for ducks and other water creatures; paved trails are popular with pedestrians during nice weather. The park hosts many events during the year, including music and art festivals. Something is almost always going on here, particularly in the summer when live music frequently fills the air. Centennial Park is home to one of Nashville's nine official dog parks, as well as marked running trails, bicycle rental stations, children's play areas, and almost anything else you would expect from a park. It's particularly glorious at sunset, with the Parthenon lit against the sky.

MAP 3: 2500 West End Ave., 615/862-8424, http://nashville.gov; sunrise-11pm daily; free

BIKE SHOPS AND RENTALS
Cumberland Transit

One of the city's most beloved independent outdoors shops, Cumberland Transit stocks and services bikes. Brands carried include Trek, Gary Fisher, and Yakima. The store also hosts how-to workshops, pint nights, and other outdoor-focused activities.

MAP 3: 2807 West End Ave., 615/321-4069, http://cumberlandtransit. com; 10am-6pm Mon.-Sat.

Shops

MUSIC ROW
CLOTHING AND ACCESSORIES
Any Old Iron

The stereotype in Nashville is that everyone wears sequins. That's not necessarily true, but if you're interested in sporting some for yourself, you want them from Andrew Clancey. The designer moved from New York to Nashville in 2014 in part because he was already dressing locals like Miranda Lambert and Taylor Swift. In 2020 he opened his Music Row shop Any Old Iron to the public. Here you'll find jackets, suits, gowns, and even face masks with sequined, stylish bling.

MAP 3: 8 Music Square S., 615/649-8499, www.anyoldiron.us; noon-5pm Thurs.-Mon.

Boutique Bella

Boutique Bella specializes in jeans. With a tremendous range of designers—including J Brand, 7 for All Mankind, AG Adriano Goldschmeid, and Rock & Republic—and an equal selection of sizes, those looking for jeans that actually fit are bound to find their Holy Grail. The boutique is cute, but not twee, particularly the perfectly adorable dressing rooms. Sale racks are fantastic.

MAP 3: 2817 West End Ave., 615/467-1471; 10am-6pm Mon.-Sat.

Native + Nomad

This local favorite specializes in men's and women's clothing, including denim and workout wear, with a boho chic emphasis. The bright boutique is well edited, with a focus on local labels. Barn-wood

accents show off denim, jewelry, and other accessories. The store has a second location in Franklin, in the **CoolSprings Galleria.**
MAP 3: 1813 21st Ave. S., 615/840-7409, http://shopnativeandnomad.com; 10am-6pm daily

Scarlett Begonia

For decades, Vanderbilt students have shopped in this boutique, which specializes in fair-trade goods. Walk by the window and inhale, and you might think it's all sweaters that smell like patchouli. There is some of that, but the merchandise is much more varied and sophisticated than the initial sniff suggests. Come here for pretty dresses, fun skirts, and jewelry in a variety of price ranges. Women's clothing is stocked in a wide cross section of sizes. Puppets, toys, and other gifts are also on the shelves.
MAP 3: 2805 West End Ave., 615/329-1272, www.scarlettbegonia.com; 10am-6pm Mon.-Sat., 1pm-5pm Sun.

UAL

Bargain-hunting fashionistas cannot skip UAL (which stands for United Apparel Liquidators). Designer samples of clothes, handbags, shoes, and jewelry are shoved onto crowded racks in this shop near the Vanderbilt campus. UAL stocks both men's and women's attire, but the women's selection is significantly larger. Label-loving shoppers can find great prices on goods, including home decor, but a little digging is involved. A second location in Hillsboro Village is smaller, with more accessories and less clothing, and there's a third in 12 South. If you

are headed to the suburbs, there's also a Brentwood outpost.
MAP 3: 2918 West End Ave., 615/340-9999, http://shopual.com; 9am-8pm Mon.-Fri., 10am-8pm Sat.-Sun.

SHOPPING DISTRICTS AND CENTERS
Edgehill Village

A former industrial laundry has become one of the city's lower-profile but more engaging retail destinations. Come here to browse small boutiques ranging from home decor to baby clothes to jewelry to wedding dresses, along with chains such as Warby Parker and J. Crew. Stop and eat tacos, enjoy ice cream, or lounge in the coffee shop. Stores are on both sides of the street and in the bigger building to the east. Street parking is mostly permit, but there are several affordable lots.
MAP 3: 1200 Villa Pl., http://edgehillvillage.com; hours vary by store

Hillsboro Village

Some complain that Hillsboro Village, which runs several blocks along 21st Avenue South, has lost its indie cred, now that many historical buildings have been replaced with new construction. True, there are more chains here than there used to be, but this is still perhaps the city's best collection of boutiques, locally owned shops, and walkable options for a shopping outing. Hillsboro Village is right next to the Vanderbilt campus and near Belmont's, so there is a slight student vibe. The shops carry clothes, jewelry, gifts, cookware, and plenty of other stuff that wouldn't be at home in a dorm room. Hillsboro Village also has restaurants, bars, dessert spots, and the renovated arthouse film destination, the Belcourt Theatre.

MAP 3: 1808 21st Ave. S.; hours vary by store

MIDTOWN AND 12 SOUTH
ANTIQUES AND VINTAGE
Antique Archaeology

The second retail location for "American Picker" Mike Wolfe, this tiny store is almost a museum for American "things." All the pieces aren't necessarily for sale, but there are stories behind all of them. There are stories, too, about the building itself, which was the Marathon Motor Works car factory. Fans of the History Channel's *American Pickers* can find fun show T-shirts as well as rub elbows with some of the show's chief "pickers." There's almost always a line, thanks to its TV reputation, but true thrifters and pickers have other favorite shops. There's also a small outpost inside the Omni Nashville Hotel in SoBro.

MAP 4: 1300 Clinton St., Ste. 130, 615/810-9906, www. antiquearchaeology.com; 10am-6pm Mon.-Sat., 11am-4pm Sun.

CLOTHING AND ACCESSORIES
✪ Planet Cowboy

In 2020, Jaylin Ramer packed up her successful New York City boot shop and moved it to Nashville, giving locals and visitors a place to buy both custom- and ready-made boots. Ramer custom designs of one-third of the stock, with price tags befitting their one-of-a-kind nature, starting around $900. The shop

Planet Cowboy

also stocks other brands, including Lugus Mercury, Rios of Mercedes, and Stallion.

MAP 4: 2905 12th Ave. S., 615/200-0991, https://planetcowboy.com; noon-6pm Mon.-Wed., 1pm-7pm Thurs.-Fri., 11am-7pm Sat., noon-4pm Sun.

Draper James

Nashville native and Academy Award-winner Reese Witherspoon launched this flagship location of her shop/lifestyle brand in her hometown. Find pillows, cocktail napkins, and more—with a Southern twist. Think J. Crew meets Kate Spade meets Southern hospitality. Women's clothes are offered in a range of sizes, from petite to plus. You'll be offered a glass of sweet tea as soon as you enter. The bright white-and-blue-striped mural on the building's exterior is popular with Instagrammers.

MAP 4: 2608 12th Ave. S., 615/997-3601, www.draperjames.com; 11am-5pm Sun.-Thurs., 10am-6pm Fri.-Sat.

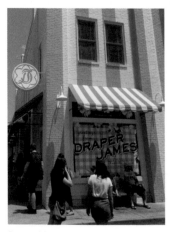

Draper James

Emerson Grace

Kimberly Lewis helped retail brands like BCBG Max Azria expand before she decided to open her own 12 South shop. Her considerable experience allowed her to design a shop with a focus on women's clothing that is stylish and well edited, and offers brands not otherwise found in Nashville.

MAP 4: 2304 12th Ave. S., 615/454-6407, www.emersongracenashville.com; 10am-5pm Mon.-Sat., noon-5pm Sun.

Hero

Claudia Robertson Fowler is one of those local stylists to the stars. For more than 25 years she's dressed Faith Hill, Trisha Yearwood, and Miranda Lambert. Come here for stylish women's clothing and accessories with a focus on timeless pieces that can be worn again and again (that's why she calls them "heroes"). The shop also has outposts in The Gulch and Franklin.

MAP 4: 2306 12th Ave. S., 615/457-1206, www.hero12s.com; 10am-5pm Mon.-Thurs., 10am-6pm Fri.-Sat., noon-5pm Sun.

Imogene + Willie

When this denim shop opened in an old gas station in 2009, it seemed like it was catering to a very niche market: a place to buy $200 jeans. But in the years since, the brand has thrived, getting into national retailers like Anthropologie, expanding into other product lines, and building a loyal local following, all by having products that are highly customizable and basically custom sewn to fit. If you have the splurge in your budget, come here to get your

SHOP LIKE A STAR

Any Old Iron

Many bona fide stars call Music City home. Not only that, they buy apparel for their stage and screen appearances in Nashville. You can emulate their style by starting at these favorite shops.

- If you have serious cash to spend, head to **Manuel Exclusive Clothier** (2804 Columbine Pl., 615/321-5444), where you can have a bedazzled rhinestone suit made just for you.

- Owned by Hank Williams Jr.'s daughter Holly, **H. Audrey** (4027 Hillsboro Pike, 615/760-5701, http://haudrey.com) is the choice for stars who want a more refined look, maybe for that talk show appearance.

- Wes Shugart at **Music City Leather** (615/ 533-4882, www.musiccityleather.com) makes one-of-a-kind cowboy boots by hand. The process takes up to a year and prices start at $5,000. Shugart takes measurements of your foot and crafts a pair in the shape, style, and color you want. You'll end up with a work of art you can wear for life.

- Designer Andrew Clancey is known for his sequined creations sold at **Any Old Iron** (8 Music Sq. S., 615/649-8499, www.anyoldiron.us). Stop by the Music Row shop to admire the shiny pieces.

- Custom-designed boots at **Planet Cowboy** (2905 12th Ave. S., 615/200-0991, https://planetcowboy.com) will set you back at least $900, but there are off-the-rack options, too, if you want something more budget-friendly.

- Want a custom-embroidered jean jacket? **Ranger Stitch** (711 Porter Rd., 615/784-8244, www.rangerstitch.com) will do it in style. There are ready-made bandanas, patches, and other stitched goods for sale, too.

pair made; they're designed to last forever. The overall vibe is accessible and welcoming.
MAP 4: 2601 12th Ave. S., 615/292-5005, http://imogeneandwillie.com; 10am-5pm Mon.-Wed., 10am-6pm Thurs.-Sat., noon-5pm Sun.

Judith Bright

Walk in the doors of this small, unassuming house, and you'll find a jewelry shop that has attracted the attention of stylists, filmmakers, and celebrities. Judith Bright trains a team of women to make reasonably

White's Mercantile

priced jewelry, including earrings, necklaces, and bracelets with gemstones. Most of the work is now done off-site, but in a small studio in this retrofitted house you can watch them switch out stones and size a piece just for you.

MAP 4: 2307 12th Ave. S., 615/269-5600, www.judithbright.com; 10am-6pm Mon.-Sat., noon-6pm Sun.

Moda

Moda's elegantly eclectic boutique features women's designer clothing, accessories, jewelry, gifts, and even a few locally made baby clothes. The atmosphere in this cute, retrofitted home is bright yet minimalist, adding to the spacious feel, and the style includes casual and the dressier side of casual. The staff are friendly and attentive without being intrusive.

MAP 4: 2511 12th Ave. S., 615/298-2271, http://modanashville.com; noon-5pm Sun.-Mon., 10:30am-6pm Tues.-Sat.

GOURMET AND SPECIALTY FOODS
Bang Candy Company

Once a food cart hawking gourmet marshmallows around town, Bang Candy Company is now a bustling sweet store and coffee shop. The shop attracts a diverse clientele, with Antique Archaeology shoppers and locals all lingering among the treats. The marshmallows and caramels are handmade in-house and include offbeat flavors such as absinthe and rose cardamom. Take home a flavored simple syrup for mixing your own cocktails.

MAP 4: 1300 Clinton St., 615/953-1065, www.bangcandycompany.com; 10am-3pm Sun.-Thurs., 10am-4pm Fri.-Sat.

HOME DECOR
White's Mercantile

White's Mercantile is owned by singer-songwriter Holly Williams. Yes, she's one of those Williams:

Country legend Hank Williams Jr. is her father and Hank Sr. her grandfather. But she's not all about rhinestones and cowboy hats. Instead, this modern general store is a curated shop stocked with stuff she loves, some of which she found while on the road touring. Look for jewelry, tasteful home decor, gifts for children, and holiday decor. Williams also owns upscale clothing shop **H. Audrey.**

MAP 4: 2908 12th Ave. S., 615/750-5379, https://whitesmercantile. com; 10am-6pm Mon.-Sat.

MUSIC
Gruhn Guitars

If you want to make your own music, head to Gruhn Guitars, a guitar shop with one of the best reputations in the music world. Founded by guitar expert George Gruhn, the shop is considered by some the best vintage guitar shop in the world. Stop in and play one of your favorites, just for fun. For 50 years shiny guitars, banjos, mandolins, and fiddles hung on the walls of the Broadway storefront near the Ryman Auditorium. In 2013 the shop moved from downtown, but the sign—and the quality—remains the same.

MAP 4: 2120 8th Ave. S., 615/256-2033, http://guitars.com; 10am-6pm Mon.-Sat.

East Nashville

Map 5

Even as East Nashville establishes itself as a major neighborhood in the city, its hip reputation remains. This vibrant area just across the Cumberland from downtown is home to stylish **vintage boutiques** and purveyors of handcrafted goods, not to mention many of the city's **tastiest restaurants** and **best watering holes.**

TOP RESTAURANTS

- Where to Eat Brunch and Meet Locals: **Margot Café and Bar** (page 131)
- Best Place to Play with Your Food: **Game Point Cafe** (page 134)

TOP NIGHTLIFE

- Best Spot to Learn Western Swing Dancing: **Honky Tonk Tuesday Nights** (page 136)
- Most Time-Honored LGBTQ Bar: **The Lipstick Lounge** (page 138)

TOP SHOPS

- Best Place to Browse for Tunes: **Grimey's New and Preloved Music** (page 141)
- Best Indie Retail Stops: **Five Points Alley Shops** (page 145) and **Shoppes on Fatherland** (page 145)

GETTING THERE AND AROUND

- Major bus routes: 4, 23, 56

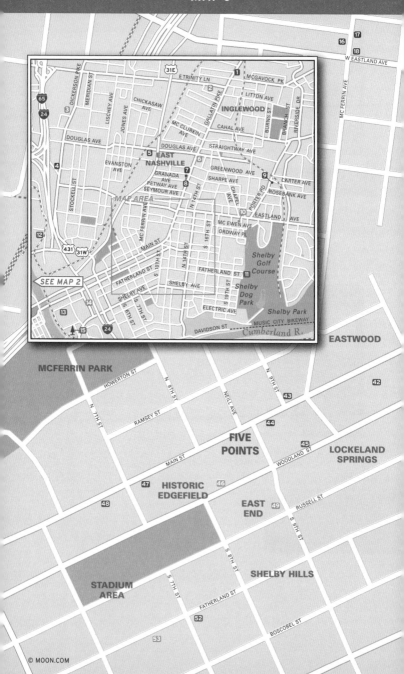

SEE MAP 6

RESTAURANTS

- **4** Shugga Hi Bakery & Café
- **7** Once Upon a Time in France
- **8** Pelican & Pig
- **9** Café Roze
- **16** Mas Tacos Por Favor
- **17** The Pharmacy Burger Parlor & Beer Garden
- **18** Lyra
- **19** Kettner Coffee Supply
- **22** Barista Parlor
- **25** Hunters Station
- **29** Margot Café and Bar
- **30** Five Points Pizza
- **34** Game Point Cafe
- **39** Lockeland Table
- **40** I Dream of Weenie
- **44** Butcher & Bee
- **47** Greko Greek Street Food
- **48** Bolton's Spicy Chicken & Fish
- **52** Sky Blue Cafe

NIGHTLIFE

- **1** Honky Tonk Tuesday Nights
- **5** Southern Grist Brewing Company
- **24** No. 308 Presents CAMP
- **26** The 5 Spot
- **31** 3 Crow Bar
- **33** By the Bottle
- **38** The Lipstick Lounge
- **42** Crazy Gnome Brewery
- **43** Smith & Lentz Brewing
- **45** The Basement East

RECREATION

- **11** Shelby Golf Course
- **12** Topgolf Nashville
- **13** Tennessee Titans
- **15** Cumberland Park

SHOPS

- **2** Grimey's New and Preloved Music
- **6** Daisy May Hat Co
- **10** Lemon Laine
- **20** The Bookshop
- **21** Star Struck Vintage Nashville
- **23** The Groove
- **27** Hip Zipper
- **28** Wags & Whiskers
- **35** Five Points Alley Shops
- **36** Fairytales Bookstore
- **37** Wonders on Woodland
- **41** Fanny's House of Music
- **46** Harlan Ruby Gift Shop
- **50** Gift Horse
- **51** Shoppes on Fatherland

HOTELS

- **3** Dive Motel & Swim Club
- **14** La Quinta Inn & Suites Downtown/Stadium
- **32** VanDyke Bed and Beverage
- **49** The Russell
- **54** The Big Bungalow

SOUTH INGLEWOOD

ROSEBANK

BARCLAY DRIVE

```
0        500 yds
0        500 m
```

DISTANCE ACROSS MAP
Approximate: 5.5 mi or 8.9 km

SEE MAP 7

MAXWELL AVE
MANSFIELD ST
CALVIN AVE
ORDWAY PL
GARTLAND AVE
FORREST AVE
CLEARVIEW AVE
WOODLAND ST
HOLLY ST
RUSSELL ST
FATHERLAND ST
LILLIAN ST
BOSCOBEL ST
SHELBY AVE
GALLATIN AVE
MAIN ST
S 10TH ST
S 11TH ST
S 12TH ST
S 13TH ST
N 14TH ST
S 16TH ST

Restaurants

PRICE KEY

$	Entrées less than $15
$ $	Entrées $15-25
$ $ $	Entrées more than $25

HOT CHICKEN

Bolton's Spicy Chicken & Fish **$**

It's a matter of local debate whether Prince's or Bolton's serves up the city's most authentic culinary specialties. Hot chicken at Bolton's is served bone-in, on a piece of white bread (soaking up the heat), with a pickle on top. And it is really spicy. It's made to order and panfrying takes time, so plan for a 20-minute wait. There's a nice patio for lounging while you do so. As its name suggests, Bolton's also serves spicy fish. There's a second location on Franklin Pike.

MAP 5: 624 Main St., 615/254-8015, www.boltonsspicy.com; 11am-7pm Tues.-Sun.

SOUTHERN

Shugga Hi Bakery & Café **$**

Sisters Sandra and Kathy cook up their mother's traditional Southern recipes in a welcoming restaurant in the quickly developing Dickerson Pike area. It's a place for chicken and waffles and Sunday brunch. Breakfasts are served with turkey sausage instead of pork. Neighborhood locals are loyal to

Bolton's Spicy Chicken & Fish

the old-fashioned cakes and pies. Call ahead to find out when live jazz music will be played.

MAP 5: 1000 Dickerson Pike, 615/928-6576, www.shuggahibakeryandcafe.com; 8am-5pm Fri.-Sat., 9am-2pm Sun.

NEW AMERICAN

✪ Margot Café and Bar $$$

This small East Nashville bistro has been serving European-style food for special occasions since before the neighborhood was hip. In fact, many of Margot Café's kitchen alumni have gone on to helm other restaurants, and most credit owner-chef Margot McCormack for starting Nashville's legit food scene. Margot Café is a reliable option for a nice dinner out, with dishes made with whatever is in season. The dishes change daily, sometimes celebrating something like Julia Child's birthday, other times demonstrating something McCormack learned on a recent vacation. The menu is well edited, the service attentive, and the space cozy.

MAP 5: 1017 Woodland St., 615/227-4668, www.margotcafe.com; 5pm-9pm Wed.-Sun.

Butcher & Bee $$

A Nashville outpost of the Charleston original, Butcher & Bee serves seasonal, shareable new American fare with global influences, including a heavy dose of Mediterranean flavors. Starters (called *mezze*) are the stars here, and the whipped feta with pita is a local obsession. The menu is heavily influenced by what's in season and inspired by chefs from around the world. Reservations are recommended for tables, but it is usually easy to grab a seat at the counter. Weekend brunch is a whirlwind of flavors. The back patio is a private outdoor oasis.

MAP 5: 902 Main St., 615/226-3322, https://butcherandbee.com; 5pm-9pm Mon.-Thurs., 11am-2pm and 5pm-11pm Fri., 10am-2pm and 5pm-11pm Sat., 10am-2pm and 5pm-9pm Sun.

Lockeland Table $$

Small farm-to-fork restaurants in Nashville aren't unusual, but Lockeland Table is a standout. This cozy eatery is great for dining with friends or on a date, and the menu takes a creative direction on Southern specialties. Check out the chowchow (pickled relish, usually including pickled peppers, tomatoes, and onions), mac and cheese, and the fried green tomato salad. The space itself has a city-meets-farm vibe and is often crowded with regulars. Make reservations before you head over.

MAP 5: 1520 Woodland St., 615/228-4864, www.lockelandtable.com; 4pm-10pm Mon.-Sat.

Pelican & Pig $$

With a full wood-fired hearth (and stacks of wood to burn out front), this small eatery fires up seasonal American specialties, accompanied by freshly baked sourdough (finished in that same hearth). Vegetable dishes are savory and flavorful enough to stand alone as main dishes. Don't skip dessert. The talented chef couple also owns **Slow Hand Coffee + Bakeshop** (1012 Gallatin Ave.) next door and know their way around a baked good.

MAP 5: 1010 Gallatin Ave.,
615/730-6887, www.pelicanandpig.
com; 5pm-10pm Tues.-Sun.

Café Roze $

When Julia Jaksic moved from New York to Nashville, she wanted to open what she thought the city was missing: an all-day café serving thoughtfully created food made fresh to order whenever you wanted. Thanks to a population of makers and musicians who work offbeat hours, the idea caught on. Now you'll wait for a table to order a vegetable bowl, creative salad, or egg dish. Roze Pony (5133 Harding Pike) is Jaksic's similar restaurant in Belle Meade on the west side of town.

MAP 5: 1115 Porter Rd., 615/645-9100,
www.caferoze.com; 8am-10pm daily

Café Roze

The Pharmacy Burger Parlor & Beer Garden $

The Pharmacy is a beer garden and burger joint that has been popular beyond anyone's expectation. In addition to an in-depth beer and burger menu, the team at The Pharmacy makes sodas by hand. The big grassy backyard beer garden is packed anytime the outdoor temperatures rise. Expect long waits on weekend nights, or check out their outpost in the Fifth + Broadway complex downtown. Park in a monitored lot or a well-lit spot, as vehicle break-ins are not uncommon in the area.

MAP 5: 731 McFerrin
Ave., 615/712-9527, www.
thepharmacynashville.com;
11am-9:30pm daily

Sky Blue Cafe $

Sky Blue looks like a coffee shop, and the coffee and bagels are decent, but this restaurant is a full-service option for breakfast and lunch. Breakfast is served all day and is one of the reasons locals love it here. The biscuit bowl, with eggs and sausage gravy, is particularly popular. The armadillo grilled cheese sandwich has cheese on both the outside and the inside. The space is sweet and cozy, with vintage tablecloths on each table and the work of local artists on the walls. The space is small and waits can be long.

MAP 5: 700 Fatherland St.,
615/770-7097, www.skybluecoffee.com;
8am-2pm Thurs.-Mon.

DINERS AND COFFEE SHOPS

Barista Parlor $

To call Barista Parlor a coffee shop is a gross understatement. It is more an art gallery where the coffee is the star. A renovated auto shop, this is a big, well-designed space with great signage from local artists, uniforms from local designers, interesting

FOLLOW THAT FOOD TRUCK!

The Peach Truck

Like every big city with a hipster population worth its salt, Nashville has scores of food trucks driving to and fro, selling gourmet delicacies from their wheel-based restaurants. These snack masters tend to show up at places with big lunch crowds, late at night after concerts, and at large public events, so you may just run into them.

Centennial Park is a popular stop for the trucks at lunchtime, but they also make it to many neighborhoods (and suburbs) throughout the week. Trucks also congregate at Nissan Stadium three hours before Tennessee Titan home games. On Saturdays, head to the Music City Food Truck Park (400 Davidson St., https://themarketplacenashville.com/food-truck-park, 11am-4pm Sat.) for a rotating selection.

- One of Nashville's first food trucks, The Grilled Cheeserie (http://grilledcheeserie.com/truck) serves delicious grilled cheese sandwiches and tomato soup. It travels all over the city, particularly to farmers markets in the summer. It became so popular, there's also now a shop in Hillsboro Village and in Hunters Station in East Nashville.
- The city's best falafel, plus other Egyptian treats, is on the truck at King Tut's (@KingTutsTruck), which can be found at 3716 Nolensville Pike and at festivals and events.
- Nashville loves The Peach Truck (900 Trinity Ln., https://thepeachtruck.com), which is exactly what it says—a truck that brings farm-fresh peaches to farmers markets and offices across the city. In peach season, you'll find them at farmers markets or at their drive-thru location in East Nashville.
- Prince's Hot Chicken has a truck permanently parked at the SoBro Complex/6th & Peabody (423 6th Ave. S., https://olesmoky.com/pages/6thandpeabody), where you can drink moonshine from Ole Smoky, too.

furniture, and attentive servers. They take coffee very seriously here and are happy to answer your questions about their pour-over style and different blends. Be patient as your caffeine fix is prepared. The folks behind Barista also have locations around town, including in Germantown, Marathon Village, and at the airport, as well as one in

The Gulch, called **Barista Parlor Golden Sound** (610 Magazine St., 615/227-4782). But East Nashville is the first and the most iconic.
MAP 5: 519B Gallatin Ave., 615/712-9766, http://baristaparlor.com; 7am-6pm daily

❂ Game Point Cafe $

The Bongo East coffee shop is transformed afternoons and evenings into a fun community center. Choose from one of more than 300 board games in the restaurant's library, each categorized by the type of game, the number of required players, and the ease of play. A game concierge will help you select the right game for your group, learn the rules, and settle disputes. The space attracts a wide variety of guests, everyone from families with kids to bachelorette parties, locals, and tourists. You can eat and drink from the café as you play; there's a suggested minimum of $10 per person applied while playing games.
MAP 5: 107 S. 11th St., www. gamepointcafe.com, 615/777-3278; 7am-2pm Mon.-Fri., 7am-4pm Sat.-Sun.

Kettner Coffee Supply $

Named after the street in San Diego where the owner used to live, Kettner is a coffee shop/remote working space/neighborhood hangout. In addition to coffee and tea, the Kettner menu offers soft-serve ice cream, baked goods, and breakfast tacos from the nearby **Redheaded Stranger** (305 Arrington, 615/544-8226, https://redheadedstrangertacos.com). Kettner connects to **The Bookshop** (1043 W. Eastland Ave.) and hosts

Game Point Cafe

Lit Club and other events with the store.
MAP 5: 1045 W. Eastland Ave., www. kettnercoffee.com; 7am-10pm daily

FOOD STANDS

I Dream of Weenie $

Long before there was a food truck craze, a nonmobile renovated VW bus captured the hearts of East Nashvillians. The lines continue, with people waiting for specialty hot dogs, chips, and drinks. There are hot dog varieties offered on a regular basis, such as the Kraut Dog (served with sauerkraut), as well as some that are offered as specials, such as the Pizza Dog. There is a grassy area where you can sit and eat your dog, but most people take their dogs to go.
MAP 5: 113 S. 11th St., 615/226-2622; 11am-3pm Mon.-Fri., 10:30am-4pm Sat.-Sun., hours vary seasonally

INTERNATIONAL

Lyra $$

Lovely Lyra bills itself as "modern Middle Eastern cuisine." Reservations are recommended, but not required, so show up and feast on the daily breads, sip creative cocktails, and share plates with friends. The happy hour offerings

(5pm-6pm Mon.-Sat.) are affordable and varied. The dining room is filled with buzz and energy and the patio is a serene oasis.

MAP 5: 935 W. Eastland Ave., 615/928-8040, www.lyranashville.com; 5pm-10pm Mon.,11am-2pm and 5pm-10pm Tues.-Sat.

Greko Greek Street Food $

With counter seating, communal tables, a small patio, and a brisk takeout business, Greko is a good problem-solver for when you want an affordable, delicious meal before seeing a concert in East Nashville or downtown. The Village Salad, with cucumber and tomato, is a particularly fresh option.

MAP 5: 704 Main St., 615/203-0251, www.grekostreetfood.com; 11am-9pm daily

Once Upon a Time in France $$

After Melvil Arnt moved to Nashville from France he realized that Music City didn't have a Parisian-style bistro and wine bar. So he convinced his parents to join him in the U.S. to open one. Their tiny East Nashville eatery is dotted with framed photos, flags, and light fixtures that they brought with them from Paris. The menu is equally legit, offering up iconic French dishes like beef bourguignon and escargot. They don't take reservations, so it'll be a wait, but there's an ample wine list, so you can sip the time away. Arnt also owns two French bars in East Nashville, The Authentique (925 Gallatin Ave.) and Overlord (2503 Gallatin Ave.). The Authentique is just across the street, so it's a great spot to wait for your table to be ready.

MAP 5: 1102 Gallatin Ave., 615/649-8284, www.onceuponatime-infrance.com; 4:30pm-9pm Wed.-Sun.

Hunters Station $

A food hall that opened in an old automotive supply shop, Hunters Station is home to about 10 local restaurants, all organized around communal seating areas (both indoor and outdoor). The complex also houses a community kitchen that small food businesses can use. Other Hunters Station restaurants serve grilled cheese, burgers, milkshakes, and tacos.

MAP 5: 975 Main St., 615/610-3396, www.huntersstation.com; 7am-9pm daily

MEXICAN
Mas Tacos Por Favor $

Mas Tacos was once known and loved for its food truck, but its physical restaurant and bar, where fans can go for tasty tacos, soups, and other Mexican delights, long ago surpassed the truck in popularity. The menu is bigger than seems possible given the tiny kitchen, with pozole, tacos, tamales, and more. You order at a window, and there's almost always a line, but it moves quickly. Enjoy a paloma or a beer while you sit back and enjoy the East Nashville people-watching.

MAP 5: 732 McFerrin Ave., 615/543-6271; 11am-9pm Tues.-Fri., 10am-9pm Sat.

PIZZA
Five Points Pizza $

This East Nashville pizzeria—founded by three locals—doles out the closest thing Nashville has to New York-style pizza. Stop by to grab it by the slice (cut from 20-inch pies) or choose a traditional stromboli or garlic knots. Whole pies feature inventive toppings such as habanero cream sauce, sliced meatballs, or vegan cheese. The kitchen staff toss the dough in the air just like pizza makers did when you were a kid . . . and it is still fun to watch.

MAP 5: 1012 Woodland St., 615/915-4174, www.fivepointspizza. com; 11am-10pm Sun.-Thurs., 11am-11pm Fri.-Sat.

Nightlife

LIVE MUSIC
COUNTRY
✪ Honky Tonk Tuesday Nights

This weekly event at the American Legion 82 is one of the most fun nights out in Music City. Before the house band, The Cowpokes, show up at this East Nashville institution dressed in full western garb, you can get some pre-show, step-by-step dance instruction to polish up your honky tonk moves. Bring cash to tip both the band and your dance teachers. This is a high-energy crowd that dresses for the occasion, with dancers often wearing suits or full skirts that twirl as they get into the action. The stage lights, costumed band, and enthusiastic crowd transform the otherwise utilitarian space. There's a full bar here.

MAP 5: 3204 Gallatin Pike, 615/228-3598, 8pm-1am Tues.; no cover, optional $10 donation

ECLECTIC
The Basement East

A sibling venue to The Basement, this club hosts music acts of all genres several nights a week in East Nashville. New Faces Night on Tuesday is a popular place to hear singer-songwriters and artists presented by East Nashville Songwriter's Club. The original Basement's street cred and connections instantly made this venue a go-to for locals wanting to hear cutting-edge music of all kinds. To the delight of the neighborhood, it was rebuilt after the March 2020 tornado.

MAP 5: 917 Woodland Ave., 615/645-9174, http:// thebasementnashville.com; showtimes and cover cost vary; doors open one hour before showtime

The 5 Spot

Fans of the old television show *Nashville* know The 5 Spot as the grungy (in terms of both decor and sound) home to indie rock wannabes. With its heavy red curtains and eclectic mix, The 5 Spot has earned the title as the go-to venue on Mondays with two-for-one drinks and its über-popular Keep on Movin' dance party featuring 1950s and '60s rock, soul, and doo-wop. The crowd is equally diverse and changes depending on the night's theme.

MAP 5: 1006 Forrest Ave., 615/650-9333, www.the5spot.club; hours and cover cost vary

BREWERIES, DISTILLERIES, AND TASTING ROOMS

Crazy Gnome Brewery

This self-proclaimed nanobrewery encourages you to bring food in from one of the neighborhood's many, many restaurants to eat as you try their beers, which include creative Tennessee concoctions such as beer made in a whiskey barrel or made with Southern-grown grains. The once-utilitarian space has been transformed with a mural of a gnome and white fairy lights. The brewery often hosts singer-songwriters for live music sessions. MAP 5: 948 Main St., 615/635-2582, www.cgbrewing.com; 3:30pm-10pm Tues.-Wed., 3:30pm-11pm Thurs.-Fri., noon-11pm Sat., noon-9pm Sun.

Smith & Lentz Brewing

This brewery's list of 14-16 lagers and ales is constantly rotating. Repeat visitors will always find something new to taste, from the California Orange Imperial IPA to the Sock Tan Pale Ale. The brewery is named for its owners, Kurt Smith and Adler Lentz, who met in Texas before moving to Nashville to go into business together. Look for taproom events such as open-mic comedy and "brew and view" movie nights. MAP 5: 903 Main St., 615/640-8761, www.smithandlentz.com; 3pm-10pm Mon.-Fri., 11am-10pm Sat.-Sun.

BARS

No. 308 Presents CAMP

This is a sleek, mod hangout with handcrafted drinks themed around national parks—and some of the proceeds even benefit the parks. This spot is the definition of a hipster hangout, with its unassuming entrance nestled next to a paint store. But for all the retro furniture, the national park theme, and the skinny jeans, CAMP is a friendly neighborhood bar that happens to be better-looking and serves better drinks. The American Samoa, honoring the park of the same name, is served in a shell-shaped bowl and features hibiscus ice cubes. Come during happy hour (5pm-7pm Sun.-Fri.), when the custom cocktails are more budget-friendly. MAP 5: 407 Gallatin Ave., 615/650-7344, http://bar308.com; 5pm-11pm Thurs., 5pm-midnight Fri.-Sat.

3 Crow Bar

Friendly and eclectic, with local eccentrics and possibly rock stars, 3 Crow Bar is the epitome of East Nashville. It is a particularly nice place to be on a sunny day when the garage door goes up and the neighborhood in all its quirkiness is on display. This is also a great time to get a bushwhacker, a Southern concoction of rum, crème de cacao, and other secret ingredients fed through a slushy machine. Rumor has it Johnny Cash spent his 70th birthday at this spot (back when it was Mike Grimes' Slow Bar). MAP 5: 1024 Woodland St., 615/262-3345, http://3crowbar.com; 11am-3am daily

By the Bottle

Housed on the first floor of Vandyke Bed and Beverage, By the Bottle is Nashville's first bottle-only wine bar. Owner Kate Cunningham knows her stuff. She selects natural

137

TENNESSEE WALTZING

In Nashville you hardly need to find a dance club to boogie. There is (quite literally) music in the streets; people will start moving whenever the mood strikes. The carillon bells play "The Tennessee Waltz" every hour on the hour at Bicentennial Mall, and it can be hard to resist the urge to start waltzing right there in public. But if you want a more structured environ, there are places to cut a rug all over town.

Plaza Mariachi

- Downtown's Wildhorse Saloon offers dance lessons every single day of the week. The lessons are free, the music is loud, and there's usually a good crowd.

- Monday nights transform East Nashville's The 5 Spot into a throwback party with swing dancing and Motown tunes. It is regularly packed and lasts into the wee hours.

- On Tuesday nights the best choice is Honky Tonk Tuesday Nights at American Legion 82, where western swing lessons take place before the band takes the stage.

- The Nashville Palace near Opryland is a good bet for line dancing without the downtown hubbub. Nearby, Country Fusion Dance Fitness (2416 Music Valley Dr., 615/679-5771, http://countryfusion.net) teaches line dancing steps in a workout class environment.

- Plaza Mariachi offers free salsa dancing classes many nights of the week.

and sustainable wines that you purchase by the bottle, and then drink with friends at a leisurely pace either inside the funky boutique hotel or in the lovely shaded courtyard garden. Most bottles are priced at $25 or $45.

MAP 5: 105 S. 11th St., no phone; 4pm-10pm Tues.-Thurs., 4pm-midnight Fri.-Sat., 2pm-8pm Sun.

PUBS
Southern Grist Brewing Company

Seasonal brews at this outfit—started by three beer-loving Nashville transplants in 2017—range from Save Play, a saison with lemongrass and orange peel, to Underbite, an imperial cream ale. Munch on thin-crust pizza from local 312 Pizza Company, soft pretzels with mustard, or beer cheese and truffles from Tempered Cafe & Chocolate. Southern Grist has a second location in The Nations on the city's west side.

MAP 5: 754 Douglas Ave., 629/203-7159, www.southerngristbrewing.com; 11am-8pm Sun.-Wed., 11am-10pm Thurs.-Sat.

LGBTQ BARS
✪ The Lipstick Lounge

There are fewer than two dozen lesbian bars left in the entire country, and The Lipstick Lounge is one of them for good reason. This is a laid-back bar with a better-than-average sound system and karaoke selection. Live music, pool, and great Tex-Mex-inspired food for brunch, and drag karaoke attract neighborhood crowds. The crowds are more mixed during the week than on the weekends, when it is mostly gay and lesbian patrons. You'll know you are in the right place when you get to the giant lip-shaped bench outside. MAP 5: 1400 Woodland St., 615/226-6343, http://thelipsticklounge.com; 6pm-3am Mon.-Fri., 10am-3am Sat.-Sun.; $5-10 cover on nights with entertainment

Festivals and Events

Music City Bowl

The Music City Bowl pits a Southeastern Conference team against a Big Ten or ACC rival. This nationally televised football game is held at Nissan Stadium. The festivities typically include a free night-before or postgame concert downtown and a parade of the collegiate athletes. Hometown team the Vanderbilt Commodores have played in the bowl several times in recent years. When that happens there is a big black and gold cheering section. East Nashville: 1 Titans Way, www.musiccitybowl.com; late Dec. or early Jan.; $25-125

Music City Hot Chicken Festival

If you know only one thing about Nashville food, it is likely that Music City loves its hot chicken. This spicy, panfried dish is at once a point of local pride and a culinary competition. Held on July 4 in East Park, this one-day eat-a-thon includes many of the city's hot-chicken purveyors frying up their best and spiciest. Come prepared to wait in line and test different recipes of the signature dish, then head downtown to watch the fireworks, which are one of the country's biggest displays. East Nashville: East Park, http://hot-chicken.com; July 4; free admission

East Nashville Tomato Art Festival

Started by the founders of the now-closed Art + Invention Gallery, the East Nashville Tomato Art Festival began as a tongue-in-cheek celebration of tomatoes and the hip, artsy vibe of East Nashville. It grew into one of the city's most iconic, beloved, and offbeat weekends. Events include a parade of tomatoes, the "Most Beautiful Tomato Pageant," biggest and smallest tomato contests, a tomato toss, a 5K run (in costume), live music, a Bloody Mary taste-off, and a tomato haiku contest. The two-day festival takes place the second weekend of August, when tomatoes are in season and the weather is hot. Costumes are encouraged, so feel free to come dressed as a tomato, or at least all in red. East Nashville: Woodland St. and 11th Ave., www.tomatoartfest.com; Aug.; free

Cumberland River Dragon Boat Festival

The Cumberland River Dragon Boat Festival is a one-day race in early September that takes place at East Bank Landing and is part of a 2,300-year-old tradition. More than 40 boats with big dragon heads and tails and 20 costumed paddlers each race each other on the water. There are plenty of river-themed activities for spectators, too, including a themed area for kids called DragonLand. Proceeds from the event benefit watershed conservation projects.

East Nashville: East Bank Landing, http://cumberlandrivercompact.org; early Sept.; free for spectators

John A. Merritt Classic

The John A. Merritt Classic, held over Labor Day, starts with a pep rally, happy hour, and high school band showcase and culminates with a football contest between the Tennessee State University Tigers and another historically Black collegiate football team at Nissan Stadium. The annual showdown is named for legendary former TSU football coach John Ayers Merritt.

East Nashville: Nissan Stadium, www.merrittclassic.com; early Sept.; $25-35

Recreation

SPECTATOR SPORTS
FOOTBALL
Tennessee Titans

You simply cannot miss the 68,000-seat Nissan Stadium, home of the NFL's Tennessee Titans. The stadium, which was finished in 1999 and renovated after the 2010 flood, towers on the east bank of the Cumberland River, directly opposite downtown. After the Titans moved to the stadium in 1999, they sold out almost every home game. But a spotty win-lose record in recent years has made tickets slightly easier to come by. If you want to see a game on short notice, your best bet is the online NFL ticket exchange, where season ticket holders can sell their seats to games they don't want to attend.

MAP 5: Nissan Stadium, 1 Titans Way, 615/565-4000, www.titansonline.com; Sept.-Dec.; tickets generally $130

Tennessee Titans at Nissan Stadium

PARKS
Cumberland Park

This 6.5-acre park is one of the city's gems and a remarkable space, nestled on the eastern bank of the Cumberland River, next to Nissan

Cumberland Park

GOLF
Shelby Golf Course
The first public golf course in Music City is still one of Nashville's favorites. Located in the popular East Nashville Shelby Park, the 18-hole course (with a 9-hole option) is particularly friendly to new golfers. It also hosts a respected junior golf program. Tee times are recommended, but not required, and can be reserved up to seven days in advance.

MAP 5: 2021 Fatherland St., 615/862-8474, http://nashville.gov; hours vary by season; $16-18/18 holes

Topgolf Nashville
Standing tall on the eastern bank of the Cumberland River is Topgolf, an outpost of a chain that has taken driving ranges to the next level. This 3,000-square-foot, three-level complex merges golf and entertainment, with 102 climate-controlled hitting bays that can accommodate up to six players each. Practice your swing, learn a new technique, listen to live music, and have a drink.

MAP 5: 500 Cowan St., 615/777-3007, http://topgolf.com; 10am-midnight daily; $30-55/hour

Stadium. It encompasses a kid-friendly rock-climbing wall, trails with native plants, misting stations, and educational information about how the Cumberland River is essential to the area's ecosystem. There are nice public restrooms and a concession stand. Right next to the park is the Riverfront Landing, an East Bank launch for canoes, kayaks, and paddleboards. The regular free parking (typically in Lot R) for both is not available when there is an event at Nissan Stadium.

MAP 5: 592 S. 1st St., 615/862-8508, www.nashville.gov; dawn-11pm daily

Shops

MUSIC
✪ Grimey's New and Preloved Music
Housed in a former church, Grimey's is one of the best places in the city to go for new and used CDs, DVDs, and vinyl. You'll find a wide selection of not just country, but also rock, folk, blues, R&B, and other genres. But Grimey's is more than a store: It's an institution. Since 1999 the staff has been amongst the city's most knowledgeable and friendly, and the clientele passionate and loyal. In-store live performances literally make the sound come alive. Music fans could spend hours here. Plan accordingly. There's a modest

bookstore space downstairs and a vintage clothing store, Anaconda Vintage (www.anacondavintage.com), in the back.

MAP 5: 1060 E. Trinity Ln., 615/226-3811, http://grimeys.com; 11am-6pm Tues.-Sat., noon-5pm Sun.

ANTIQUES AND VINTAGE
Hip Zipper

This East Nashville vintage stalwart is so packed with gems from days gone by that it can be hard to work your way around the racks. Working through the inventory is part of the fun, though. Hip Zipper was hip and here before the rest of the neighborhood was. Come here to find men's and women's vintage clothing, handbags, and accessories. Goods are also available for rent, if you're in town for a music video, film, or other production.

MAP 5: 1008 Forrest Ave., 615/228-1942, http://hipzipper.com; 11am-7pm daily

Star Struck Vintage Nashville

Star Struck Vintage is, like many other East Nashvillians, a New York transplant. This vintage store is in a funky strip mall that makes it seem like it would be smaller than it is. Inside you will find 3,000 square feet of goods packed onto shelves and racks. The focus is on clothing from the 1920s to the 1980s. You'll find velvet dresses, fringed jackets, concert t-shirts, and lettermen jackets. Be prepared to spend some time going through all the inventory.

MAP 5: 604 Gallatin Pike, 615/679-9675, www.starstruckvintage.com; 11am-6pm Tues.-Sat.

BOOKS
The Bookshop

Owner Joelle Herr, who, earlier in her career, worked for Avalon Travel Publishing, built this tiny but mighty bookstore based on her good instincts and professional experience. Herr selects everything that graces these pretty, well-designed shelves, with a mix of fiction, nonfiction, local interest, and children's books. The Bookshop connects through an inner hallway to next-door-neighbor Kettner Coffee Supply (1035 W. Eastland Ave., 7am-3pm daily). Kettner is a coffee shop with a few delicious menu items (including soft-serve ice cream) and space to host The Bookshop's Lit Club, silent book club, and other events.

MAP 5: 1043 W. Eastland Ave., 615/485-5420, www.herbookshop.com; 10am-7pm Mon.-Fri., 10am-6pm Sat., 10am-5pm Sun.

CLOTHING AND ACCESSORIES
Daisy May Hat Co

Hand-crafted, beaver-felt headwear is the focus at Daisy May Hat Co. These fedora-esque hats are not fast fashion. They are not the cheap cowboy hats you'll find at souvenir shops. They are investment pieces, featuring contrasting piping and colored bands, that you'll have forever and will remind you of the Nashville aesthetic. Daisy May also sells belts and other accessories. The wallpapered shop displays each hat on vintage and custom displays, showing off their one-of-a-kind nature.

SHOP LOCAL

One of Nashville's charms is the creativity apparent in every corner of the city, not just its music venues. This is particularly evident in its boutiques, which stock one-of-a-kind and locally made items. If you're looking or a souvenir to take home or a gift that will make your friends want to plan a return trip with you, check out one of these top shops. If you're more into browsing than buying, that's fun, too. Shopkeepers love to talk about their wares and the city that gives them inspiration.

- **Gift Horse** and **Tenn Gallon Hat:** Located in the Shoppes on Fatherland in East Nashville, these two stores run by the same owners carry locally produced art, jewelry, and Tennessee-themed items with a modern aesthetic. Letterpress fans should stop by to flip through the stacks of colorful posters.

- **Daisy May Hat Co:** A hand-blocked wool hat can last a lifetime. Find your stylish millinery purchase at this East Nashville studio and shop.

- **Planet Cowboy:** Whether you lean toward flashy colors or understated texture, you can have custom cowboy boots that reflect your personality designed at this 12 South boutique.

- **Any Old Iron:** Sequins are the signature look of many a Nashville star. Pick up your own head-turning outfit by stopping at this Music Row shop helmed by designer Andrew Clancey.

- **ABLE:** Sleek leather goods, clothing, and jewelry are the end product at this boutique in The Nations, but the mission is to help craftswomen around the globe earn a living wage.

- **Nisolo:** Explore the light, airy showroom for the fashionable, eco-friendly, fair wage shoe brand in their Buchanan Street outpost.

- **Music Valley Handmade:** Connected to the Texas Troubadour Theatre, near the Opryland resort, local artist and craftspeople display their wares in this gift shop. Come for picture frames, small art objects, soaps, candles, and jewelry.

MAP 5: 1100 Douglas Ave., no phone, https://daisymayhats.com; 10:30am-6pm daily

MAP 5: 1110 Woodland St., 615/226-5300; 11am-5pm Sat. and by appointment

Wonders on Woodland

Wonders on Woodland inhabits the front room of this East Nashville house. It is stocked with a well-curated selection of jewelry and other collectibles in a mix of mid-century and Victorian styles (yes, they can go together well). The jewelry comes in a range of costs and styles. It is a great place to find a quirky gift for quirky people.

GIFTS
Lemon Laine

Book a $65 appointment at this East Nashville skincare stop and you'll get a custom analysis of your skin and skincare routine, facial oil mixed just for you, a free drink or two, and an experience that goes beyond just grabbing a container of moisturizer. Lemon Laine is a destination for locals as well as bachelorette parties in town for group fun.

MAP 5: 1900 Eastland Ave., Ste. 102, 629/702-6940, www.lemonlaine.com; 11am-7pm Mon.-Sat., noon-5pm Sun.

Gift Horse

Located in the Shoppes on Fatherland, this sweet, hip shop stocks plenty of cards and art prints from local makers, contemporary jewelry, T-shirts, and other small gifts such as mugs, pins, and notebooks. Everything is well designed and well merchandised, making for fun browsing. They also own the adjacent **Tenn Gallon Hat,** which is focused on quality Tennessee-themed gifts and souvenirs.

MAP 5: 1006 Fatherland St., no phone, http://gifthorsenashville.com; noon-6pm Mon.-Tues., 10:30am-6pm Wed.-Sat., noon-4pm Sun.

Harlan Ruby Gift Shop

It's a family affair at Harlan Ruby, an umbrella for several creative businesses run by a mother and her daughters. You'll be delighted by the surprises in this modern party supply and gift shop, stocking locally made artwork, housewares, and hipster greeting cards, plus a "balloon bar" with unusual options like unicorns, cacti, margarita glasses, and oh-so-trendy rose gold letters and numbers. The youngest daughter (who is school-age) runs Hankabee Button Co., which is a part of the shop.

MAP 5: 805 Woodland St. #301, 615/955-0565, www.harlanruby.com; 10am-4pm Mon.-Sat.

KIDS
Fairytales Bookstore

This bookstore is kid heaven. It has what children—and adults—need to express themselves in most every art form. The books are wonderful, but there are toys, games, and crafting supplies, too. Everything is touchable, and there's a secure play area for trying things out. There's a quiet room with a couch and a cup of tea for parents needing a break. They also host events: story time and art classes for kids and adults.

MAP 5: 1108 Woodland St., 615/915-1960; 10am-4pm Mon.-Fri., 11am-5pm Sat.-Sun.

MUSIC
Fanny's House of Music

In another city, Fanny's might be considered an unusual place. It's a woman-owned, guitar-centered music store with a vintage clothing shop mixed in. But in Nashville, it's par for the course. The staff can help you find a guitar that's comfortable for you to play, regardless of gender or size. There are new, used, and vintage guitars and gear, and the guitar techs do a superb job of getting the road dings out of your axe. There are almost always folks sitting around jamming while you shop.

MAP 5: 1101 Holly St., 615/750-5746, http://fannyshouseofmusic.com; 11am-5pm Mon.-Sat.

The Groove

The Groove stocks some CDs, but mainly it's all about the vinyl, new and used. The folks behind the counter know what they're doing, so the records are in the right genre. In contrast with many stores for record diggers, this is a bright and airy place in a sunny house. Instead of smelling like dust and basement, it smells faintly of incense. They have a turntable listening station and host live bands.

MAP 5: 1103 Calvin Ave., 615/227-5760, http://thegroovenashville.com; 11am-6pm Wed.-Sat., noon-5pm Sun.

PETS

Wags & Whiskers

Wags & Whiskers carries holistic dog and cat food and offers self-serve dog-washing stations. The washing stations are big metal tubs set at a height that won't break your back. They also stock a cornucopia of treats, including dog-safe bones in the freezer. Wags & Whiskers is a little tricky to find, on the back side of vintage purveyor Hip Zipper, in the basement, but it's worth the trip. Look for other locations in 12 South and West Nashville.

MAP 5: 1008 Forrest Ave. (back of building), 615/228-9249, www.wagsandwhiskersnashville.com; 10am-8pm Mon.-Fri., 10am-6pm Sat., noon-5pm Sun.

SHOPPING DISTRICTS AND CENTERS

✪ Five Points Alley Shops

A collection of quirky shops nestled near East Nashville's 5 Points intersection, Five Points Alley Shops (also called The Idea Hatchery or 1108 Shops at Woodland) is a good destination for one-of-a-kind goods you won't find at home. Expect locally made crafts, a bookstore with a local bent, home goods, vintage clothes for men and women, letterpress stationery, and more.

MAP 5: 1108 Woodland St., http://theideahatchery.net; hours vary by store and season

✪ Shoppes on Fatherland

Some of the tiny stores on the Shoppes on Fatherland strip are hip to the point of humor. It can be somewhat surreal, like an episode of *Portlandia*. But beyond silliness is a nice community of more than 20 local businesses primarily selling handmade goods and repurposed vintage items. There's a fun energy in these East Nashville businesses. Hours vary by store, but weekends are when you'll see locals strolling by and hanging out. Some businesses pop up just for the holiday season, while others are stalwarts that have been here for years. You'll always be able to find something new. A number of local shops have started here to test the retail waters before moving to bigger (more expensive) spaces.

MAP 5: Fatherland St. between 10th St. and 11th St., 615/227-8646, www.fatherlanddistrict.com; hours vary by store

Music Valley

Map 6

The home of the **Grand Ole Opry** and **Opry Mills,** Music Valley is designed for tourists. Here you'll find kitschy attractions, **family-friendly restaurants,** affordable hotels and motels, plus a few true gems that locals secretly love.

TOP SIGHTS

- Most Renowned Venue: **Grand Ole Opry House** (page 149)
- Best Escape: **Gaylord Opryland Resort** (page 150)

TOP NIGHTLIFE

- The Radio Show that Started It All: **Grand Ole Opry** (page 153)

TOP RECREATION

- Where to Make a Splash: **SoundWaves** (page 155)

GETTING THERE AND AROUND

- Major bus routes: 34

Pennington Bend

MUSIC CITY CIR

1
2

RUDY'S CIR 3

4
5 6

Willie Nelson and
Friends Museum/8
Cooter's 9 11
7 10

MCGAVOCK PIKE

155

MUSIC VALLEY DR

PENNINGTON BEND RD

WESTERN HILLS DR

SPRINGHOUSE LN

Gaylord
Springs
Golf
Links

Cumberland
River

Haysboro

OPRYLAND DR

PENNINGTON BEND RD

SEE MAP 5

MOSS ROSE DR

OPRY MILLS DR

Cumberland
River

Gaylord
Opryland
Resort

12

13
14

OPRYLAND DR

OPRYLAND DR

Music Valley

MCGAVOCK PIKE

Grand Ole
Opry House

15 16

KIMBERLY DR

Rosebank

OPRY MILLS DR

17

Opry
Mills

DONNA HILL DR

Two
Rivers
Lake

155

Two Rivers
Golf Course

TWO RIVERS PKWY

18

© MOON.COM

DISTANCE ACROSS MAP
Approximate: 1.9 mi or 3.0 km

0 — 0.25 mi
0 — 0.25 km

SIGHTS
8 Willie Nelson and
Friends Museum
9 Cooter's
13 Gaylord Opryland Resort
15 Grand Ole Opry House

RESTAURANTS
4 Nashville Coffees
10 Scoreboard Bar & Grill
11 Semper Sliders

NIGHTLIFE
6 The Troubadour Nashville
7 The Nashville Palace
16 Grand Ole Opry

RECREATION
12 SoundWaves
17 General Jackson
Showboat
18 Wave Country

SHOPS
5 Dashwood Vintage

HOTELS
1 Best Western Suites
near Opryland
2 Courtyard by
Marriott Opryland
3 Hyatt Place
Nashville-Opryland
14 Gaylord Opryland Resort

Sights

✪ Grand Ole Opry House

The most famous broadcast in the city (if not the country) can trace its roots to October 1925, when Nashville-based National Life and Accident Insurance Company opened a radio station in town. Its call letters (both then and now), WSM, stood for "We Shield Millions," the company's motto.

WSM hired George D. "Judge" Hay, a radio announcer who had worked in Memphis and Chicago, to manage the station. Hay—who, while in Chicago, had announced one of the nation's first live country radio shows—planned to create a similar such program in Nashville.

On November 25, 1925, Hay invited a 78-year-old fiddler, Uncle Jimmy Thompson, to perform live on Saturday night over the radio waves. The response was electric, and WSM continued to broadcast live old-time music every Saturday night. In May 1927, the program developed the name the Grand Ole Opry, practically by chance. Hay was segueing from the previous program of classical opera to the barn dance. "For the past hour, we have been listening to music taken largely from Grand Opera. From now on, we will present the Grand Ole Opry," he said. The name stuck. By 1939, the Opry gained a slot on the nationwide NBC radio network, allowing it

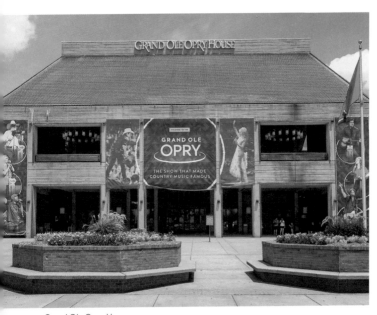

Grand Ole Opry House

Grand Ole Opry signage

to reach a national audience every week.

Always a live audience show, the Opry has been performed at several different venues over the years. It started in the WSM studio, then moved to the Hillsboro Theater (now the Belcourt), the Dixie Tabernacle on Fatherland Street, and the War Memorial Auditorium downtown. In 1943 it moved to the Ryman Auditorium, where it remained until 1974, when National Life built a new 5,000-seat auditorium in Music Valley, a rural area northeast of Nashville. The first show from the new Opry House was broadcast on March 16, 1974. After the 2010 Nashville flood, the Opry House was renovated and expanded. For a few months each year—typically between mid-November until after New Year's—the Opry returns to the Ryman stage and the Opry House hosts family-friendly holiday shows.

As its home base has changed, so, too, has the music that flows from the Opry's stage. Today it is a showcase for all types of country and country-inspired music, including bluegrass, folk, gospel, honky-tonk,

and zydeco. The Opry remains one of the most esteemed and celebrated institutions in American music.

The Opry performs at least two times a week, Friday and Saturday, with additional shows on Tuesday night most weeks. The Opry also offers a **backstage tour.** Daytime tour tickets go on sale two weeks in advance and are generally offered every 15 minutes. If you are buying tickets to a show, you can also purchase a post-concert backstage tour led by docents, where you'll get to see dressing rooms, learn lots of Opry history, and hear plenty of juicy stories about performers and their backstage behavior (and even see a performer or two in the flesh). One of the highlights of the guided tour is getting to go onstage and have your photo taken under the lights. Even if you don't think of yourself as a fan of country music, seeing the Opry is an essential Nashville experience.

MAP 6: 2802 Opryland Dr., 615/871-6779, www.opry.com; daytime tours vary; post-show tour 9:30pm Tues. and Fri.-Sat.; tours from $35 adults, $30 children

✪ Gaylord Opryland Resort

The massive Gaylord Opryland is Nashville's only true resort, a place that locals and tourists alike come to spend a few hours, regardless of whether or not they spend the night. Opryland is a head-turner: The resort operates its own nurseries so that it can fill its mammoth glass atriums and conservatories with lush, non-native flora like orchids. Regardless of the weather outside, you can walk miles of brightly lit footpaths, check out a 40-foot waterfall, or take a ride on flatboats that float along an artificial river. Kids love SoundWaves, the indoor-outdoor water park.

Also in the resort complex are restaurants (20 of them!), bars, shops, nightclubs, and wholesome, family-friendly live musical performances. A full-service spa offers serious relaxation, and there are multiple swimming pools for lounging. If you prefer your fun on the greens, the resort-affiliated Gaylord Springs Golf Links is across the street, featuring a 6,842-yard Larry Nelson-designed 18-hole, par 72 course. Seasonal events bring people in all year, but "A Country Christmas" is the showstopper. In November and December, the resort is bedecked with lights and offers a walk-through ice sculpture experience, ice tubing, and ice skating.

You could spend a weekend in Opryland without stepping outside at all. You'll miss a lot of authentic Music City if you do that, but stopping in for one of the many diversions can be a pleasant addition to a larger Nashville itinerary.

MAP 6: 2800 Opryland Dr., 615/889-1000, http://www.marriott.com

Willie Nelson and Friends Museum

The front of the Willie Nelson and Friends Museum is designed to look like a roadside stand. Inside, it's packed with memorabilia from Nelson's career, showcasing items that once belonged to the artist, including his golf bag, a replica of his tour bus, and the guitar he played during his first performance on the Grand Ole Opry. The gift shop is popular for Nashville mementos. True country fans will enjoy a quick visit here, but it isn't a go-out-of-your-way destination.

MAP 6: 2613A McGavock Pike, 615/885-1515, http:// willienelsonmuseum.com; 9am-6pm Sun.-Thurs., 9am-8pm Fri.-Sat.; $10, free for children under 12

Cooter's

If you're in the mood for Music Valley's signature kitsch, head straight for Cooter's, a gift shop and museum dedicated to the *Dukes of Hazzard* television show. This stop features a mind-boggling array of toys, ornaments, and model cars manufactured in the 1970s to profit off the Dukes' wild popularity. You can also see one of the bright-orange Dodge Chargers that became the Dukes' icon. In the gift shop, buy a pair of "official" Daisy Dukes or any number of themed souvenirs. Cooter's is operated by Ben Jones, who played Cooter, the affable sidekick mechanic, in the original television series.

MAP 6: 2613 McGavock Pike, 615/872-8358, http://cootersplace.com; 9am-7pm daily; free

Cooter's

Restaurants

PRICE KEY

$	Entrées less than $15
$ $	Entrées $15-25
$ $ $	Entrées more than $25

BURGERS

Semper Sliders $

A bright green shipping container in a shopping center parking lot may not sound like the most glamorous place to grab a bite. But owner Zac Jenkins makes it one of the tastiest. Jenkins appeared on The Food Network's *Great Food Truck Race* and has perfected his slider game. Try the brisket sliders and the tots, and don't sleep on the white cheddar mac 'n' cheese. Seating is offered inside a tent (complete with fans) or outside at picnic tables.

MAP 6: 2416 Music Valley Dr., 615/434-2614, www.sempersliders.com; 11am-2pm and 5pm-8pm Tues.-Thurs., 11am-8pm Fri.-Sat.

DINERS AND COFFEE SHOPS

Nashville Coffees $

This family-owned coffeeshop (seriously, the kids may even take your order) serves locally roasted coffee, as well as scones, muffins, and other baked goods. There are a few tables if you want to sit and plot out your day. If local coffee is your thing, this is the best bet near the Opryland complex.

MAP 6: 2416 Music Valley Dr. #143, 615/970-7337, www.nashvillecoffees.com; 6am-4pm Mon.-Fri., 8am-4pm Sat., 9am-3pm Sun.

HOT CHICKEN

Scoreboard Bar & Grill $$

This sports bar and eatery is a surprisingly solid option for curbing a hot chicken craving. Besides the usual pub grub, there are barbecued meat salads, burgers, and catfish and steak dinners. While Scoreboard is no traditional chicken shack, many locals swear by the hot chicken, in the form of bites, tenders, or bone-in breast on Texas toast.

MAP 6: 2408 Music Valley Dr., 615/883-3866, www.scoreboardbar.net; 11am-3am daily

DINE IN DONELSON

Stopping for a bite in Music Valley is convenient if you're headed to the Opry House for a show or to The Troubadour Nashville to go dancing. But if you don't want to eat inside the Gaylord Opryland Resort or the Opry Mills mall, your choices for good eats are limited. Consider hopping in the car to check out Donelson, a hip neighborhood four miles south (about a 10-minute drive). The neighborhood is lined with restaurants, bars, and coffee shops. Donelson is about the same distance north of Nashville International Airport, so it can be a good stop for a meal on your way out of town, too. Here are a few spots to try:

- **Caliber Coffee** (2513 Lebanon Pike, 615/679-9013, www.calibercoffeeco.com): Head to the drive-thru for breakfast sandwiches and coffee.
- **Homegrown Taproom** (2720 Old Lebanon Rd., 629/888-9180, http://homegrownnashville.com): Craft beers and scratch-made sandwiches are on the menu at this locally owned taproom. Sunday brunch is a good way to start the day.
- **MirkoPasta** (2264 Lebanon Pike, 615/882-7990, http://mirkopastanashville.com): Chicken marsala, pastas, and great breads make this a reliable Italian food outing.
- **Nectar: Urban Cantina** (206 McGavock Pike, 615/454-2277, www.nectarcantina.com): A combination of Mexican and Southern dishes means you'll find creations like a hash brown taco. Nectar has a full bar, smoothies and coffee in the morning, and a popular patio with lawn games.
- **Party Fowl** (2620 Lebanon Pike, 615/988-2179, http://partyfowl.com): Watch whatever game is on, drink adult slushies, and eat hot chicken at this outpost of the local chain.
- **Phat Bites** (2730 Lebanon Pike, 615/871-4055, www.phatbites.com): Vegetarian-friendly foods, daily hummus specials, plus live music and a full bar at night make this a local hangout.
- **TennFold Brewing** (2408 Lebanon Pike, 615/727-7577, www.tennfold.com): Some breweries have food as an afterthought, but the pizzas here are worthy on their own. The dog-friendly patio is a good place to sample the craft beers.

Nightlife

LIVE MUSIC
COUNTRY AND BLUEGRASS

TOP EXPERIENCE

✪ Grand Ole Opry

If there's one thing you really must do while in Nashville, it's see the Grand Ole Opry. Really. Even if you think you don't like country music, consider it a must. Since 1925, this weekly radio showcase of country music has drawn crowds to Nashville. Every show at the Opry is still broadcast live on WSM, a Nashville AM radio station. Shows are also streamed online, and some are televised on cable. But nothing beats the experience of being there. Often there is an additional Tuesday evening show.

Since this is a radio broadcast, shows start and end right on time. Every Opry show is divided into

Grand Ole Opry

30-minute segments, each of which is hosted by a different member of the Opry. This elite country music fraternity includes dozens of stars that you've heard of and others you haven't. The host performs two songs; one at the beginning of that half-hour segment and one at the end. In between they will introduce two or three other performers, each of whom will sing about two songs. In between segments, the announcers read radio commercials and stagehands change the set. Each year, usually from mid-November to early January, the Opry returns to the Ryman stage and the Opry House hosts family-friendly holiday shows.

MAP 6: 2804 Opryland Dr., 800/733-6779, www.opry.com; shows Tues. and Fri.-Sat.; prices vary, typically $55-110

The Nashville Palace

The Nashville Palace is an old-school restaurant, nightclub, and dance floor across from the Gaylord Opryland Resort. If your image of Nashville is line dancing as you've seen in movies, this place is more likely to meet your mental image than anywhere else in town, including Lower Broad. The big restaurant and bar has several rooms adorned with country decor (one even has a giant guitar-shaped mass of Christmas lights on the ceiling). Live music is on tap daily, plus free dance lessons, so you can try line dancing and two-step for yourself.

MAP 6: 2611 McGavock Pike, 615/889-1540, www. thefamousnashvillepalace.com; 11am-midnight Sun.-Mon., 11am-2am Tues.-Sat.; cover cost varies by event

The Troubadour Nashville

Once called the Texas Troubadour Theatre, this historic space is now a bar playing live classic country music, offering line-dancing lessons and a large dance floor where you can cut a rug. A full bar serves beer, wine, and cocktails, plus a few snacks like pizza. Connected to the bar is **Music Valley Handmade,** a gift shop with Nashville-themed items. The building also houses the **Green Hornet tour bus** that Ernest Tubb used between 1970-1979. The bus has been restored so that you can walk through it and see what life was like on the road for country's biggest stars. There's no cover charge for most shows, but don't forget to tip the band and your dance teachers. Midnite Jamboree, the famed weekly radio show that used to take place here, is now broadcast downtown at the **Ernest Tubb Record Shop.**

MAP 6: 2416 Music Valley Dr., no phone; 6pm-10pm daily, cover cost varies by event

Recreation

General Jackson Showboat

TOURS

General Jackson Showboat

Gaylord Opryland's *General Jackson* showboat offers campy, big-budget-style musical shows on the stage of a giant riverboat as it lumbers down the Cumberland River. Show dates and times vary by season but typically include midday lunch and evening dinner cruises. A smaller boat, the *Music City Queen,* offers tailgating cruises before Titans football games. Because of the meal and the live entertainment, these cruises aren't necessarily the best way to see the river, as you're focused on the stage, rather than the scenery.

MAP 6: 2812 Opryland Dr., 615/889-1000, http://generaljackson.com; showtimes generally noon and 7pm daily; $30-135

AMUSEMENT PARKS

✪ SoundWaves

While primarily designed for overnight guests of the **Gaylord Opryland Resort,** the mammoth SoundWaves indoor/outdoor water park is available for nonguests and is jam-packed with fun and sun. No detail has been overlooked: You can eat, drink, and lounge, or plunge in the water all day. The park includes a 315,000-gallon outdoor wave pool with a giant LED movie screen, several giant indoor corkscrew water slides, a lazy river, adult-only pools and cabanas, kids' pools, a surfing simulator, food trucks, live music, and more. Party rooms for groups are available for four-hour blocks, with all-day access to the park. Much of the park is indoors, so even when the weather isn't cooperating,

FIND A BARGAIN AT OPRY MILLS

Opry Mills

Opry Mills (433 Opry Mills Dr., 615/514-1000, http://oprymills.com), a discount mall in Music Valley, is the city's most maligned favorite destination. Locals love to hate it, in part because it replaced the old Opryland amusement park on this same site and because it is so popular. It's one of the area's leading tourist attractions, and the lines for the parking lot back up along Briley Parkway around Christmas and during back-to-school shopping season in summer.

If you're looking for an upscale shopping experience or you're familiar with other national-brand outlet malls, you don't need to come here. But if good deals on name-brand merchandise appeal to you, Opry Mills is the mall for you. Brands include Disney, Lego, Coach, Kate Spade New York, Ann Taylor, H&M, and Torrid. It also has a 20-screen movie theater, IMAX, and a mammoth Bass Pro Shops with all sorts of outdoor equipment. The Nashville outpost of Madame Tussauds Wax Museum (515 Opry Mills Dr., 615/485-4867, www.madametussauds.com/nashville) is worth a visit even if you aren't otherwise interested in the mall. It's the only Madame Tussauds with a focus on music. If you're killing time before the Grand Ole Opry, you can pop over to Opry Mills and while away an hour or two.

the park's atrium makes it feel sunny and warm. Discounts are available for Tennessee residents.
MAP 6: 2800 Opryland Dr., 615/458-6802, www.soundwavesgo. com; 10am-8pm Mon.-Fri., 9am-8pm Sat.-Sun.; $40-55 pp

Wave Country

When the summer gets hot, as it does in Tennessee, locals line up to take their kids to Wave Country. Located near Music Valley, this water park has exciting slides, a wave pool, and sand volleyball courts, as well as a play area for smaller kids. Wave Country is managed by Metro Parks.
MAP 6: 2320 Two Rivers Pkwy., 615/885-1092, www.nashville.gov/parks; 11am-5pm Mon.-Thurs., 10am-6pm Fri.-Sat., 11am-6pm Sun. May-Aug.; $12 adults, $10 children ages 3-12, children under 3 free

Shops

ANTIQUES AND VINTAGE

Dashwood Vintage

Part of the Music Valley Village shopping center north of the Gaylord Opryland Resort, Dashwood Vintage will woo fans of midcentury modern decor. The shop features lots of retro lamps, art, furniture, and other home goods, all looking as if they came directly off the set of *Mad Men*. Vintage vinyl albums and live houseplants round out the offerings.

MAP 6: 2416 Music Valley Dr., 615/712-7091, www.dashwoodtn.com; 10am-4pm Tues.-Sat., 10am-3pm Sun.

South Nashville

Map 7

South Nashville is a collection of smaller neighborhoods and doesn't have quite the cohesive vibe as some other parts of the city. In fact, it can be hard to define the borders between areas like Chesnut Hill and Wedgewood-Houston. But South Nashville makes up for this with worthy destinations: the **Nashville Zoo at Grassmere,** innovative **art galleries and maker spaces,** and the best **international cuisine** in the city.

TOP SIGHTS

- Best Place to Honor the Black Soliders who Protected Nashville: **Fort Negley Park** (page 161)
- Collection Most Likely to Rev Your Engine: **Lane Motor Museum** (page 162)

TOP RESTAURANTS

- Place for World-Class Dining: **Bastion** (page 164)
- Transformative Dining Experience: **Plaza Mariachi** (page 166)

TOP NIGHTLIFE

- Best Spot for Beer: **The Ranch Taproom + Brewery** (page 167)

TOP RECREATION

- Best Reason to Board a Train to Nowhere: **Tennessee Central Railway** (page 170)

TOP SHOPS

- Where to Buy Iconic Western Wear: **Manuel Exclusive Clothier** (page 171)

GETTING THERE AND AROUND

- Major bus route: 52

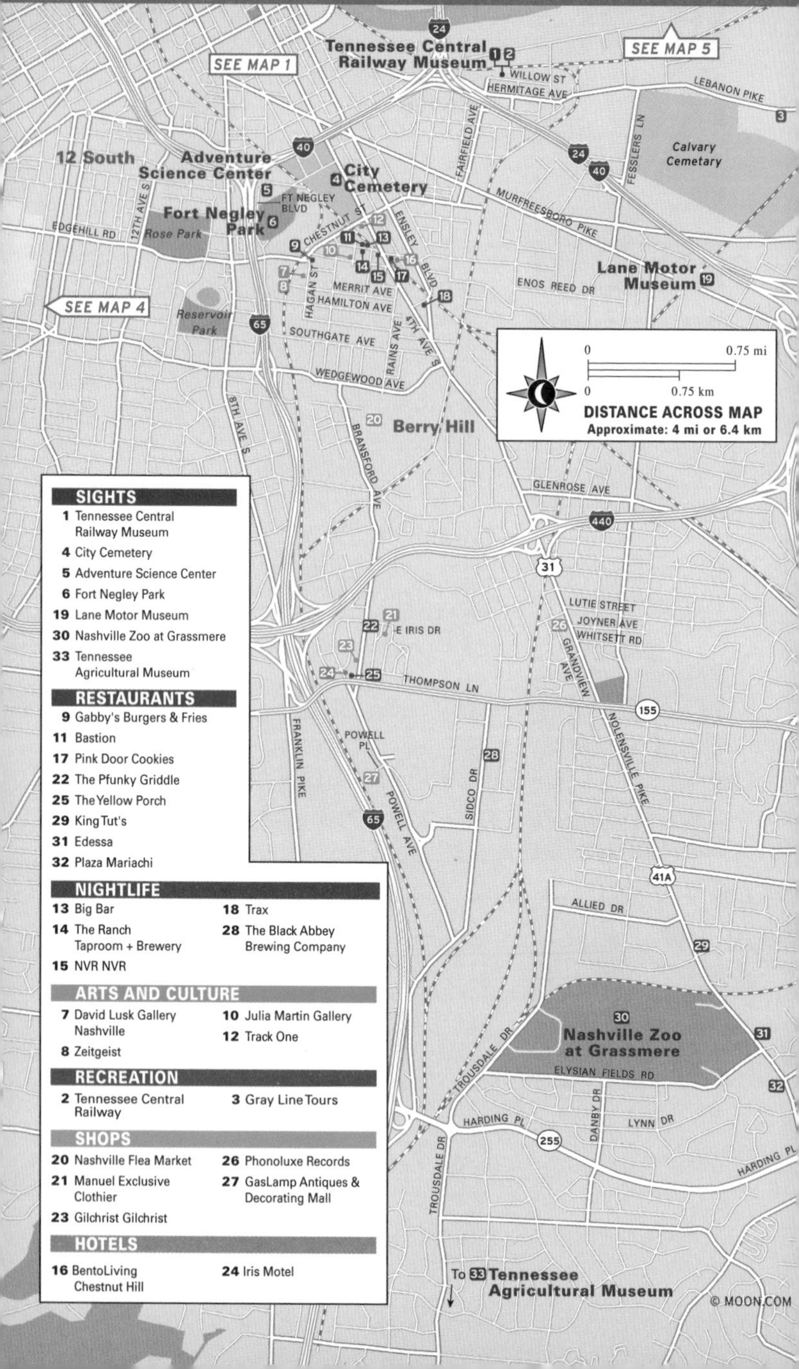

SEE MAP 1

Tennessee Central
Railway Museum

SEE MAP 5

WILLOW ST
HERMITAGE AVE

LEBANON PIKE

FAIRFIELD AVE

24

40

Calvary
Cemetery

12 South

Adventure
Science Center

City
Cemetery

FT NEGLEY
BLVD

FORT NEGLEY
PARK

Rose Park

EDGEHILL RD

MURFREESBORO PIKE

CHESTNUT ST

9

10

11

13

12

ENSLEY BLVD

Lane Motor
Museum

19

14   15   16
17

ENOS REED DR

SEE MAP 4

HAGAN ST

MERRIT AVE

18

65

HAMILTON AVE

RAINS AVE

SOUTHGATE AVE

4TH AVE S

Reservoir
Park

WEDGEWOOD
AVE

9TH AVE S

BRANSFORD AVE

Berry Hill

20

| 0 | | 0.75 mi |
| 0 | | 0.75 km |

DISTANCE ACROSS MAP
Approximate: 4 mi or 6.4 km

GLENROSE AVE

440

31

LUTIE STREET

JOYNER AVE

WHITSETT RD

26

E IRIS DR

22   21

23

24   25

THOMPSON LN

GRANDVIEW AVE

155

POWELL PL

27

28

SIDCO DR

NOLENSVILLE PIKE

65

FRANKLIN PIKE

POWELL AVE

41A

ALLIED DR

29

Nashville Zoo
at Grassmere

30

31

ELYSIAN FIELDS RD

32

TROUSDALE DR

SIDCO DR

DANBY DR

LYNN DR

HARDING PL

255

HARDING PL

To 33 **Tennessee
Agricultural Museum**

© MOON.COM

Sights

Adventure Science Center

While the hands-on educational programs available at the Adventure Science Center are designed for children, there's plenty to entertain adults, too. Interactive exhibits explore how the body works, the solar system, and other scientific areas. Perhaps the most popular attraction is the multi-story climbing tower in the building's center, which features a giant guitar and other instruments and is always covered in enthusiastic visitors. The center's 164-seat **Sudekum Planetarium** (http://sudekumplanetarium.com; $7 adults, $6 children) is the largest planetarium in Tennessee. It offers a variety of popular space-themed shows, gravity-suspending rides, and exhibits about spaceflight, the moon, and the solar system.

MAP 7: 800 Fort Negley Blvd., 615/862-5160, www.adventuresci.com; 10am-3pm Thurs.-Mon., 10am-6pm Sat.; $25 adults, $20 children

City Cemetery

Right below Fort Negley Park is the old City Cemetery. Opened in 1822, City Cemetery is the final resting place of many of Nashville's most prominent early citizens, including founder James Robertson; William Driver, the U.S. Navy captain who named the flag "Old Glory"; Mabel Lewis Imes and Ella Sheppard, members of the original Fisk Jubilee Singers; and 14 Nashville mayors. During the Civil War, the cemetery was contracted to bury more than 15,000 Union and Confederate dead, though they were later reinterred in different cemeteries.

Pamphlets and signage on-site will help you along a self-guided tour. The grounds are tended to by the Master Gardeners of Davidson County, so they are often in bloom. Guided tours are available by appointment and tell the history of Nashvillians who are buried at this historical site. Note there is only one entrance and exit, which is at an awkward angle from 4th Avenue South if you are driving. Be patient at the intersection.

MAP 7: 1001 4th Ave. S., http://thenashvillecitycemetery.org; dawn-dusk daily, guided tours by appointment; free

TOP EXPERIENCE

✪ Fort Negley Park

Early in the Civil War, the Union army determined that taking and holding Nashville was a critical strategic link in their victory. So after Nashville fell in 1862, the Federals wasted no time fortifying the city against attacks. One of the city's forts was Fort Negley, built between August and December 1862 on St. Cloud Hill south of the city center.

That effort was not without enormous cost. Fort Negley owes its existence to the 2,768 men who were enrolled to build it. Most were Black people, some free and some enslaved, who were pressed into service by the Union army. These men felled trees, hauled earth, and cut and laid limestone for the fort.

161

They slept in the open and enjoyed few, if any, comforts while they labored. Between 600 and 800 men died while building the fort, due to terrible working conditions, injury, and more. One historian suggests that working on the fort was as deadly as going to the battlefield would later be for African American soldiers. Of the Black workers who toiled at the fort, only 310 received payment. It is likely that the remains of some of these Black laborers are buried at Fort Negley.

When it was completed, Fort Negley was the largest inland masonry fortification in North America. It was never challenged. Fort Negley was abandoned by the military after the war, but it remained the cornerstone of one of Nashville's oldest African American communities, now known as Cameron-Trimble. During the New Deal, the Works Progress Administration rebuilt large sections of the crumbling fort, and it became a public park.

In 2019 the site was named a UNESCO Slave Route Destination for its effort to document the work of both enslaved and free Black workers. Explore the **visitors center** (noon-4pm Tues.-Fri., 9am-4pm Sat., free) to learn the story of the fort. It includes a museum about the fort and Nashville's role in the Civil War, as well as a sizable gift shop. There is a paved loop trail around the base of the fort, plus raised boardwalks through the fortifications themselves. Some of the boardwalks need repair, so heed signage if a certain path is closed. The total distance of the paths inside the park is less than a mile, and

Fort Negley Park

the exterior paths are wheelchair-accessible. Historical markers tell the story of the fort's construction and detail its military features, and wildflowers bloom on the hillside. Fort Negley is one of the great places to take in a view of Music City.
MAP 7: 1100 Fort Negley Blvd., 615/862-8470, http://nashville.gov; dawn-dusk daily; free

✪ Lane Motor Museum
Kids and adults alike relish coming to this one-of-a-kind, off-the-beaten-track museum. Here you'll find all manner of automobiles, from early hybrids and steam engines to a car that's so small it can be "reversed" merely by picking it up with a lever and putting it down facing the other direction. The amphibious cars are always a delight, too.

The museum, based in the old Sunbeam Bakery, has the largest collection of European cars and motorcycles in the country. In fact, the collection is so big that not everything is on view at all times. Glass dividers allow you to watch the restoration of antique automobiles in progress. There's a decent play area for small kids who need a break.

MAP 7: 702 Murfreesboro Pike, 615/742-7445, www.lanemotormuseum. org; 10am-5pm Thurs.-Mon.; $12 adults, $8 seniors, $3 children ages 6-17, children under 6 free

Nashville Zoo at Grassmere

Nashville Zoo at Grassmere

See familiar and exotic animals at the Nashville Zoo at Grassmere, one of the largest zoos in the country. Many of the zoo's animals live in habitats that are designed to emulate their native surroundings, like Lorikeet Landing, Gibbon Islands, and Bamboo Trail. The zoo's meerkat exhibit, featuring the famously quizzical animals, is one of its most popular, as is the Tiger Crossroads exhibit. The Wild Animal Carousel is an old-time carousel with 39 different brightly painted wooden animals.

The zoo is located at Grassmere, the onetime home and farm of the Croft family. The historical Croft farmhouse has been preserved, its gardens replicated, and is open for guided tours March through mid-October.

MAP 7: 3777 Nolensville Pike, 615/833-1534, www.nashvillezoo.org; 9am-6pm daily mid-Mar.-mid-Oct., 9am-4pm daily mid-Oct.-mid-Mar.; $18-21 adults, $14-17 children ages 2-12; children under 2 free, $8 parking

Tennessee Agricultural Museum

The two-story Tennessee Agricultural Museum celebrates the ingenuity and dedicated labors of farm life from the 17th to the 20th centuries. Operated by the Tennessee Department of Agriculture and set on the department's pleasant South Nashville campus, the museum depicts various facets of Tennessee farm life. It has exhibits about clothes washing, blacksmithing, coopering, plowing, weaving, and more. Outside, there is a small kitchen garden with heirloom vegetables, along with replicas of a log cabin, one-room schoolhouse, and outdoor kitchen. A short self-guided nature trail illustrates the ways that settlers used various types of native Tennessee trees. Visitors can

Tennessee Agricultural Museum

always see the historical exhibits on their own in this welcoming and educational space. Hands-on demonstrations are typically offered on summer Saturdays and by advance appointment for groups with a small fee, but the knowledgeable staff are available to answer any questions at any time. The museum is inside the bucolic Ellington Agricultural Center, a 207-acre site with walking trails and an iris garden.

MAP 7: 440 Hogan Rd., 615/837-5197, http://tnagmuseum.org; 9am-4pm Mon.-Fri.; self-guided tour free

Tennessee Central Railway Museum

Railroad enthusiasts should make a detour to the Tennessee Central Railway Museum. This institution is best known for its special railroad excursions that are part tour, part performance. The museum houses an extensive collection of railroad equipment, paraphernalia, and a jaw-dropping model railroad. Dedicated volunteers restore and care for the collection and are more than willing to chat about railways and run the miniature trains on their indoor loops, with sound effects, raising and lowering bridges, and more. The museum is in a largely industrial area between the interstate and the railroad tracks, one block north of Hermitage Avenue and east of Fairfield Avenue. It's a quick drive from downtown or East Nashville. (For details on themed railway tours that depart from the museum, see page 170.)

MAP 7: 220 Willow St., 615/244-9001, www.tcry.org; 9am-3pm Tues.-Sat.; free

Restaurants

PRICE KEY

$	Entrées less than $15
$ $	Entrées $15-25
$ $ $	Entrées more than $25

NEW AMERICAN
✪ Bastion $$$

The first thing to know about Bastion is that it's divided into two spaces. The left side is the **Big Bar,** which is an offbeat, hip, popular people-watching spot with nice art, good nachos, and great drinks. The right side is the 24-seat restaurant. Tables here are at a premium as the restaurant has repeatedly made best-of lists across the country. When you arrive, you'll be given a piece of paper with an à la carte list of dishes made from fresh ingredients. Part of the experience that chef Josh Habiger created is watching the food being prepared and getting to talk to the staff about the concepts behind the food. The room is designed to feel like you are in someone's living room, complete with a turntable playing music. Allow enough time to fully engage in the experience of eating here. Make pre-paid reservations online (up to four weeks in advance). The five-course, choose-your-own-adventure meal ($90 pp) is a great way to experience Bastion.

Bastion

MAP 7: 434 Houston St., Ste. 110, 615/490-8434, www.bastionnashville. com; 5:30pm-8:30pm Wed.-Sat.

The Yellow Porch $$

Located in a cute, comfortable house in Berry Hill, The Yellow Porch serves solid American cuisine, with good salads, appetizers, and entrées, not to mention a quality wine list and satisfying desserts. The staff is friendly and welcoming. A small, covered porch is nice for outdoor dining, although it looks out on a traffic-heavy street.

MAP 7: 734 Thompson Ln., 615/386-0260, www.theyellowporch. com; 11am-3pm and 5pm-9pm Mon.-Thurs., 11am-3pm and 5pm-10pm Fri.-Sat.

DINERS AND COFFEE SHOPS

Gabby's Burgers & Fries $

Gabby's is a lunch spot in the rapidly changing Wedgewood-Houston neighborhood. Locals love this tiny place for its grass-fed beef patties, handmade black bean burgers, and sweet potato fries. Expect a wait, as the place is small, and more likely than not you'll sit at the counter to eat. Police officers, active military, and firefighters receive 20 percent off their bills.

MAP 7: 493 Humphreys St., 615/733-3119, http:// gabbysburgersandfries.com; 10:30am-2:30pm Mon.-Fri., 11am-2:30pm Sat.

Pink Door Cookies $

Pink Door Cookies, nestled on the first floor of the **BentoLiving Chestnut Hill** hotel, is smaller than some closets. But from this tiny space, Mathew Rice creates big flavors, baking a delicious rotating section of cookies. Some are offbeat (pink lemonade), others are classics (brownie). Check out the floor, which was created by scattering

165

brightly colored sprinkles into the epoxy.

MAP 7: 321 Hart St., Ste. 309, no phone, www.pinkdoorcookies.com; noon-6pm Tues.-Sun.

The Pfunky Griddle $

This Berry Hill restaurant has a gimmick: Order pancakes, eggs, and breakfast potatoes, and you're served the ingredients to cook at your own table, which is outfitted with a hibachi-style grill. The potatoes are particularly well-seasoned, and pancakes are all-you-can-eat with your choice of toppings and two kinds of batter. There are sandwiches and other dishes prepared in the kitchen, should you not want to make your own food. The menu includes many gluten-free options. Waits for a table can be long on the weekend.

MAP 7: 2800 Bransford Ave., 615/298-2088, www.thepfunkygriddle. com; 8am-2pm Tues.-Fri., 7am-2pm Sat.-Sun.

KURDISH
Edessa $

While many of Nashville's Kurdish eateries are casual takeout spots, Edessa offers a more upscale dining experience. Cozy booths and attentive service accompany the dishes of beef and lamb, lentil and bean soups, and salads. The hot and cold appetizers feature some Turkish delicacies, as well as popular Middle Eastern dishes like falafel and tabbouleh. The owners of Edessa also have a restaurant in

the Assembly Food Hall at Fifth + Broadway.

MAP 7: 3802 Nolensville Pike, 615/837-2567, www.edessarestauranttn. net; 11am-8:30pm daily

EGYPTIAN
King Tut's $

The best falafel in Nashville is served from this food truck that is permanently parked on Nolensville Pike. The owners bult a lovely patio where you can enjoy Egyptian dishes, including salads, sandwiches, and full plates. The environment is laid-back and welcoming. Look for the bright red truck toward the back of the parking lot.

MAP 7: 3716 Nolensville Pike, 615/944-3735, http://kingtutsnashville. com; 4pm-9pm Thurs.-Sun.

MEXICAN
✪ Plaza Mariachi $

This Mexican marketplace features a number of restaurants mixed with grocery stores, clothes shops, and other services. Dining highlights include Argentinean steak house Tres Gauchos and a walk-up ceviche bar called El Ceviche Loco. Come at night and you can take free dance lessons, and even during the day there's often live music. The atmosphere can seem a little like a cruise ship—lots of flashing lights and faux scenic backdrops—but the food is fun, affordable, and festive.

MAP 7: 3955 Nolensville Pike, 615/373-9292, www.plazamariachi. com; 11am-9pm Tues.-Thurs., 11am-1am Fri.-Sat., 11am-10pm Sun.

Nightlife

BREWERIES, DISTILLERIES, AND TASTING ROOMS

The Black Abbey Brewing Company

Three Nashville home brewers founded this brewery in 2013 to focus on Belgian-inspired ales that are both unique and accessible. Tours of the brewing operation (1pm-4pm Sat.; $10, book online or at the brewery) include a pint glass and a 16-ounce pour of one beer. The interior has a monastery-like vibe, where arched wooden insets showcase brewery merch. Food trucks often visit on the weekends, making it a fine spot to grab a snack with your beer.

MAP 7: 2952 Sidco Dr., 615/755-0070, www.blackabbeybrewing.com; 2pm-8pm Sun.-Fri., noon-8pm Sat.

✪ The Ranch Taproom + Brewery

The women-owned Jackalope Brewing Company makes multiple year-round beers, seasonal beers, and some limited editions, too. This was the first craft brewery in Nashville to can their beers. Their taproom, called The Ranch, is a fun outdoor patio that welcomes dogs. Hang out and play shuffleboard as you taste beers that include seasonal stouts and IPAs. Nosh on small bites like pretzels, salami, and cheese plates, or bring in food from other restaurants in the neighborhood.

MAP 7: 429 Houston St., 615/873-4313, https://jackalopebrew.com; 2pm-10pm Wed.-Thurs., noon-10pm Fri.-Sat., noon-6pm Sun.

BARS

Big Bar

Here you'll find two completely different (but equally worthy) businesses at one spot. To the right is Bastion, a reservations-only, sit-down dining experience. To the left is Big Bar, a fun bar with funky artwork, tiered seating, crafted cocktails, and two varieties of nachos. Come here to play darts, hang out with friends, or have a drink before heading out to dinner.

MAP 7: 434 Houston St., Ste. 110, 615/490-8434, www.bastionnashville. com; 5pm-midnight Sun.-Thurs., 5pm-1am Fri.-Sat.

NVR NVR

You'll hear the railroad go by as you sit at an outdoor table at NVR

NVR NVR

LITTLE KURDISTAN

Nashville has a population of about 15,000 Kurdish American residents, more than any other city in the United States. Many of these people came to Nashville as refugees beginning in the late 1970s, fleeing political upheaval, genocide, and the dictatorship of Saddam Hussein. They hail from the Kurdish region of the Middle East, which overlaps the borders of Iran, Iraq, Syria, and Turkey; the Kurds are the largest ethnic group in the world without their own fully autonomous land.

Edessa Restaurant

While Kurdish people live all over the Nashville area, the community is concentrated in South Nashville, near an area referred to as Little Kurdistan (Nolensville Pike and Elysian Fields Ct.). The best way to experience Nashville's Kurdish culture is by having a meal at some of the community's many restaurants. Here are some of the best picks:

- Edessa Restaurant (3802 Nolensville Pike, 615/837-2567, www.edessanashville. com) offers the best Kurdish sit-down dining experience in the city.
- Named for the celebration of spring that many Kurds observe, Newroz Market (393 Elysian Fields Ct., 615/333-0037) is a go-to shop for black tea, baklava, halal meats, and groceries. Walk to the back to find House of Shawarma, a sandwich counter.
- Azadi International Food Market and Bakery (391 Elysian Fields Ct., 615/315-0904) provides the community with fresh-baked bread made in the brick oven behind the shop. You can grab meat or cheese-topped breads, *sambusa* (a samosa-like snack), and shawarma.
- Botan Market (4905 Edmondson Pike, 615/942-9398) is a market stocked with fresh-baked bread and baklava, delicious hummus, plus bulk spices, halal meats, and groceries.

NVR (pronounced "Never Never"). This is a hip, casual bar where you can listen to live music and sip reasonably priced drinks. The tequila sangria is a particular favorite. This is one of the few bars in the city without any TVs. To find it, look for the neon sign that reads "BAR."

MAP 7: 413 Houston St., 615/649-8475, www.nevernevernashville.com; 4pm-2am Mon.-Fri., 4pm-3am Sat., 11am-2am Sun.

LGBTQ BARS

Trax

For a low-key evening of shooting pool or a happy hour stop before dinner, Trax is the place to go. The patio is a nice place to sit in warm weather. Trax has wireless Internet and big-screen televisions but little in the way of ambience. The back parking lot is well lit, a perk when leaving in the wee hours.

MAP 7: 1501 Ensley Blvd., 615/742-8856, https://trax-gay-bar. business.site; noon-3am daily; no cover

Arts and Culture

GALLERIES

David Lusk Gallery Nashville

David Lusk Gallery started in Memphis in 1995, but now, with a second location in the state capital next to Zeitgeist, it is a pivotal part of the thriving Wedgewood/Houston art scene. It makes sense, given the fact that Lusk has gravitated to transitional neighborhoods throughout his career. The gallery focuses on the works of emerging artists, many—but not exclusively—from the South. Expect to see paintings, photography, and sculpture. MAP 7: 516 Hagan St., 615/780-9990, http://davidluskgallery.com; 10am-5pm Tues.-Sat.; free

Julia Martin Gallery

Artist Julia Martin opened her eponymous gallery in an old railroad house, and from it she fuses the historical with the contemporary. Martin has an eye and sense of what makes Nashville the dynamic city it is, and she cultivates relationships with artists who bring their sensibilities about Nashville to their work. Some of Martin's own work can be seen in the Noelle hotel downtown. MAP 7: 444 Humphreys St., 615/336-7773, www.juliamartingallery.com; noon-6pm Sat. or by appointment; free

Track One

In what once was a feed and seed warehouse built by Nashville Decatur Railroad in 1924 to serve nearby farming communities, Track One is a retail/arts/hipster paradise in Wedgewood-Houston. There are a number of galleries in this renovated space, and many artists call Track One their studio. Hours vary, but the monthly WeHo Art Crawl (www.wehoartsnashville.com) on the first Saturday of the month is a good time to see lots of open doors. MAP 7: 1201 4th Ave. S., no phone, https://trackonenashville.com; hours vary; free

Zeitgeist

For years Zeitgeist was the cornerstone—literally and figuratively—of Hillsboro Village, attracting talented artists and well-heeled collectors. In 2013 the gallery moved to a bigger, reclaimed historical space with Manuel Zeitlin Architects and helped welcome an artistic community to the Wedgewood-Houston neighborhood. Now the space is the cornerstone of this neighborhood. The exhibited art changes monthly, depending on which artists the gallery is featuring. MAP 7: 516 Hagan St., 615/256-4805, http://zeitgeist-art.com; noon-4pm daily or by appointment; free

Recreation

TOURS

✪ Tennessee Central Railway

The Tennessee Central Railway Museum offers an annual calendar of sightseeing and themed railway rides in central Tennessee, including kids' trips, Old West shoot-outs, and murder mysteries. Excursions include fall foliage tours, Christmas shopping expeditions, and trips to scenic small towns. All trips run on the Nashville and Eastern Railroad, which runs east, stopping in Lebanon, Watertown, Cookeville, or Monterrey. These tours are not just train rides, but well-organized volunteer-led events. You might get "robbed" by a Wild West bandit (the cash goes to charity) or taken to a scenic winery. The volunteers know their railroad trivia, so feel free to ask questions. The cars vary depending on what is available, but one car doubles as a gift shop and another as a concession stand, though you are welcome to bring your own food on the train. Trips sell out early, so book your tickets well in advance. MAP 7: 220 Willow St., 615/244-9001, http://tcry.org; tour times vary; $42-160 adults, $21-38 children

Gray Line Tours

Nashville's largest tour company, Gray Line, offers more than 20 different sightseeing tours of the city. The three-hour Discover Nashville tour includes entrance to the Ryman Auditorium and the Country Music Hall of Fame and stops at other city landmarks. The three-hour Homes of the Stars tour takes you past the current and former homes of stars, including Garth Brooks and Trisha Yearwood, Taylor Swift, Reese Witherspoon, and Dolly Parton. A one-hour downtown trolley tour and a downtown walking tour are also available. MAP 7: 1307 Lebanon Pike, 615/883-5555 or 800/251-1864, http://graylinetn.com; tour times vary; $25-141 adults, $15-71 children

Shops

ANTIQUES AND VINTAGE

GasLamp Antiques & Decorating Mall

Just south of the Berry Hill neighborhood you'll find one of the city's largest and most popular antiques malls. It may be squeezed between big-box stores, but its wares are anything but. It has more than 150 vendors, many of them local interior designers, and a great selection of all types of antiques. MAP 7: 100 Powell Pl., Ste. 200, 615/297-2224, http://gaslampantiques.com; 10am-6pm Mon.-Sat., noon-6pm Sun.

FLEA MARKETS

Nashville Flea Market

Nashville's largest flea market takes place on the fourth weekend of every month at the Fairgrounds Nashville. It's a bargain lover's dream, with thousands of sellers peddling clothes, crafts, and all sorts of vintage and used housewares, often at lower prices than you'd find in bigger cities. The fairgrounds are on 4th Avenue, south of downtown. Admission is free; parking is $5.

MAP 7: 500 Wedgewood Ave., 615/862-5016, www.thefairgrounds. com; 8am-5pm Fri., 7am-5pm Sat., 7am-4pm Sun. fourth weekend Jan.-Feb., 8am-5pm Fri., 7am-6pm Sat., 7am-4pm Sun. fourth weekend Mar.-Nov., 8am-5pm Fri., 7am-6pm Sat., 7am-4pm Sun. third weekend Dec.

HOME DECOR

Gilchrist Gilchrist

Shopkeepers say country/pop singer and Nashville favorite Taylor Swift is a fan of the vintage finds with a shabby chic patina in this Berry Hill storefront. When it comes to furniture, expect to find real antiques, not items made to look old, most of which are in the beige and white color family. There are also new lampshades, picture frames, and other goods that would be easier to pack in a suitcase.

MAP 7: 2823 Bransford Ave., 615/385-2122, www.gilchristgilchrist. com; 10am-5pm Mon.-Sat.

MUSIC

Phonoluxe Records

Phonoluxe Records owner Mike Smyth has always marched to the beat of his own drum. He never lost faith in vinyl, so in the 1990s, when everyone started buying CDs, he stocked up on LPs. Now that people remember why they loved vinyl in the first place, he has the stock to attract collectors and music lovers. The location is a bit out of the way if you are staying downtown, and the hours can be eccentric, but this only increases the romance. Smyth pulls gems from his own vault every week, so it's worth checking back regularly. All genres are represented.

MAP 7: 2609 Nolensville Pike, 615/259-3500; 10am-7pm Fri.-Sat., noon-6pm Sun.

CLOTHING

✪ Manuel Exclusive Clothier

The name says it all: Manuel Exclusive Clothier. Manuel Cuevas goes by just his first name, and he's the man who outfits all the stars with their stage-worthy blingiest clothing. The cowboy shirts start at $750 and jackets at more than $2,000, so this isn't the place for an impulse buy. This is the place to go to show that you've made it. You can stop by to admire the work even if you can't order your own Manuel suit . . . yet.

MAP 7: 2804 Columbine Pl., 615/321-5444; 9am-6pm Mon.-Fri. or by appointment

Greater Nashville

Map 8

Nashville's suburbs and outlying areas offer compelling reasons to jump in the car and explore. From the window you'll see Middle Tennessee's **rolling hills** along the **Natchez Trace Parkway** or by paddling on **Percy Priest Lake.** For a more manicured experience, the art and flora at **Cheekwood** are a must.

TOP SIGHTS

- Most Immersive Gardens:
  Cheekwood (page 176)

TOP RESTAURANTS

- Must-Eat Biscuit: **The Loveless Cafe** (page 179)
- Best Place to Feel the Burn: **Prince's Hot Chicken Shack** (page 179)

TOP NIGHTLIFE

- Best Listening Room: **The Bluebird Cafe** (page 183)

TOP RECREATION

- Most Scenic Way to Stretch Your Legs:
  Natchez Trace Parkway (page 189)

TOP SHOPS

- Best Place to Make Kids' Dreams Come True: **Phillips Toy Mart** (page 198)

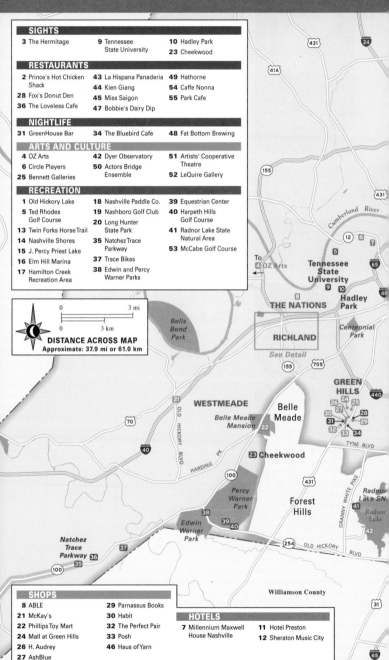

SIGHTS

3 The Hermitage
9 Tennessee State University
10 Hadley Park
23 Cheekwood

RESTAURANTS

2 Prince's Hot Chicken Shack
28 Fox's Donut Den
36 The Loveless Cafe
43 La Hispana Panaderia
44 Kien Giang
45 Miss Saigon
47 Bobbie's Dairy Dip
49 Hathorne
54 Caffe Nonna
55 Park Cafe

NIGHTLIFE

31 GreenHouse Bar
34 The Bluebird Cafe
48 Fat Bottom Brewing

ARTS AND CULTURE

4 OZ Arts
6 Circle Players
25 Bennett Galleries
42 Dyer Observatory
50 Actors Bridge Ensemble
51 Artists' Cooperative Theatre
52 LeQuire Gallery

RECREATION

1 Old Hickory Lake
5 Ted Rhodes Golf Course
13 Twin Forks Horse Trail
14 Nashville Shores
15 J. Percy Priest Lake
16 Elm Hill Marina
17 Hamilton Creek Recreation Area
18 Nashville Paddle Co.
19 Nashboro Golf Club
20 Long Hunter State Park
35 Natchez Trace Parkway
37 Trace Bikes
38 Edwin and Percy Warner Parks
39 Equestrian Center
40 Harpeth Hills Golf Course
41 Radnor Lake State Natural Area
53 McCabe Golf Course

0   3 mi
0   3 km

DISTANCE ACROSS MAP
Approximate: 37.9 mi or 61.0 km

SHOPS

8 ABLE
21 McKay's
22 Phillips Toy Mart
24 Mall at Green Hills
26 H. Audrey
27 AshBlue
29 Parnassus Books
30 Habit
32 The Perfect Pair
33 Posh
46 Haus of Yarn

HOTELS

7 Millennium Maxwell House Nashville
11 Hotel Preston
12 Sheraton Music City

Sights

☼ Cheekwood

Plan to spend a full morning or afternoon at Cheekwood, so you can experience the full scope of this magnificent art museum and botanical garden. Galleries in the Cheekwood mansion house the museum's American and European collections, including some excellent contemporary art. Cheekwood has the largest public collection of works by Nashville artist William Edmondson, the sculptor and stoneworker. The museum usually displays items from its permanent collection as well as traveling exhibitions from other museums. Many exhibits have special ties with Nashville.

But Cheekwood is far more than just an art museum. The mansion overlooks hundreds of acres of gardens and woods, and it is easy to forget that you are near a major American city when you're there. Walk the mile-long Carell Woodland Sculpture Trail past works by 15 internationally acclaimed artists, or stroll past the water garden to the Japanese garden. There are dogwood gardens, an herb garden, a delightful boxwood garden, and much more. Wear comfortable shoes and pack a bottle of water so that you can enjoy the grounds in comfort.

Cheekwood owes its existence to the success of the coffee brand

Cheekwood

THE SCULPTURE OF WILLIAM EDMONDSON

The first African American artist to have a one-man show at the Museum of Modern Art in New York was Nashville-born sculptor William Edmondson (1874-1951). Edmondson was born in the Hillsboro area of Nashville. He worked for decades as a laborer on the railroads, a janitor at the Women's Hospital, and in other similar jobs before discovering his talent for sculpture in 1929. Edmondson told *The Tennessean* that his talent and passion were God-given: "God appeared at the head of my bed and talked to me, like a natural man, concerning the talent of cutting stone He was about to bestow. He talked so loud He woke me up. He told me He had something for me."

A prolific sculptor, Edmondson worked exclusively with limestone, and he created angels, women, doves, turtles, rabbits, and other "varmints." He also made tombstones. Edmondson never learned to read or write, and he called many of his works "mirkels" because they were inspired by God.

In the 1930s, Louise Dahl-Wolfe, a photographer for *Harper's Bazaar* magazine, brought Edmondson and his work to the attention of Alfred Barr, the director of the Museum of Modern Art. Barr and other trustees of the museum admired what they termed as Edmondson's "modern primitive" work, and they invited him to display a one-man show at the museum in 1938. In 1941, the Nashville Art Museum put on an exhibit of Edmondson's work.

Edmondson continued to work until the late 1940s, when he became ill with cancer. After his death in 1951 he was buried in an unmarked grave at Mount Ararat Cemetery in Nashville. The city park at 17th Avenue North and Charlotte Avenue is named in honor of Edmondson.

Some of Edmondson's work is on display at Cheekwood.

Maxwell House. During the 1920s, Leslie Cheek and his wife, Mabel Wood, invested in the new coffee brand being developed by their cousin, Joel Cheek. Maxwell House proved to be a success and earned the Cheeks a fortune, which they used to buy 100 acres of land in West Nashville. The family hired New York residential and landscape architect Bryant Fleming to create a 30,000-square-foot mansion and neighboring gardens. Cheekwood was completed in 1933.

Leslie Cheek lived in the mansion just two years before he died, and Mabel lived there for another decade before deeding it to her daughter and son-in-law, who later offered it as a site for a museum and garden. Cheekwood opened to the public in 1960.

MAP 8: 1200 Forrest Park Dr., 615/356-8000, http://cheekwood.org; 9am-5pm Tues.-Sun.; $20 adults, $18 seniors, $13-16 students and children, $5 parking

Hadley Park

Founded in 1912, Hadley Park is believed to be the oldest public park developed for African Americans in the South and, most likely, the United States. The park got its start when Fisk University president George Gates requested that the city buy land and create a park for its Black citizens. This was in the era of segregation, so other city parks were not open to Black people. The request was granted, and the park opened in July 1912. An old farmhouse was converted into a community center, and benches and a playground were installed. It is now home to a state-of-the-art gym and fitness center, computer labs, meeting rooms, and tennis courts.

MAP 8: 1037 28th Ave. N., 615/862-8451, www.nashville.gov; dawn-11pm daily

The Hermitage

East of the city is The Hermitage, Andrew Jackson's plantation home. The Hermitage is where Jackson retired following his two terms as president of the United States, and it is where he and his wife, Rachel, are buried. Following President Jackson's death, The Hermitage remained in family hands until 1853, when it was sold to the state of Tennessee to pay off the family's debts. It opened as a museum in 1889. Many of the furnishings are original, and even the wallpaper in several rooms dates back to the years when Andrew Jackson called it home.

The site's tour and museum focus not only on Jackson and the construction and decoration of the mansion, but also the enslaved Black people who were forced to work here. Curators and archaeologists have studied The Hermitage to learn about the hundreds of enslaved men and women who made the plantation profitable and successful for so many years. The tour of the grounds takes visitors to Alfred's Cabin, which was occupied until 1901 by Alfred Jackson, who had been enslaved at The Hermitage. (Alfred is buried near Andrew Jackson on the grounds.) To learn even more about the enslaved people who lived at The Hermitage, take an add-on wagon tour (Apr.-Oct., $12). The tours also cover Jackson's enforcement of the

The Hermitage

Trail of Tears, one of his most brutal legacies, which forced more than 16,000 Native Americans from their homes. In 2016 The Hermitage was added as an official stop on the Trail of Tears.

Visitors to The Hermitage first watch a video and then can continue on to the museum. The audio tours of the grounds include a kids' version narrated by Jackson's pet parrot. Guided tours of the mansion are included with admission. Plan on spending at least three hours here to make the most of your visit. Try to come when the weather is good, so you can take in the grounds and not just the residence.

MAP 8: 4580 Rachel's Ln., 615/889-2941, http://thehermitage.com; 8:30am-6pm daily mid-Mar.-mid-Oct., 9am-5pm daily mid-Oct.-mid-Mar.; $24 adults, $21 seniors, $15 children ages 5-12

Tennessee State University

Founded in 1912 as the Agricultural and Industrial State Normal College for Black students, Tennessee State University is now a comprehensive university with more than 9,000 students. In 1979, as a result of a court order to desegregate the state's universities, TSU merged with the

Nashville campus of the University of Tennessee. Today TSU's student body is 75 percent Black.

Walking through the leafy, brick-building campus, which takes up more than 500 acres in North Nashville, you'll pass the historical President's Residence, the columned McWherter Administration Building, and the modern Lawson Hall. Campus tours are offered twice daily on weekdays during the school year.

MAP 8: 3500 John A. Merritt Blvd., 615/963-5000, www.tnstate.edu; 24 hours daily; campus tours 10am Mon.-Thurs. May-Aug., 10am and 2pm Mon.-Fri. Sept.-Apr.; free

Restaurants

PRICE KEY

$	Entrées less than $15
$ $	Entrées $15-25
$ $ $	Entrées more than $25

BARBECUE AND SOUTHERN

✪ The Loveless Cafe $$

The Loveless Cafe is an institution, and some may argue it's a state of mind. But this little café-that-could is increasingly a destination, too, not only for Nashville visitors but also for those touring the heartland of Tennessee. The Loveless got its start in 1951 when Lon and Annie Loveless started to serve good country cooking to travelers on Highway 100. Over the years the restaurant changed hands, but Annie's biscuit recipe remained the same, and it was the biscuits that kept Nashvillians, including many famous ones, coming back for more. In 1982, then owner George McCabe started the Hams & Jams mail-order business, and in 2003 the Loveless underwent a major renovation that expanded the kitchen and dining rooms and added additional shops in the rear. The biscuits are fluffy and buttery, the ham salty, and the eggs, bacon, and sausage will hit the spot. The supper and lunch menu has expanded to include Southern standards like fried catfish and chicken, pit-cooked pork barbecue, pork chops, and meat loaf, as well as a few salads. Loveless is about 20 miles (32 km) from downtown Nashville; plan on a 30-minute drive out TN-100. Once you get out of the congestion of the West End, it's a pretty trip, and close to the northern terminus of the Natchez Trace Parkway. Loveless also operates a food truck, which can be seen at events around town.

MAP 8: 8400 TN-100, 615/646-9700, www.lovelesscafe.com; 7am-9pm daily

HOT CHICKEN

✪ Prince's Hot Chicken Shack $

Out of all the food that you eat in Music City, you'll likely still be dreaming about Prince's Hot Chicken when you get home. "Hot chicken" is panfried chicken that is also spicy, and it is special to Music City. Prince's serves three varieties: mild, hot, and extra hot. Most

HOT CHICKEN!

Nashville's most lauded food experience is not to be found in a fine restaurant or even at a standard meat-and-three cafeteria. It is served on a plate with a slice of Wonder bread and a pickle chip. It is hot chicken, a very spicy panfried delicacy, made with bone-in breast and secret spices.

Legend goes that in the 1930s a woman made an extra spicy dish to punish her philandering boyfriend. But it turned out that he *liked* it extra hot, and both Prince's Hot Chicken Shack and a national obsession were born.

A growing number of shops specialize in this regional treat: Hattie B's Hot Chicken; 400 Degrees (3704 Clarksville Pike, 615/244-4467, www.400degreeshotchicken.com);

Nashville hot chicken

Prince's Hot Chicken Shack, the most famous hot chicken shack, which has the longest lines; and Bolton's Spicy Chicken & Fish. Each has its special spices, but the basic idea is the same. Order it as spicy as you can take it, but not so hot that you can't enjoy the flavor. Panfrying takes time, so you're likely to wait wherever you go. Party Fowl is a good choice for those who want to drink with their spicy food. Scoreboard Bar & Grill is your best bet for hot chicken near the Gaylord Opryland Resort.

The Music City Hot Chicken Festival (www.hot-chicken.com), held each year on July 4 in East Nashville, is the best place to compare lots of different recipes, as countless vendors offer up their own takes on the dish. For more on hot chicken, its history, and the connection to appropriation, redlining, and real estate, read Rachel Louise Martin's book, *Hot Hot Chicken: A Nashville Story*.

uninitiated will find the mild variety plenty spicy, so beware. It is served with slices of white bread—perfect for soaking up that spicy chicken juice—and a pickle slice. You can add a cup of creamy potato salad, coleslaw, or baked beans if you like. Your food is made to order, and Prince's is very popular, so the wait often exceeds 30 minutes. Take heart, though—Prince's chicken is worth it. Get a fix in South Nashville or at Prince's food truck in the SoBro Complex/6th & Peabody (423 6th Ave. S.). A

location at Nashville International Airport is also in the works. MAP 8: 5814 Nolensville Pike, 615/801-9388, www.princeshotchicken. com; 11am-10pm Mon.-Sat.

NEW AMERICAN

Hathorne $$

The building that houses Hathorne used to be the meeting room for the former church next door, and that friendly gathering-place vibe permeates this lovely American eatery. The vegetable dishes are particularly creative, drawing inspiration and

NOT JUST FOR VEGETARIANS

Nashville, with its hot chicken and its meat-and-threes, historically hasn't been known as a vegetarian paradise. But as its food scene in general has become more varied, so have the vegetarian options. Here's a look at some of the more interesting options for those looking for a plant-based meal (or two). Don't worry, omnivores—everyone will find something to eat at these spots.

- AVO (3 City Ave., #200, 615/329-2377, www.eatavo.com): The entire menu at this quirky local favorite is plant-based, raw, and gluten-free. The AVOcado margarita (made with avocado, aged tequila, cilantro, and lime) is the talk of the town.

- Graze (1888 Eastland Ave., 615/686-1060, www.grazenashville.com): This "plant-based bistro and bar" is at home in East Nashville, serving dinner as well as weekend brunch. Here, the cheese is made from cashews, the hot chicken sandwich is made with meat-free tempeh, and the banh mi is filled with seitan. There are also a handful of juices and smoothies for those looking for sustenance in liquid form.

- Wild Cow (1000 Fatherland St., 615/262-2717, http://thewildcow.com): With its tongue-in-cheek name, this East Nashville joint is all about vegetarian and vegan fare made with organic and locally sourced ingredients when possible. Choose from salads, tacos, and bowls filled with grains or greens.

- Sunflower Cafe (2834 Azalea Pl., 615/457-2568, www.sunflowercafenashville.com): This Berry Hill house is home to a vegetarian cafeteria-style restaurant with a changing selection of entrées and sides served in meat-and-three style, albeit without the meat. Many of the offerings are vegan and gluten-free as well. There's also the related Sunflower Bakehouse (2414 Lebanon Pike) close to Opryland.

seasonings from Southern, Japanese, and Irish traditions. Owner John Stephenson used to be the chef at the shuttered (but beloved) Family Wash; sometimes you'll see a few Family Wash recipes on the menu, particularly at brunch.

MAP 8: 4708 Charlotte Ave., 629/888-4917, www.hathornenashville.com; 5pm-10pm Mon.-Thurs., 5pm-10:30pm Fri.-Sat., 10am-2pm Sun.

ITALIAN
Caffe Nonna $$$

For some of the best Italian food in Nashville, head west to the neighborhood of Sylvan Park, where you'll find Caffe Nonna. Inspired by chef Daniel Maggipinto's own *nonna* (grandmother), the café serves rustic Italian fare. Appetizers include salads and bruschetta, and entrées include the divine Lasagna Nonna,

made with butternut squash, ricotta cheese, spinach, and sage. The service at Caffe Nonna is friendly and attentive, and the atmosphere is cozy, but the space is small. Call ahead for a table.

MAP 8: 4427 Murphy Rd., 615/463-0133, www.caffenonna.com; 5pm-9pm Mon.-Thurs., 5pm-10pm Fri.-Sat.

NEW AMERICAN
Park Cafe $$$

Park Cafe is Sylvan Park's reliable upscale dinner-out spot, with a small but solid menu of meats and poultry. Typically at least one vegetarian-friendly item is on the menu. Park Cafe offers an impressive happy hour, with specials on both food and drinks, that draws in the locals. The space is dark in a cozy way, great for a date or an intimate chat. Parking can be challenging on Murphy Road on the weekends.

MAP 8: 4403 Murphy Rd.,
615/383-4409, http://parkcafenashville.
com; 4pm-10pm Mon.-Sat.

VIETNAMESE
Kien Giang $

Just west of the Kroger grocery store, in a strip mall near the K&S World Market, is one of Nashville's favorite Vietnamese restaurants. The ambience is not fancy, and the service can be slow, but the spring rolls, pho, and other dishes are flavorful. Bring cash: Kien Giang does not accept credit cards. (Note: Using the address "5300 Charlotte Pike" may work better in some GPS systems.)

MAP 8: 5845 Charlotte Pike,
615/353-1250; 11am-8pm Tues.-Sun.;
cash only

Miss Saigon $

A renovation made Miss Saigon seem swanky in comparison to its neighbors, all of whom are worthwhile Vietnamese eateries in this area of town. Miss Saigon is in a strip mall on a hill off Charlotte Avenue; it can be easy to miss the driveway. But when you arrive, you'll find more than ample parking, friendly staff, and a fresh menu with tasty spring rolls, banh mi sandwiches, and many types of pho. Miss Saigon is usually buzzing, but there's rarely a wait for a table.

MAP 8: 5849 Charlotte Pike,
615/354-1351, www.misssaigontn.com;
10am-9pm Wed.-Mon.

SWEETS
Bobbie's Dairy Dip $

Go back in time to this old-fashioned burger and ice cream

shop. Walk up to the window, order, and then sit at one of the few picnic tables until your shake or sundae is ready. On summer nights the place is packed with families, couples on date night, and others enjoying the simplest of pleasures. Hours vary based on the weather. A hot spell may encourage them to open their doors (er, windows) in early March.

MAP 8: 5301 Charlotte Ave.,
615/463-8088; 11am-7pm Mon-Tues.
and Thurs., 9am-9pm Wed., 11am-10pm
Fri.-Sat., noon-5pm Sun. spring-fall

Fox's Donut Den $

In general, eating at a joint that is known for its signage as much as it is for its food is a bad idea. But at Fox's Donut Den, you get to take in the old-time neon sign that graces Hillsboro Pike (and was part of a rezoning debate in Green Hills) and eat a tasty doughnut at the same time. The sweet breakfast treat of your choice is a matter of personal preference, but the apple fritters are a local favorite.

MAP 8: 3900 Hillsboro Pike,
615/385-1021; 5am-10pm Mon.-Thurs.,
5am-midnight Fri., 6am-midnight Sat.,
6am-10pm Sun.

La Hispana Panaderia $

La Hispana Panaderia is one of the city's great bakery bargains. People flock here from across town for inexpensive bread and pastries that are as good as at the finest European bakery. Favorites include the crunchy white bread and their dense cookies and sweet tres leches cakes, craved by the most ardent sweet tooth.

MAP 8: 6208 Charlotte Pike,
615/645-9723; 6am-9pm daily

Nightlife

LIVE MUSIC

LISTENING ROOMS
✪ The Bluebird Cafe

The Bluebird Cafe is where Nashville's real music magic happens. It's an unassuming room, small and, depending on the night, a bit cramped, but when people talk about how they heard so-and-so play in Nashville, odds are pretty good that it was here. The Bluebird is famous for its songwriters' nights, open mics, and performances in the round. Musicians aren't up on a stage—they are right there, with you. Since it is a small room, reservations are required, and this is not the place to plan to talk to your neighbor while the music plays. You will be shushed. Not every performer on the calendar is someone recognizable, but odds are they've written something that is. It's worth the risk to find out. The Bluebird is all ages, except for its 10 bar seats, which are only for those 21 and older.

If you can't get tickets to the Bluebird, try The Listening Room Café (618 4th Ave. S., 615/259-3600, https://listeningroomcafe.com). It has a similar songwriter-in-the-round vibe but is larger and has more availability.

MAP 8: 4104 Hillsboro Pike, 615/383-1461, http://bluebirdcafe.com; 5:30pm-midnight Mon. and Fri.-Sat., 5pm-midnight Tues.-Thurs. and Sun.; cover varies

BREWERIES, DISTILLERIES, AND TASTING ROOMS
Fat Bottom Brewing

This brewery, one of several in The Nations neighborhood, focuses on beer, but it's also a spot for great food. Seasonal salads, good burgers, a cheese and charcuterie plate, and other better-than-bar-fare options make up the menu, making Fat Bottom a good destination for a meal with your beer. Each of the flagship beers has a Vargus-girl-style icon to distinguish it. The brewery also houses The Reserve, a 3,000-square-foot event space. The 45-minute brewery tour (6pm Fri., 2pm and 3pm Sat.; $10, book online) includes four beer tastes and a souvenir glass to take home.

MAP 8: 800 44th Ave., 615/678-5895, http://fatbottombrewing.com; 4pm-10pm Mon.-Thurs., noon-11pm Fri., 10:30am-11pm Sat.,10:30am-9pm Sun.

BARS
GreenHouse Bar

The name doesn't lie. You'll be sipping your specialty drinks and beers amid hanging plants and under the transparent ceiling of an actual greenhouse. This is a laidback spot with long hours where you can have a drink and enjoy lots of oxygen, thanks to all those plants. The bar shares space with a catering company, so there's also a menu of salads, soups, and sandwiches. To find

NASHVILLE'S CRAFT BREWERY SCENE

Music City has seen its craft beer scene grow into something interesting in recent years. Here's a list of places to stop for a local ale (and in some cases, a taproom tour) if you crave a cold one while in town.

- Bearded Iris Brewing (101 Van Buren St., 615/928-7988, www.beardedirisbrewing.com)
- The Black Abbey Brewing Company (2952 Sidco Dr., 615/755-0070, www.blackabbeybrewing.com)
- Czann's Brewing Company (4909 Indiana Ave., 615/748-1399, www.czanns.com)
- Fat Bottom Brewing (800 44th Ave., 615/678-5895, http://fatbottombrewing.com)
- Jackalope Brewing Company (429B Houston St., 615/873-4313, http://jackalopebrew.com)
- New Heights Brewing Company (928 Rep. John Lewis Way S., 615/490-6901, www.newheightsbrewing.com)
- Rock Bottom Brewery (111 Broadway, 615/251-4677, www.rockbottom.com)
- Southern Grist Brewing Company (1201 Porter Rd., 629/203-7159, www.southerngristbrewing.com)
- Smith & Lentz Brewing (903 Main St., no phone, www.smithandlentz.com)
- TailGate Brewery (811 Gallatin Ave., 629/203-7152; 7300 Charlotte Pike, 615/861-9842; 1538 Demonbreun St., 629/702-5914, www.tailgatebeer.com)
- Tennessee Brew Works (809 Ewing Ave., 615/436-0050, www.tnbrew.com)
- Yazoo Tap Room (900 River Bluff Dr., 615/891-4649, http://yazoobrew.com)

the GreenHouse Bar, look for the Green Hills Kroger and take a left. Its location means you'll find more locals than tourists. The back parking lot is tiny, but there are others nearby, and Uber and Lyft are always good options for a night out on the town.

MAP 8: 2211 Bandywood Dr., 615/385-4311, www.greenhousenash.com/greenhouse-bar; 8am-3am Mon.-Sat., 10am-3am Sun.

Arts and Culture

GALLERIES

Bennett Galleries

From a two-story building in the heart of Green Hills, Bennett Galleries shows the work of contemporary artists away from the concentration of other galleries in town. Works range from abstract to figurative, with an emphasis on painting and sculpture. Bennett also offers framing services for those pieces you pick up elsewhere.

MAP 8: 2104 Crestmoor Rd., 615/297-3201, www.bennettgalleriesnashville.com; 9:30am-5:30pm Mon.-Fri., 9:30am-5pm Sat.; free

LeQuire Gallery

Sculptor Alan LeQuire is known for two iconic Nashville works: *Musica,* the Music Row sculpture contro-versial for its unclad figures, and *Athena*, the massive golden goddess at the Parthenon. His Sylvan Park gallery is more diverse, exhibiting both his own work and that of other sculptors. In addition to having works on display, LeQuire Gallery also teaches classes and workshops for those who want to get in touch with their artistic side.

MAP 8: 4304 Charlotte Ave., 615/298-4611, www.lequiregallery.com; 10am-3pm Tues.-Sat.; free

PERFORMANCE VENUES

Dyer Observatory

A working space observatory oper-ated by Vanderbilt University, Dyer Observatory has emerged as a pop-ular venue for music. **Bluebird on the Mountain** ($135 per vehicle, up to 8 guests), working with The Bluebird Cafe, brings live music to this dramatic and one-of-a-kind spot. Imagine a night of fine music enjoyed under the stars with the fresh air and the atmosphere of the forest all around you. Dyer is oper-ated by the university but is not lo-cated on campus.

MAP 8: 1000 Oman Dr., Brentwood, 615/373-4897, http://dyer.vanderbilt. edu; 9am-4pm Tues.-Thurs. Mar.-Nov.; additional hours vary by event

Oz Arts

Founded in 2013 by Nashvillians who wanted to give back to the city that welcomed them as immigrants, Oz is a multiuse performance space with an emphasis on contemporary arts. Spoken word, music, perfor-mance art, film, and contemporary dance are often on the schedule.

Yes, the location is on the far west side of town. But Oz presents some of the most cutting-edge perfor-mances in the city and should be on your radar regardless of what the map says.

MAP 8: 6172 Cockrill Bend Cir., 615/350-7200, http://ozartsnashville.org; hours and cost vary by event

THEATER

Actors Bridge Ensemble

New theatrical works are given the spotlight by the Actors Bridge Ensemble, a theater company for both new and seasoned actors. The ensemble brings provocative and new plays to theaters across Nashville and hosts performances at Belmont University's Troutt Theater Complex and the Darkhorse Theater. The ensemble approach means everyone gets to try every-thing, from acting to lighting to manning the box office.

MAP 8: Darkhorse Theater, 4610 Charlotte Ave., 615/498-4077, http:// actorsbridge.org; show and class times vary; general admission $10-20

Artists' Cooperative Theatre

Artists' Cooperative Theatre, or ACT 1, is an organization dedicated to bringing theatrical gems, both classic and modern, to Nashville audiences. Founded in 1989, ACT 1 has presented productions of more than 90 of the world's greatest plays, using both classical and mod-ern plays to describe and comment on the human condition. Each year the theater puts on 4-7 productions. Past productions have included *Dr. Horrible's Sing-Along Blog, The Night of the Iguana, Noises Off,* and *The Pirates of Penzance.*

MUSIC CITY ROOTS

For nearly a century, the Grand Ole Opry has been the standard-bearer for multi-act live radio shows. But in 2009 Music City Roots (MCR, 615/669-1627, http://musiccityroots.com) was created, based on the same idea of many artists playing, interspersed with interview segments and on-air live commercials, except with an Americana music focus designed to bring in younger audiences. And, just like the Opry, Music City Roots has had many homes, including The Loveless Cafe and the Factory at Franklin. In 2022 MCR got its first permanent home, in suburban Madison. The Roots Barn will be adjacent to Historic Amqui Station (303 Madison St., 615/891-1154, http://amquistation.org), a former railroad stop that was essential for musicians traveling to Music City. The late, great Johnny Cash preserved Amqui Station after rail service stopped.

The Roots Barn accommodates up to 1,000 people and has room for plenty of dancing. The two-plus-hour multiple-act show includes live interview segments with the musical guests. You'll see a cross-section of musicians, from the well-known to the up-and-coming. CDs from most of the performers are available at the show. Stay till the very end for the jam, when all the night's performers cram onstage for one last jam session. It's a good idea to buy your tickets online in advance.

MAP 8: Darkhorse Theater, 4610 Charlotte Ave., http://act1online.com; showtimes and ticket prices vary

Circle Players

Circle Players is the oldest nonprofit, all-volunteer arts association in Nashville. As a community theater, all its actors, stagehands, directors, and other helpers are volunteers. The company stages four or five performances every year at a variety of theater locations around the city. Performances include classic theater, plus stage adaptations of popular cinema and literature.

MAP 8: Z. Alexander Looby Theater, 2301 Rosa Parks Blvd., 615/332-7529, www.circleplayers.net; showtimes vary; $15-20

Festivals and Events

Tin Pan South Songwriters Festival

Many Nashville music events celebrate the performers. But the Tin Pan South Songwriters Festival honors the people who come up with the lyrics for all those great tunes. So while you may not recognize most of the names on the lineup, you're sure to get a good introduction to the people behind the famous words. Typically held the last week of March or first week in April, Tin Pan South, organized by the Nashville Songwriters Association International, schedules performances at venues across the city, primarily downtown, including City Winery, and 3rd & Lindsley.

Citywide: www.tinpansouth.com; late Mar. or early Apr.; $10-20 tickets available at the door for each show, limited number of $100 fast access passes available online prior to festival

Call it the Banksy effect: In recent years many of Nashville's blank spaces, such as the sides of buildings in alleys, have been transformed into canvases of color.

The Nashville Walls Project (www.nashvillewallsproject.com) started in 2013 to put high-quality works of art in places where people could appreciate them and interact with them without going to a museum. Perhaps the most striking is on the side of a silo—160 feet tall—a sepia-toned portrait of a man who lived in the neighborhood for more than 90 years. It is visible from the interstate. Some of these works do change over time, so the best way to find one is to check the map online and wander to your heart's and eyes' content.

Other artists have used walls as their medium, too. Favorites among the selfie crowd include: the *Wings* (giant white angel wings) in The Gulch; Hillsboro Village's dragon; DCXV's red, white, and blue "I Believe in Nashville" signs, which are in several places in the city, including 12 South and Marathon Village; and Draper James's striking blue and white stripes. Several companies will take you on a tour of the murals, stopping at some of the most Instagrammable. Check with Nashville Mural Tours (www.nashvillemuraltours.com) and Mint Julep Tours (http://mintjuleptours.com/nashville).

Nashville Fashion Week

Nashville's creative class isn't just musically inclined. There's a rich fashion design community. And the first week of April is the time to see it in all its runway glory during Nashville Fashion Week. Events take place across the city all week, ranging from runways to workshops to parties with the city's best-dressed folks.

Citywide: www.nashvillefashionweek.com; early Apr.; $50-73 for general runway tickets, $30-500 for special events

Nashville Film Festival

Film lovers throughout the country look forward to the Nashville Film Festival, which has been held in Nashville for more than 50 years. Founded in 1969 as the Sinking Creek Film Celebration, this is now an event with Academy Award qualifying status. These days more than 20,000 people attend the weeklong event, which includes film screenings, industry panels, and lots of parties. Lots of locals volunteer to help put on the event, which screens many regional films not shown at other festivals.

Citywide: www.nashvillefilmfestival.org; Oct.; packages $295-495, individual tickets $15-20

Iroquois Steeplechase

For something a little different, plan to attend the Iroquois Steeplechase at Percy Warner Park. Held on the second Saturday of May, the race is the nation's oldest continuously run weight-for-age steeplechase in the country. Fans in sundresses or suspenders and hats enjoy watching some of the top horses in the country navigate the racecourse (but unlike at the Kentucky Derby there is not betting on these races). A general admission ticket gets you a seat on the hillside overlooking the stadium. Pack a blanket, food, and drinks (and mud boots if it has rained recently, which is not uncommon), and you'll have an excellent day. Various tailgating tickets ($550-600) are available and are priced according to how good the view is from the parking spot. If you want to tailgate, you'll need to buy tickets well in advance.

Greater Nashville: Percy Warner Park, 7311 TN-100, 800/619-4802, www.iroquoissteeplechase.org; May; tickets $75 with add-on options

Recreation

Percy Warner Park

PARKS

Edwin and Percy Warner Parks

The largest city parks in Tennessee, Edwin and Percy Warner Parks, also known as **The Warner Parks,** are a 2,600-acre oasis of forest, fields, and quiet pathways just 9 miles (14.5 km) southwest from downtown Nashville. Nashvillians come here to walk, jog, ride bikes and horses, and much more. The parks offer scenic drives, picnic facilities, playgrounds, cross-country running trails, an equestrian center, bridle trails, a model-airplane field, and athletic fields. Percy Warner Park is also home to the Harpeth Hills Golf Course, and Edwin Warner Park has a nature center that provides year-round environmental education. The nature center also hands out maps and other information about the park.

MAP 8: 7311 TN-100, 615/370-8051, http://nashville.gov; dawn-11pm daily; free

Hamilton Creek Recreation Area

Most of the access areas on J. Percy Priest Lake are managed by the U.S. Army Corps of Engineers, but Metro Nashville operates Hamilton Creek Recreation Area, on the lake's western shore. Locals dock their boats at the sailboat marina, and this is a pretty spot from which to watch regattas and other sailing events. Storage for boats and paddleboards is available at a nominal fee for locals. This is also the site of Nashville Paddle Company, Music City BMX, and a challenging community-maintained mountain bike trail. A playground and traditional park offerings (room for Frisbee and picnic tables) round out the offerings.

MAP 8: 2901 Bell Rd., 615/862-8472, http://nashville.gov; sunrise-sunset daily (security gate open 6:30am-9:30pm); free

GREEN IN THE CITY

Nashville has a remarkable network of connected green spaces thanks to its greenways (615/862-8400, http://nashville.gov/greenways). The master plan is for this linear system to eventually connect the entire city. Today there are more than 190 miles (306 km) of paved pathways and primitive trails used by bicyclists, runners, and dog walkers, all of which connect different parts of the city to each other. The greenways run through the city's prettiest natural areas and, in places, along the Cumberland River. Some greenways include nature centers and other educational facilities. For the most part, the routes are clean and safe. The long-term plan is for every Nashville resident to live within 1 mile of a greenway. Good maps are available for download from Greenways for Nashville (http://greenwaysfornashville.org) as well as from the official website.

HORSEBACK RIDING
Equestrian Center

Those who love horses are fans of the Equestrian Center in The Warner Parks, best known for the annual Iroquois Steeplechase Horse Race it hosts each May. But a 10-mile (16-km) bridle path is open to horseback riding year-round. Because these trails are the only public horse trails in the county, they are crowded, and your horses need to share the trails with dogs, runners, and walkers. **MAP 8:** 2500 Old Hickory Blvd., 615/370-8051; dawn-11pm daily; free for 1-9 horses, $44 permit for 10-25 horses

Twin Forks Horse Trail

Hikers and horseback riders alike appreciate this 18-mile (29-km) trail located in the East Fork Recreation Area on the southwestern shore of J. Percy Priest Lake. The trail, which dips into the Stones River, is wooded and well maintained and perfect for horseback riding, but the emphasis is on the trail, not the vistas. If what you really want is views of the water, select a different vantage point. Come prepared: This trail can be muddy after a rainstorm.

MAP 8: J. Percy Priest Lake, 3737 Bell Rd., 615/889-1975, www.percypriestlake.org; 24 hours daily; free

HIKING AND BIKING
Long Hunter State Park

The state of Tennessee operates this park on the eastern shore of J. Percy Priest Lake. It offers mountain biking trails, both a 2-mile (3.2-km) loop and a 4-mile (6.4-km) loop. In addition, there are several hiking trails around the lake, with good vantage points and views of the water. Boats are available for rent during the summer season. Camping, both group and backcountry, is available.

MAP 8: 2910 Hobson Pike, Hermitage, 615/885-2422, http://tnstateparks.com; 7am-sunset daily; free

✪ Natchez Trace Parkway

The primary destination for cyclists around Nashville is the Natchez Trace Parkway, a historic two-lane, 444-mile (715-km) blacktop scenic drive that runs from Nashville and journeys south through the Tennessee and Mississippi countryside, eventually terminating in

189

Natchez Trace Parkway

Natchez, Mississippi. The parkway, which is a designated bike route, is closed to commercial traffic, and the speed limit is strictly enforced, making it popular for biking. Cycling the Trace can be an afternoon outing or a weeklong adventure.

The National Park Service maintains three campgrounds along the Trace, plus five bicyclist-only campsites with more modest amenities. The northernmost bike campsite is at the intersection of the Trace and TN-50, about 36 miles (58 km) south of Nashville. When biking on the Trace, ride in a single-file line (cars are encouraged to move to the opposite lane when safe to give cyclists plenty of room) and always wear reflective clothing and a helmet.

Each mile of the Trace is well-marked, and periodically there are turnouts from the road with signage about the spot and its history. Most stops have picnic tables and shade. A few have restrooms and other amenities. Highlights on the Trace near Nashville include the striking **Double Arch Bridge** (milepost 438) and the historic **Gordon House and Ferry site** (milepost 407.7).
MAP 8: TN-100 at McCrory Ln., 800/305-7417, www.nps.gov/natr; 24 hours daily; free

Radnor Lake State Natural Area
Just 7 miles (11.5 km) southwest of downtown Nashville, Radnor Lake State Natural Area provides a natural escape for visitors and residents of the city. Spanning 85 acres, Radnor Lake was created in 1914 by the Louisville and Nashville Railroad Company, which impounded Otter Creek to do so. The lake was built to provide water for the railroad's steam engines. By the 1940s, the railroad's use of the lake ended, and 20 years later the area was threatened by development. Local residents, including the Tennessee Ornithological Society, successfully rallied against

development, and Radnor Lake State Natural Area was established in 1973.

Around the lake are 6 miles (10 km) of hiking trails, and Otter Creek Road is closed to vehicular traffic and open to bicycles and walkers. The lake is not open to paddling or other recreation, and because this is a wildlife area, dogs are not allowed on the trails. A nature museum at the visitors center (8:30am-noon and 1pm-4pm daily) describes some of the 240 species of birds and hundreds of species of plants and animals that live at Radnor. The Barbara J. Mapp Aviary Education Center (http://radnorlake.org) houses non-releasable birds of prey.

MAP 8: 1160 Otter Creek Rd., 615/373-3467, http://tnstateparks.com; 6am-sunset daily; free

BIKE SHOPS AND RENTALS

Trace Bikes

Trace Bikes is in The Shoppes on the Harpeth. This is a picture-perfect spot for getting out and riding a bike on the lovely Natchez Trace or anywhere on the west side of town. Bikes and gear are also available for sale, and the shop leads biking events.

MAP 8: 8080B TN-100, 615/646-2485, http://tracebikes.com; 10am-6pm Mon.-Fri., 10am-5pm Sat., noon-6pm Sun.; bike rentals $65/day

GOLF

Harpeth Hills Golf Course

Nestled in Percy Warner Park, Harpeth Hills is a public course with a solid reputation. It was designed in 1965 and renovated in 1991. Golfers can appreciate the natural beauty

Radnor Lake State Natural Area

TRAVELING THE NATCHEZ TRACE PARKWAY

Just to the west of Nashville is one of the National Park Service's little-known gems. The Natchez Trace Parkway is a 444-mile (715-km) ribbon of green connecting three states and 10,000 years of military, Native American, musical, and U.S. history. As you walk (or drive or ride) in the footsteps of the Native Americans, Kaintuck boatmen, soldiers, preservationists, and others, it's impossible not to feel connected to their journeys.

The first people to travel what is now considered the Natchez Trace were probably Choctaw and Chickasaw people, who made the first footpaths through the region. Early European settlers quickly identified the importance of a land route from Natchez to Nashville. In 1801, the Natchez Trace opened as an official post road between the two cities. One historian characterized the diverse array of people who used the Trace as "robbers, rugged pioneers, fashionable ladies, shysters, politicians, soldiers, scientists, and men of destiny, such as Aaron Burr, Andrew Jackson, and Meriwether Lewis." By 1820, more than 20 inns, referred to as "stands," were open. Many were modest—providing food and shelter only.

Then came the years of disuse and neglect. Steamboats, railways, and new roads rendered the Trace obsolete. Although it faded from use, the Natchez Trace was remembered. In 1909, the Daughters of the American Revolution in Mississippi started a project to mark the route of the Trace. The marker project continued for the next 24 years and eventually caught the attention of Mississippi Rep. Thomas J. Busby, who introduced the first bills in Congress to survey and construct a paved road along the route of the old Natchez Trace.

It took nearly another century for the project to be completed. In 1996 the final leg of the parkway was completed, and in 2005, sections near Jackson and Natchez, Mississippi (now some of the most traveled), were paved.

Today the parkway follows the general path of the old, sunken, unpaved Natchez Trace; in a few places, they fall in step with each other. These spots are great for hikes and photographing the landscape. More than 100 miles (160 km) of the parkway lie within Tennessee, and one of the beauties of the Trace is that you can feel like you are fully immersing yourself in it, whether you drive a few miles or the whole thing. The Trace is popular with cyclists and motorcycle riders, as well as drivers.

The Trace runs along the Western Highland Rim through Davidson, Williamson, Hickman, Maury, Lewis, and Wayne Counties. The **National Park Service** (800/305-7417, http://nps.gov/natr) publishes a foldout map and guide to the parkway. For more detailed information on the breadth and depth of opportunities on the Trace, see *Moon Nashville to New Orleans Road Trip,* a guide to all 444 miles (715 km) and more.

of the surrounding parks while they hit the links. Affordable lessons are available at many of Metro Nashville's public courses, including this one.

MAP 8: 2424 Old Hickory Rd., 615/862-8493, http://nashville.gov; hours vary based on season; $26-34/18 holes

McCabe Golf Course

The city's Sylvan Park area is home to the public McCabe Golf Course, a large 27-hole course. Built in 1942, the course is challenging enough for regular golfers but accessible for those who are new to the sport. There's also a driving range with target greens. Tee times can be reserved up to seven days in advance.

MAP 8: 100 46th Ave. N., 615/862-8491, http://nashville.gov; hours vary based on season; $26-34/18 holes

Nashboro Golf Club

Larger bunkers and water hazards dot the 6,887 yards in this private golf course, which is open to the public. The course was designed by Benjamin J. Wihry. A clubhouse and a pro shop can meet all your associated golfing needs.

MAP 8: 1101 Nashboro Blvd., 615/367-2311, www.nashborogolf.com; hours vary based on season; $40-50/18 holes

Ted Rhodes Golf Course

In 1992 this North Nashville golf course was renovated, thanks to a design by Gary Roger Baird. The greens run along the banks of the Cumberland River, which means pretty views and lots of wildlife alongside the putting greens and fairways. The 18-hole course is an easy one to walk, making it a good choice for a little extra exercise. Tee times can be reserved up to seven days in advance.

MAP 8: 1901 Ed Temple Blvd., 615/862-8463, http://nashville.gov; hours vary based on season; $26-34/18 holes

WATER SPORTS
MARINAS AND LAKES
Elm Hill Marina

Boating, fishing, and water sports are among the most popular activities on J. Percy Priest Lake. Elm Hill Marina is the marina closest to downtown Nashville and, as such, one of the busiest. Lots of locals rent slips and have their boats docked here. But even if you don't have a boat of your own, you can rent one. The pontoon boats ($285-475/half day) are popular with the bachelorette party crowd. Renting a 14-foot trolling motor fishing boat for two hours costs $30. Elm Hill also has an outdoors store and a restaurant with typical seaside fare.

MAP 8: 3361 Bell Rd., 615/889-5363 office, 615/739-9100 rentals, http://elmhillmarina.com; office and boathouse 9am-6pm daily, boat rentals until 6pm daily

J. Percy Priest Lake

J. Percy Priest Lake

J. Percy Priest Lake was created in the mid-1960s when the U.S. Army Corps of Engineers dammed the Stones River east of Nashville. The lake is a favorite destination for fishing, boating, swimming, paddling, and picnicking. Access to this lake sprawling over 14,200 acres is provided through more than a dozen different parks and entry points on all sides of the lake. Many of these areas bear the names of communities that were inundated when the lake was created.

CANOEING ON THE HARPETH

With its location just west of Nashville, and easy access from I-40, this stretch of the Harpeth River is one of the most popular places to canoe, kayak, and paddleboard in the area. In Harpeth River State Park (1230 Cedar Hill Rd., Kingston Springs, http://tnstateparks.com) alone there are nine access points for getting on the water; many outfitters are set up to make it a breeze to float down this scenic stretch of river. There's no commercial development on these river banks, so you really feel like you are out in the wilderness, despite the proximity to town and the fact that you don't have to do any hiking or hauling of gear: The outfitters do it all. The Class I river is generally an easy paddle, although water levels do fluctuate based on rain and other issues—too little water and the river isn't deep enough; too much and swift water and flooding are risks. Check river conditions before you go. While the river is open to the public, some of the river banks are private property: Paddlers should abide by posted regulations and, of course, never litter in the water or on its banks.

TIP-A-CANOE

Tip-a-Canoe (1279 US-70, Kingston Springs, 800/550-5810, www.tip-a-canoe.com; hours and prices vary by season; $50 for 2 hours for 2 people) has been offering canoe and kayak rentals on the Harpeth River on the west side of town since before the Narrows of the Harpeth was a state park. All that experience has paid off. Boat rentals include shuttle service from where you get off the river back to the beginning, where your car is parked. Shuttles are also available (for a fee) for those who have their own boats.

MUSIC CITY CANOE

Music City Canoe (1203 US-70, Kingston Springs, 615/952-4211, www.canoemusiccity.com; hours and prices vary by season; $45 per canoe) offers a variety of floats down the Harpeth, with trips and shuttles allowing you to opt for 2- to 9.5-mile routes on the Harpeth River on the west side of town. This is a large operation; you won't be floating alone on a sunny weekend.

FOGGY BOTTOM CANOE

Foggy Bottom Canoe (1270 US-70, Kingston Springs, 615/952-4062, www.foggybottomcanoe.com; hours and prices vary by season; trips up to 5 hours $36-40) generally offers floats down the Harpeth River between April and November in either canoes or kayaks. There are no set departure times; they aim to shuttle you as soon as you arrive and are ready to go.

The lake's visitors center, operated by the U.S. Army Corps of Engineers, is at the dam site on Bell Road (at exit 219 off I-40 heading east from downtown Nashville). There you will find a lake overlook and one of four marinas on the lake. To rent a boat, head to Elm Hill Marina, about 1 mile south on Bell Road.

MAP 8: 3737 Bell Rd., 615/889-1975, www.percypriestlake.org; 24 hours daily; free

Old Hickory Lake

One of two lakes formed by the damming of the Cumberland River (the other is J. Percy Priest), Old Hickory is named after Andrew Jackson, whose plantation was nearby. The lakeshore is home to eight marinas, an arboretum, and more than 40 places to launch a boat (or paddleboard) and get out on the water or just sit on the banks and fish. There are beaches, picnic areas, and sailboat marinas, as well as two campgrounds.

MAP 8: 876 Burnett Rd., Old Hickory, 615/822-4846, http://www.lrn.usace.army.mil; 24 hours daily; free

STAND-UP PADDLEBOARDING

TOP EXPERIENCE

Nashville Paddle Co.

Middle Tennessee's flatwater lakes and rivers are perfect for paddling. Nashville Paddle Company offers stand-up paddleboard (SUP) instruction and lessons for both adults and kids. Lessons take place at the company's boathouse at Hamilton Creek Recreation Area on J. Percy Priest Lake. Rentals are also available for those who want to take boards or a kayak and go for a weekend. With more than a dozen yoga teachers, Nashville Paddle Co. offers SUP yoga as well as SUP fitness classes, which are workouts that use both land and water to get your core in tip-top shape. (Full disclosure: The author of this book is one of the owners of Nashville Paddle Co.). Dogs are welcome for an additional $5 fee.

MAP 8: Hamilton Creek Recreation Area, 2901 Bell Rd., 615/682-1787, http://nashvillepaddle.com; daily May-Sept., hours vary; $30-45 for classes, lessons, and rentals

AMUSEMENT PARKS

Nashville Shores

Nashville Shores is a great destination for a hot summer day. This water and amusement park features miles of sandy beaches along the shore of J. Percy Priest Lake, pools, water slides, and water sports. Admission to the park

Nashville Paddle Co.

includes the opportunity to take a 15-minute lake cruise on *The Shoreliner*, which looks like an old steamboat and has a paddle wheel in the back.

MAP 8: 4001 Bell Rd., 615/889-7050, www.nashvilleshores.com; May-Sept., hours vary; $50 adults, $30 seniors and children under 48 inches tall, children 2 and under free, $10 parking

Shops

BOOKS
McKay's
Originally based in Knoxville, McKay's encourages readers to return books, CDs, and DVDs for store credit after they've read or listened to or watched them. That means the mammoth Nashville location is always buzzing with sellers as well as buyers. McKay's has a fun energy and is cleaner and better organized than most used bookstores. The space is large—and also includes some electronics—so allot plenty of time to browse.
MAP 8: 636 Old Hickory Blvd., 615/353-2595, www.mckaybooks.com; 10am-9pm Sun.-Fri., 9am-9pm Sat.

Parnassus Books
Located in a strip mall across from the Mall at Green Hills, Parnassus is known for its famous co-owner, novelist Ann Patchett. This independent bookstore specializes in a well-edited selection, personal service, and literary events for both kids and adults. The shop isn't huge, but it's chock-full of new and local books. It also hosts many literary events.
MAP 8: 3900 Hillsboro Pike, Ste. 14, 615/953-2243, http://parnassusbooks. net; 10am-6pm Mon.-Sat., noon-6pm Sun.

CLOTHING AND ACCESSORIES
ABLE
The idea behind ABLE is that by selling ethically made leather goods, clothing, and jewelry, it enables the women who make the pieces to help themselves out of poverty. The business is headquartered in The Nations neighborhood on the west side but works with women across the globe. Designs are sleek, modern, and timeless.
Map 8: 5022 Centennial Blvd., 571/723-4836, www.livefashionable. com; 10am-7pm Mon.-Sat., noon-5pm Sun.

Habit
This little white cottage, with whitewashed floors and a bright country loft feel, satisfies casually sophisticated tastes. Habit's owners find the best of new and known clothing designers, including Joie, Rebecca Taylor, and Ella Moss, to offer lovely selections to their discriminating customers.
MAP 8: 2209 Bandywood Dr., 615/292-9399; 10am-5:30pm Mon.-Sat.

H. Audrey
This women's clothing boutique, owned by renowned singer-songwriter Holly Williams (Hank

Jr.'s daughter), aims to fill a niche in Nashville for the well-heeled. The store is aimed at clients who shop at Barney's, Saks, and Bergdorf's—or would, if they had Nashville locations. The clothing here could take you from work to a red-carpet event. The shop is exquisitely edited with an eye for detail. Upstairs, a small loft space showcases portraits of renowned musicians by equally renowned photographers.

MAP 8: 4027 Hillsboro Pike, 615/760-5701, http://haudrey.com; 10am-6pm Mon.-Sat., noon-5pm Sun.

The Perfect Pair

For people who love the pursuit of the perfect shoe, there's no better place than this well-edited shop. High-fashion pumps and flats meet the quintessential Music City boots on these shelves. The inventory is limited, so you leave feeling like what you've purchased won't be worn by everyone in town. The shop also stocks jewelry and handbags, but shoes are what makes The Perfect Pair a regular stop for those who are well-heeled.

MAP 8: 4103 Hillsboro Cir., 615/385-7247, www. theperfectpairnashville.com; 10am-5:30pm Mon.-Sat.

Posh

One of the city's hippest clothing shops, Posh stocks a large selection of clothing for both men and women, as well as a drool-worthy shoe department, handbags, and other accessories. The back room's sales area is a bargain hunter's dream. Regular prices can be on the higher end. Fashions are stylish and run the gamut from casual to a

Haus of Yarn

GET OUTDOOR GEAR

If you're continuing onward from Nashville on an outdoor adventure, such as the 444-mile (715-km) trip down the Natchez Trace, you'll need to stock up. These are the best places in the area to find high quality camping and hiking gear, waterproof supplies, water bottles, and everything else you might need. The salespeople at these spots know the area well.

- **Bass Pro Shops at Opry Mills** (323 Opry Mills Dr., 615/514-5200, http://basspro.com)
- **Binks Outfitters** (4015 Hillsboro Pike, 615/298-1700, www.binksoutfitters.com)
- **Cumberland Transit** (2807 West End Ave., 615/321-4069, http://cumberlandtransit.com)
- **Friedman's Army/Navy Surplus & Outdoors** (2101 21st Ave. S., 615/297-3343, www.friedmansarmynavyoutdoorstore.com)
- **Patagonia** (601 Overton St., 615/747-2535, www.patagonia.com)
- **Mountain High Outfitters** (1800 Galleria Blvd, Franklin, 615/465-6447, http://mountainhighoutfitters.com)

night on the town. There's another location in **Hillsboro Village** (1801 21st Ave. S., 615/383-9840) with the same hours.

MAP 8: 4027 Hillsboro Pike, 615/269-6250, www.poshonline.com; 10am-7pm Mon.-Sat., noon-5pm Sun.

CRAFTS
Haus of Yarn

Both local knitters and those from out of town flock here. Haus of Yarn's large, well-stocked shop offers things stores in bigger cities don't. The shelves are filled with some of the country's best selection of yarns. The staff are avid knitters, so there are hundreds of shop samples that help you visualize what the yarns will look like in a finished garment.

MAP 8: 265 White Bridge Rd., 615/354-1007, http://hausofyarn.com; 10am-2pm Mon.-Sat.

HOME DECOR
AshBlue

Imagine a shop that carries everything from fine jewelry to funky furniture to garden accessories—that's AshBlue. People come here for everything from bridal registries to hostess gifts. If you're visiting Music City via airplane, you'll likely have to ship your finds home, because you're not going to want to limit yourself to what will fit in a carry-on.

MAP 8: 2170 Bandywood Dr., 615/383-4882, http://ashblue.com; 10am-6pm Mon.-Sat.

KIDS
✪ Phillips Toy Mart

Phillips Toy Mart is the sort of toy store both children and adults dream about. They not only have the nostalgia factor on their side with lava lamps, Lincoln Logs, and Tinker Toys, but they also stock modern crazes like Baby Shark toys and board games galore. Not to be missed is the model train setup in the back, which most likely will enchant grandpa and grandson into starting a train set together. Phillips is also old-school enough to carry a full selection of kites, from beginner to stunt, and model-making supplies.

MAP 8: 5207 Harding Pike, 615/352-5363, http://phillipstoymart.com; 9am-5:30pm Mon.-Sat.

SHOPPING DISTRICTS AND CENTERS

Mall at Green Hills

The signature shopping mall in Nashville is the Mall at Green Hills, an indoor mall about a 15-minute drive south from downtown Nashville along Hillsboro Road. Stores include Macy's, Brooks Brothers, Tiffany & Co., and Nordstrom. The mall has spawned additional shopping opportunities nearby, including the upscale Hill Center, so this is a good place to head if you're in need of just about anything. Call the concierge (615/298-5478, ext. 0) to find out if your favorite store is here. The parking lot can get crowded on weekends, but the mall offers free valet service, which makes it doable. The mall includes a movie theater and a number of decent restaurants, too.

MAP 8: 2126 Abbott Martin Rd., 615/298-5478, www.shopgreenhills.com; 10am-9pm Mon.-Sat., noon-6pm Sun.

WHERE TO STAY

Music City's status as a tourist hot spot may be most noticeable in its hotel room rates. Nashville has grown from a city with no shortage of

The Joseph

places to stay to one with a premium on accommodations.

The good news is, the greater Nashville area has more than 53,000 (and growing) hotel rooms, with options for places to sleep ranging from historical downtown hotels to standard chain motels to nontraditional options (short-term rentals in homes and apartments). Many seemingly standard hotels have quirky Music City touches, such as recorded wake-up calls from country stars or guitar-shaped swimming pools. The first urban Margaritaville hotel and the third Virgin Hotel in the United States have both opened their doors in Nashville.

The tougher-to-swallow news is that many of these new hotels are luxury properties. Room rates may be as high as other major cities, and deals aren't always easy to come by.

CHOOSING A HOTEL

The bulk of the city's hotels are concentrated in three areas: **downtown**, **Midtown** (near Vanderbilt), and **Music Valley** (near Opryland), but options are everywhere, from East Nashville to the airport. This chapter highlights a selection of top places across the city, but there are many more chain hotels citywide. For more options, plus a guide to nearby campgrounds, see http://visitmusiccity.com.

As is the case anywhere, prices fluctuate based on the time of year and scheduled events. Summer and winter holidays are in-demand times for Nashville hotel rooms. If you intend to come to town for the music

HIGHLIGHTS

✪ **BEST IMMERSIVE CITY VIBE:** Sit among the mid-century modern details in the lobby at **The Fairlane** and watch the people of Nashville go by (page 202).

✪ **BEST PLACE TO EXPERIENCE A SENSE OF HISTORY:** Important things happened and important people stayed at the **Hermitage Hotel,** but it's Gene Autry's horse who has the best tale. You get a feel for the significance of this place just by walking into the lobby (page 202).

✪ **WHERE TO LIVE THE GOOD LIFE:** Catering to your every travel need, the staff at **The Joseph** will make it vacation to remember (page 207).

✪ **BEST PLACE TO RECORD YOUR MESSAGE:** A small podcast studio inside **The Russell** provides locals and guests the opportunity to record without distraction (page 212).

✪ **BEST BARGAIN NEAR DOWNTOWN:** Just across the river and near Nissan Stadium, **La Quinta Inn & Suites Downtown/Stadium** offers budget prices from a prime location (page 213).

✪ **BEST RESORT:** Other hotels in town, even the nicest ones, are just that: hotels. Gaylord Opryland Resort is a full-on resort, with enough attractions, including a water park, to allow you to fill a weekend without leaving the property (page 213).

PRICE KEY

$	Less than $150 per night
$ $	$150-300 per night
$ $ $	More than $300 per night

Gaylord Opryland Resort

Because one of Nashville's few drawbacks is a lack of a robust 24/7 public transportation system, that old real estate saw of location, location, location applies to selecting the right place to stay. Here are some suggestions for figuring out which part of town is best suited to you.

TO SAVE SOME CASH: Stay in Music Valley or near the airport, which are likely to have the cheapest options.

TO BE NEAR THE NIGHTLIFE SCENE: Stay in downtown, near Lower Broad, in SoBro, or The Gulch.

TO SEE THE COMMODORES PLAY: Stay in Midtown, near the Vanderbilt University campus.

TO BE NEAR GAYLORD OPRYLAND: Stay at the resort or somewhere in Music Valley or near the airport and you'll reduce your commute time by at least 30 minutes (but you'll have a drive to see most of the city's attractions).

A GREAT SPOT FOR A BACHELORETTE PARTY: Pick a place with multiple bathrooms and bedrooms but shared common areas, such as BODE Nashville.

A NEIGHBORHOOD FEEL: Pick a boutique hotel in East Nashville, where you'll be close to restaurants and bars and can walk across the pedestrian bridge to get downtown.

extravaganzas CMA Music Fest or Bonnaroo in June, book your rooms at least a year in advance. Other music festivals can also put a strain on hotel availability, as can football (NFL and college) and college basketball games. The rates in this chapter are based on double occupancy in such high seasons.

Downtown   Map 1

✪ The Fairlane $$$

Downtown has lots of new hotels that were born out of old, renovated buildings. But The Fairlane is different for its 1970s retro feel. The old bank building has carpeted floors, midcentury furnishings, and one-of-a-kind furniture. Beds have cup holders in the headboards, and service is impeccable. There's an on-site coffee and bagel shop, a cheese shop, and a restaurant with an outdoor patio. The lovely lobby is the place to set up if you enjoy people-watching. The gym (called "Jim") features Peloton bikes. The Fairlane is walking distance to Printers Alley, the Ryman, and Lower Broad.
MAP 1: 401 Union St., 615/988-8511, www.fairlanehotel.com

✪ Hermitage Hotel $$$

The Hermitage Hotel has been sheltering travelers in downtown Nashville for more than a century. The 122-room hotel was commissioned by prominent Nashville citizens and opened for business in 1910, quickly becoming the favorite gathering place for the city's elite. Prominent figures including Al Capone, Gene Autry, and

ALTERNATIVES TO HOTELS

Not every trip calls for a traditional hotel. Sometimes the best way to see Music City is by booking a guest room or a condo. These options are sometimes more economical than a hotel, particularly for groups, who may appreciate having a kitchen and not eating every meal out. Other options, like campgrounds or even quirky "art farms," give you a chance to see the city from a different perspective.

Airbnb (www.airbnb.com) and VRBO (www.vrbo.com) list options across the city. Many of these locations have the advantage of being in neighborhoods where locals live, rather than in tourist-heavy areas. (East Nashville and 12 South are especially good bets for being within walking distance of some restaurants and shops.) There are plenty of houses and condos, often with free parking and Wi-Fi, available for those who want to stay awhile. Look for places that tout a short-term rental permit, so you know the listing is legit. Just remember to be respectful of the neighbors, who may not be crazy about having loud visitors partying next door.

If you're the outdoorsy type, Hipcamp (www.hipcamp.com) is a resource for cabins, camping spots, RV sites, and other places to sleep where the view matters. Most of these tend to be outside Davidson County, but many suburbs are an easy drive to the city.

Scarritt-Bennett Center (1027 18th Ave. S., 615/340-7500, www.scarrittbennett.org, from $79) is a religious conference center near the Vanderbilt campus and Music Row. There are 125 spartan rooms in three former residence halls that can be rented like hotel rooms, and many standard hotel amenities, including wireless Internet, are provided. However, bathrooms are shared with other guests. The lovely grounds are the appeal of Scarritt-Bennett, along with the meditative vibe you get from just being there.

Creature Camp (via Hipcamp) and Rancho de Barnes (www.ranchodebarnes.com) are art farms, featuring the work of two artists. Book a night at either of these offbeat locales and you'll be able to check out the artwork, pet goats, play with chickens, and see the stars.

seven U.S. presidents have stayed at the Hermitage Hotel, not to mention some of country music's biggest names and even Gene Autry's horse. Its location near the state capitol meant it was the site of important debates, including that which ultimately gave women the right to vote in 1920. Guests enjoy top-of-the-line amenities, including 24-hour room service, pet walking, valet parking, and laundry services. Rooms are furnished in an opulent, if old-school, style. Many rooms have clear views of the capitol and the city that has grown up around the hotel. If modern and minimalist is your vibe, this might not be the place for you, but nevertheless, it is worth walking in and checking out the lovely lobby. In a nod to state pride, you can choose to have $2 from your room rate contributed to the Land Trust for Tennessee. The on-site restaurant and bar, Drusie & Darr, is overseen by celebrity chef Jean-Georges Vongerichten.

MAP 1: 231 6th Ave. N., 615/244-3121, www.thehermitagehotel.com

Holston House $$$

This art deco beauty, built in 1929, has a boutique hotel feel, but the benefit of being part of the Hyatt chain is that it has lots of major hotel amenities. The decor includes some Nashville touches without being overly country music kitsch. The breakfast and lunch counter is a throwback to a different time. The

Nashville is a city rich in heritage. To experience some of that history for yourself, choose to stay somewhere that has a past.

Hermitage Hotel

Among the most famous historical lodgings is downtown's **Hermitage Hotel.** Opened in 1910, the hotel has been at the center of historic events from the very beginning. In 1914 it hosted the National American Woman Suffrage Association's national convention, playing a role in women's right to vote. Presidents, senators, and movie and music stars have stayed there, and for eight years pool legend Minnesota Fats lived (and played) there. Luckily, you don't have to be famous to stay at the Hermitage.

Built in 1929, **Holston House** has since been remodeled with all the necessary modernization but kept its art deco vibe intact. Of particular interest is the original decorative facade with its scrolling columns, the interior hexagon light fixtures, and the neon marquee over the front doors. Velvet furniture and high lobby ceilings complete the 1920s feel.

Built in the 1930s, the **Noelle** combines new art and modern aesthetics with its appreciation of period architecture and design. The lobby features high ceilings with arched windows that flood the marble-accented space with natural light. The building, which is a prime example of Classical Revival style, includes crown molding and other period millwork.

A restored 19th-century railroad station, **Union Station Hotel** is an example of Richardsonian-Romanesque elegance. Train schedules still adorn the lobby as decor, and the guest rooms have cathedral ceilings, stylish furnishings, and a subtle art deco touch, not to mention expansive marble vanities in the bathrooms. The track level of the hotel once held two alligator ponds, but today the luxury hotel is alligator-free.

Built in 1865, the small **Germantown Inn** is one of the neighborhood's oldest buildings. From the outside you can appreciate its brick Federal-style facade. The interior has been updated, so you get to relax in sumptuous rooms decorated with bright pops of color.

generous number of outlets in the lobby means you can work as long as you need without your laptop losing juice, and the rooftop pool is perfect for when you need a break or a view. **MAP 1:** 118 7th Ave. N., 615/392-1234, http://holstonhousenashville.hyatt.com

Noelle $$$

Nashville's über-creative class has come together in this 220-room luxury hotel in the former Noel Place hotel building that dates from the 1930s. The artwork in the rooms and public spaces is by Bryce McCloud of Isle Printing, who also runs a print shop/art gallery on the hotel's ground floor. The rooms are on the small side (think New York, not Nashville) but are packed with original art and thoughtful touches, such as blackout shades. Two of the places to eat and drink—Makeready Libations & Liberation and The

Trade Room lobby bar—are open to the public. The rooftop deck is for hotel guests only, while Hidden Bar downstairs is open to the public. On the ground floor, check out Drug Store Coffee and the fashionable Keep Shop, which is stocked with apparel, jewelry, and art made by local artisans.

MAP 1: 200 4th Ave. N., 615/649-5000, http://noelle-nashville.com

Omni Nashville Hotel $$$

Opened in 2013, the Omni is adjacent to the 1.2-million-square-foot Music City Convention Center. It has more than 80,000 square feet of meeting and event space, more than 800 guest rooms, plus easy access to the convention center, the Country Music Hall of Fame, restaurants, and other attractions south of Broadway. Don't miss the cool displays of musicians' costumes in the hallway that connects Hatch Show Print to the hotel. Amenities include several on-site restaurants, a fitness center, a rooftop pool deck, and a seriously indulgent spa.

MAP 1: 250 Rep. John Lewis Way S., 615/782-5300, www.omnihotels.com

Renaissance Nashville Hotel $$$

North of Broadway, this hotel stands 25 stories, making views of the city below one of its charms. The Renaissance's 673 rooms offer web TV, hair dryers, ironing boards, crisp linens, coffeemakers, and business services. High-speed wired Internet access is available for a fee. The fitness center is next door to an indoor heated swimming pool, whirlpool, and sauna. Daily valet parking is $45.

lobby bar at Noelle

MAP 1: 611 Commerce St.,
615/255-8400, http://marriott.com

Thompson Nashville $$$

The Thompson offers Nashville a
lot of things that seem at odds with
one another: It is in the heart of
The Gulch, but still quiet enough
to sleep. It's in a modern high-rise,
but feels like a small, boutique hotel.
Enjoy pet-friendly rooms with hardwood floors, midcentury modern-
style furnishings, honor bars with
local spirits, Bluetooth speakers,
and rain showers. The Thompson
is one of the hotels celebrities are
likely to book. Everyone from the
Jonas Brothers to Michelle Obama
has stayed here.

MAP 1: 401 11th Ave. S., 615/262-6000,
www.thompsonhotels.com

21c Museum Hotel Nashville $$$

In 2017 Nashville welcomed 21c
Museum Hotel, a 124-room hotel
with a contemporary art museum
inside. The public can tour the
museum for free (and everyone
should—this collection is superla-
tive). Perks for guests include free
Wi-Fi, free bottled water, smartphone docking stations, bathrobes,
and more original art in every
room. Some suites have lovely balconies with city views. The hotel
also features a bar and restaurant
frequented by locals, seven suites
with terraces and a spa, and a vibrant downtown atmosphere.

MAP 1: 221 2nd Ave. N., 615/610-6400,
www.21cnashville.com

Union Station Hotel $$$

One of Nashville's most notable
downtown hotels is the 125-room

Union Station Hotel

Union Station Hotel, located in what
was once the city's main train station. Distinctions include magnificent ironwork and molding and an
impressive marble-floored great hall
that greets guests, contributing to
what makes this one of the National
Trust's Historic Hotels of America.
One of Nashville's great old buildings, the hotel has high ceilings and
lofty interior balconies, and amenities include a fitness center, wireless
Internet, plasma televisions, com-
plimentary morning newspapers,
and room service. Packages include
a recording session at the Ryman
and other Nashville-centric perks.
It's remarkable how cozy and quiet
the spaces inside feel, just steps from
the traffic and sounds of Broadway.

MAP 1: 1001 Broadway, 615/726-1001,
www.unionstationhotelnashville.com

Holiday Inn Express Nashville-Downtown $$

Across Broadway from the Frist
Center for the Visual Arts, the
Holiday Inn Express offers a com-
fortable compromise between value

and location. Amenities include an on-site fitness room, free wireless Internet, a business center, and a guest laundry. Guest rooms have desks and coffeemakers. Suites have refrigerators and microwave ovens. All guests enjoy free continental breakfast, and on-site valet parking is available for $42. The Holiday Inn is about five blocks away from the Lower Broadway honky-tonk action.

MAP 1: 920 Broadway, 615/244-0150, www.ihg.com

Hotel Indigo Nashville $$

Housed in the restored historical American Trust and Nashville Trust building, the Hotel Indigo is one of downtown Nashville's oft-overlooked hotels. This boutique hotel is on the north side of downtown, making it convenient to the Tennessee Performing Arts Center, the courthouse, and other government buildings. Business travelers will have their needs met with high-speed Internet access, an on-site restaurant (which often has live music), and a nearby FedEx business center. There's a small on-site fitness center, or pay extra to use a nearby full gym. Valet parking is $40 per day. The hotel's pet-friendliness is clearly conveyed by a doghouse in the lobby.

MAP 1: 301 Union St., 615/891-6000, www.ihg.com

✪ The Joseph $$$

This SoBro hotel provides one of Nashville's most luxurious experiences. Owned by the Pizzuti family, the hotel is stocked with artwork from their personal collection. From the driveway to the check-in desk to the rooftop bar, you'll be wowed by contemporary artworks that rival many museums. The service, views, and food are beyond compare, including at Yolan, the fine-dining Italian restaurant hemled by Chef Tony Mantuano. Valet parking is the only option; it costs $52 a day.

MAP 1: 401 Korean Veterans Blvd., 615/248-1990, www.thejosephnashville.com

BODE Nashville $$

This former apartment building is now a convenient, stylish, limited-service hotel that makes a good option for families and groups. There are multiple bedrooms and bathrooms in each apartment-style room, as well as kitchens so you can eat at "home." Some rooms have guitars, foosball tables, and other entertainment options. There's an on-site coffee shop and bar, occasional live music, and on-site parking. The location is an easy walk to downtown attractions, but is a bit removed from the Broadway noise.

MAP 1: 401 2nd Ave. S., 844/431-2633, www.bode.co

Germantown and Capitol View

Map 2

The Germantown Inn

The Germantown Inn $$$

One of the oldest buildings in historic Germantown, this two-story, Federal-style house constructed in 1865 has been transformed into an inspired six-bedroom luxury boutique inn, with a remarkable garden, rooftop decks and views, and an ambience that combines modern amenities with original charm. Once known in the neighborhood as the Wallman House (for the building's first owner, H. H. Wallman, a prominent shoemaker), today the inn is an oasis in an urban environment. Eat breakfast in the light-filled lobby, sleep in a luxurious, quiet bedroom, and walk to many Germantown and downtown attractions. The staff is attentive but not overbearing.

MAP 2: 1218 6th Ave. N., 615/581-1218, www.germantowninn.com

Towneplace Suites Nashville Downtown $$

Located in between Bicentennial Mall and downtown, this all-suites hotel is a comfortable, modest option for folks on a budget who want to be in on the action. Each suite has a small kitchenette, perfect for saving leftovers and making quick meals. There's an on-site coffee-shop and a rooftop resataurant that offers a view of the city from an unusual vantage point. Parking is $38 per day.

MAP 2: 310 Gay St., 615/551-8880, www.marriott.com

Music Row

Map 3

Hutton Hotel $$$

This artsy hotel near the Vanderbilt campus offers an easy commute to Music Row and downtown. But regular visitors stay here less for the great location and more for the ambience. It's designed for creative types: There are on-site recording studios, a writing room, and a 300-seat concert venue called Analog, which is popular with locals. Room decor includes funky lamps, patterned carpets, sleek white linens, and a Fender guitar that you can plug into an iPad and play to your heart's content.

MAP 3: 1808 West End Ave., 615/340-9333, www.huttonhotel.com

Kimpton Aertson Hotel $$$

Opened in 2017, this 180-room hotel rises next to the Vanderbilt campus. Perks include free bike rentals (also available to nonguests), an 8th-floor pool deck with cabanas, and a 17th-floor indoor/outdoor event space. Enjoy free coffee and tea in the morning in the lobby (cutely referred to as the living room). Henley, the swanky first-floor restaurant, is a favorite of locals (don't skip the cocktail list). Kimpton hotels are well known for their pet-friendliness; there's no extra charge for pet beds, mats, or water bowls in your room.

MAP 3: 2021 Broadway, 615/340-6376, www.aertsonhotel.com

Loews Vanderbilt Hotel $$$

This pet-friendly 340-room hotel on West End Avenue is close to Centennial Park and Hillsboro Village. Many rooms have views of the Nashville skyline; premium rooms provide guests with access to the concierge lounge, continental breakfast, and evening hors d'oeuvres. All guests can enjoy a fine fitness room (or ask about in-room fitness sessions), spa, art gallery, and gift shop. The parking garage includes charging stations for electric vehicles. If you want to stay here during a Vanderbilt reunion or graduation weekend, reserve well in advance.

MAP 3: 2100 West End Ave., 615/320-1700, www.loewshotels.com

Nashville Marriott at Vanderbilt University $$$

You can't get closer to Vanderbilt University than the Marriott Nashville Vanderbilt. Set on the northern end of the university campus, the Marriott has 301 guest rooms, 6 suites, and plenty of meeting space. It is across West End Avenue from Centennial Park, home of the Parthenon, and a few steps from Vanderbilt's football stadium. It has an indoor pool, a full-service restaurant, a concierge lounge, an ATM, a fitness center, and a business center. Plan ahead if you want a room during a Vanderbilt game weekend or parents' weekend.

MAP 3: 2555 West End Ave., 615/321-1300, http://marriottvanderbilt. com

Aloft West End $$

This hotel has changed names and ownership over the years, but it has remained a favorite of visitors to the Vanderbilt area. The lobby's café is more of a Nashville-style listening room than a traditional hotel lobby coffee shop. It hosts regular singer-songwriter nights, attracting locals who come to support their favorite musicians. The hotel offers free Wi-Fi and amenities that travelers welcome, such as dry cleaning and both valet ($34 per day) and self-parking ($30 per day).

MAP 3: 1719 West End Ave., 615/329-4200, www. aloftnashvillewestend.com

Holiday Inn Nashville-Vanderbilt $$

The closest hotel to Vanderbilt football stadium and Centennial Park, this renovated hotel has clean, if small, guest rooms, as well as an excellent bar with live music seven days a week. Free Wi-Fi, shuttle service downtown, an outdoor pool, and a fitness center round out the offerings, but the location—walking distance to all the Vanderbilt campus must-sees—makes this hotel in demand for reunions and graduations. Parking is $22 per night if you do it yourself and $25 per night for valet (don't bother looking for street parking near campus during the school year).

MAP 3: 2613 West End Ave., 615/327-4707, www.ihg.com

Virgin Hotels Nashville $$

When it opened in 2020, this Music Row hotel became only the third Virgin property in the United States. The building features floor-to-ceiling windows with jawdropping views from almost every angle. The pet-friendly hotel boasts a first-floor restaurant, bar, and coffee shop, and a reputation for being a good place to have a good time. Don't miss the swanky rooftop Pool Club; it's a popular destination even in winter, when you can curl up by the fireplace. Look for the signature red staircase; a version appears in all Virgin hotels.

MAP 3: 1 Music Sq. W., 615/667-8000, https://virginhotels.com/nashville

Music City Hostel $

The Music City Hostel is set amid doctors' offices, restaurants, and commercial buildings in between downtown and Vanderbilt. The low-slung, 1970s-style building looks like nothing much on the outside, but inside it is cheerful, welcoming, and a comfortable home base for budget travelers. The hostel offers the usual dorm-style bunk-bed accommodations (coed or female-only), as well as a handful of private apartments. You can also have a private bedroom with private bath plus shared kitchen and common room. Common areas include a large kitchen, dining room, reading room, cable TV room, computer with Internet access, an outdoor grill, and a coin laundry. Parking is free, and the hostel is within walking distance of restaurants, a bus stop, car rental agency, post office, and hospitals, but a bus or car would be best for getting downtown. Note: You must have a residence at least 60 miles (100 km) outside of Nashville to stay here.

MAP 3: 1809 Patterson St., 615/497-1208, http://musiccityhostel.com

Midtown and 12 South   Map 4

Daisy Hill Bed and Breakfast $$

Stay in a 1925 Tudor home that has a spot on the National Register of Historic Places. Tucked into a brick house near Hillsboro Village and the Vanderbilt and Belmont campuses are three guest rooms, each with its own European decor (Scottish, French, and Scandinavian). Amenities include fireplaces and a family-style breakfast with an emphasis on local produce. Cancellation policies differ during Titan game weekends and other big events, so check when making reservations during these times.
MAP 4: 2816 Blair Blvd., 615/297-9795, www.daisyhillbedandbreakfast.com

Linden Manor Bed and Breakfast $$

Housed in a 19th-century Victorian house, this bed-and-breakfast has private baths in every room and other amenities that B&Bs sometimes lack, such as cable TV and Wi-Fi. The guest rooms at this cheerful yellow-brick home on a corner lot have stylish furniture and hardwood floors, while the separate carriage house offers even more privacy. One room has a private whirlpool, and another has a fireplace.
MAP 4: 1501 Linden Ave., 615/298-2701, http://nashville-bed-breakfast.com

East Nashville   Map 5

The Big Bungalow $$

A Craftsman-style early-1900s town house, The Big Bungalow offers three guest rooms, each with its own private bath and television. Guests have shared access to a computer, microwave, and refrigerator. Common areas are comfortable and stylish, with tasteful decor and hardwood floors. Host Ellen Warshaw prepares breakfast for her guests and occasionally puts on in-the-round concerts in her living room. She is also a licensed masseuse and sometimes offers discounted massage rates with the room. This is a pet-free facility. Children over 10 are welcome. It is about seven blocks from the John Seigenthaler Pedestrian Bridge, which takes you to the heart of downtown.
MAP 5: 618 Fatherland St., 615/256-8375, http://thebigbungalow.com

VanDyke Bed and Beverage $$

The name tells you all you need to know. Van Dyke is a liquor-themed hotel with an open-air bar that connects guest rooms to the East Nashville neighborhood outside its doors. Each of the luxury hotel's eight rooms is named after a different beverage: Champagne, whiskey, wine, beer, tequila, and rum, with decor and specific glassware appropriate to that drink. Only the two rooms on the ground floor are wheelchair accessible; higher levels and the rooftop bar are not, so plan accordingly when making reservations. Some rooms have bunk beds for bachelorette parties or family groups. While the hotel serves food and drinks in the bar, this isn't a full-service establishment: You'll be carrying your own bags, and before check-in you'll be directed to an app to use to open your room door.

MAP 5: 105 S. 11th St., 615/730-5023, www.vandykenashville.com

✪ The Russell $

You'll be able to tell that this East Nashville building used to be a church by the restored stained-glass windows and the repurposed church pews as headboards. The lobby is a stunner, thanks to those windows, reading areas stocked with books from The Bookshop, and a podcasting studio. There's no elevator for humans to the second floor (although there is one for luggage). The Russell donates a portion of each room rate to homelessness ministries in the city, including supporting Shower Up, a truck that provides hot showers for the unhoused. Like many smaller, boutique hotels, the 23-room Russell offers what they call in the business "limited service." There's help if and when you need it, but you'll be carrying your own bags and going out to eat. The owners of The Russell are also the minds behind The Gallatin Hotel (2510 Gallatin Ave., 615/861-1634). The brightly colored Gallatin is a bigger property, with more rooms with bunk beds and more parking, and the same mission to help the less fortunate in Music City.

MAP 5: 819 Russell St., 615/861-9535, www.russellnashville.com

The Gallatin Hotel

Dive Motel & Swim Club $

Dickerson Pike runs northeast of downtown and is home to used car lots and sculptures marking its history on the Buffalo Trace. But in the 1950s and '60s, celebs such Hank Williams Jr. hung out in the motel swimming pools that were clustered along it. The retro Dive Motel brought one of these motels back to life, with mid-century, Palm Springs-inspired decor and disco balls in every room. Amenities are limited, but the hip scene (at the pool during the day and the bar at night) is top-notch and attracts locals every weekend.

MAP 5: 1414 Dickerson Pike, 615/650-9103, www.thedivemotel.com

✪ La Quinta Inn & Suites Downtown/Stadium $

When La Quinta opened this modern hotel across from Nissan Stadium in 2021, it was just what Nashville needed. It's on the east bank of the river, but walking distance from downtown (and with great views of downtown, too). The spacious rooms include couches and desks as well as high ceilings and lots of natural light. The pet-friendly hotel has its own parking garage. Rates are higher during downtown events and on game days but are still a bargain for the location.

MAP 5: 315 Interstate Dr., 615/795-0077, www.wyndhamhotels.com/laquinta

Music Valley   Map 6

✪ Gaylord Opryland Resort $$$

The Gaylord Opryland Resort is more than just a hotel. The 2,882-room luxury resort and convention center is built around a nine-acre indoor garden with 20 different restaurants (the place is so big there is an app to help you navigate indoors). The large rooms have desks, lounge chairs, and plenty of closet space. Rooms opening out onto the mammoth atrium have balconies that feel like they're outdoors (except with climate control); you'll even hear the sounds of the indoor waterfall in the background. Service is impeccable. Press the "consider it done" button on the phone in your room, and any of your needs will be met. Guests can buy onetime or daily passes on the downtown shuttle for about $20 per person round-trip or $40 for three days, and the airport shuttle costs $38 round-trip. Self-parking is $32, and valet parking is $40 per day.

MAP 6: 2800 Opryland Dr., 615/889-1000, http://www.marriott.com

Courtyard by Marriott Opryland $$

This 87-room hotel offers all the basic amenities, as well as a few pluses: It is close to the mammoth Opryland complex and offers shuttles to and from the resort as well as the airport. Convention-goers and others who are on a budget but attending an event at Opryland can save by staying here.

MAP 6: 125 Music City Cir., 615/882-9133, http://marriott.com

Hyatt Place Nashville-Opryland $$

After the Gaylord resort, this is perhaps Music Valley's nicest hotel property, and if you ask for a room that faces the resort, you may even be able to see Opryland's famous holiday lights in season. This hotel caters to folks who want to take in the Music Valley attractions, with free shuttles (and friendly shuttle drivers) to the Gaylord resort, Grand Ole Opry, the airport, and Opry Mills mall. For a small fee there's even a shuttle that will take you downtown. The hotel offers a 24-hour fitness center, free wireless Internet, 24-hour room service, HDTVs, and other better-than-average amenities.

MAP 6: 220 Rudy's Cir., 615/872-0422, http://nashvilleopryland.place.hyatt.com

Best Western Suites near Opryland $

The all-suite Best Western Suites near Opryland is a comfortable compromise between the luxury of the Gaylord Opryland Resort and the affordability of a motel. Each of the hotel's 100 suites has a couch, desk, Internet access, coffee/tea maker, microwave, ironing board, and refrigerator. Rooms with whirlpool tubs are available. Take advantage of the on-site fitness room, 24-hour business center, outdoor pool, free continental breakfast, and weekday newspaper. The Best Western is along a strip of motels and restaurants about 1 mile from the Grand Ole Opry and other Opryland attractions.

MAP 6: 201 Music City Cir., 615/902-9940, http://bestwestern.com

South Nashville   Map 7

BentoLiving Chestnut Hill $$

This pet-friendly, suite-style hotel in the Wedgewood-Houston neighborhood is a good choice for travelers who plan to stay more than a day or two. Rooms have kitchens, balconies, and living areas as well as bedrooms and bathrooms. Downstairs you'll find a better-than-average convenience store where you can buy groceries to cook in your room, or a bottle of wine for enjoying on the rooftop lounge. The lounge hosts regular live music, and the on-site gym is spacious and good for yoga as well as cardio and weightlifting. There are a few small shops on the first level of the building. Don't skip visiting Pink Door Cookies, which makes delicious, brightly colored sweets.

MAP 7: 321 Hart St., 629/231-4001, https://bentochestnuthill.com

Iris Motel $

This is a no-frills, clean, stylish, and safe place to stay while in Nashville. Its Berry Hill location puts it close to a few bars, restaurants, and shops, as well as many recording studios. Berry Hill is about four miles south of downtown, so it's relatively quick to get to most of the city's major attractions. The hotel is a contactless property: You'll check in online and

let yourself into your room using an app. Staff are available by text message if needed, but for the most part you'll be on your own. Rooms have patios, coffeemakers, TV, and places to put your stuff.
MAP 7: 656 W. Iris Dr., 615/669-1295, https://theirismotel.com

Greater Nashville   Map 8

Hotel Preston $$

Hotel Preston is a boutique hotel near the airport. Youthful energy, modern decor, and up-to-date rooms set this property apart from the crowd. Rooms are stocked with Tazo tea and Starbucks coffee, and amenities include a 24-hour fitness center and free airport shuttle. The "You-Want-It-You-Got-It" button in each room beckons the 24-hour room service, and whimsical extras, including a lava lamp, pet fish, and a pillow menu, are available by request when you check in. High-speed Internet is an extra add-on. Two restaurants—including the Pink Slip bar and nightclub, which features a sculpture by local artist Herb Williams—provide food and entertainment.
MAP 8: 733 Briley Pkwy., 615/361-5900, www.hotelpreston.com

Millennium Maxwell House Nashville $

Located in MetroCenter, just off the interstate and north of downtown, the Maxwell House is one of Nashville's overlooked budget hotels. The common areas are light, airy, and clean, but there's nothing fancy. Amenities for the 287-room hotel include a fitness center and outdoor pool, free Wi-Fi, and a business center. A free shuttle takes you to most of the city's main attractions. Free parking is ample, and the hotel often offers discounted government rates on rooms.
MAP 8: 2025 Rosa L. Parks Blvd., 615/259-4343, www.millenniumhotels.com

Sheraton Music City $

The Sheraton Music City is another good option for business travelers who want to be in the Music Valley area but don't need (or want) the full-on resort amenities of the Gaylord. This is a very large convention hotel, with plenty of meeting room space, plus amenities for leisure travel, like both indoor and outdoor swimming pools. Spa services are available, and the free shuttle to the airport is a nice perk. There is a charge for wireless Internet access. Self-parking is free. Security ensures that only guests drive onto the property at night.
MAP 8: 777 McGavock Pike, 615/885-2200, http://starwoodhotels.com

DAY TRIPS

Nashville's geographic location (within one day's drive for about half of the country's population) is one of the reasons it's such a good road-trip destination.

Jack Daniel's Distillery

And the inverse is true, too. Nashville is a great place from which to set off on an awesome day trip, because so much is nearby. In almost every direction there's something worth seeing. True Middle Tennessee doesn't have the high-profile scenic reputation of, say, the nearby Smoky Mountains, but the landscape is rural, rolling, and pure relaxation. If you're planning to be in Nashville for a week or more, take the time to get in the car and explore some nearby attractions.

Chief among these must-sees are suburban Franklin and Leiper's Fork, upscale communities that are a mecca for both history buffs and shoppers (how many destinations can say that?); Mammoth Cave National Park; and the recreation paradise of Land Between the Lakes. All of them are easily accessed from Nashville by car. Much of the drive is on efficient interstates, but of course, taking the back roads is often more interesting.

PLANNING YOUR TIME

Tennessee is a long state. From east to west, the Volunteer State stretches 432 miles (695 km). If you're looking for a little adventure outside of Nashville, Middle Tennessee (plus a few excursions over the state line into Kentucky), offer opportunities to see the countryside.

If you have limited time to explore, no worries. Just one day is ample (though you'll leave wanting more) to check out Franklin and Leiper's Fork

HIGHLIGHTS

✪ **MOST UPDATED BLAST FROM THE PAST:** The 1937-era **Franklin Theatre** has been renovated with modern amenities, but that old-world charm remains (page 221).

✪ **BEST PLACE TO LEARN ABOUT POST-WAR LIFE FOR BLACK SOUTHERNERS: McLemore House** was the first home in the area owned by a formerly enslaved person after the Civil War (page 221).

✪ **BEST PLACE TO FIND A TREASURE WORTH SHIPPING HOME:** Leiper's Fork's **Serenite Maison** is the pick of local celebs looking for drool-worthy antiques and decor (page 231).

✪ **MOST ICONIC DISTILLERY:** Small-batch whiskey is enjoying a renaissance, but **Jack Daniel's Distillery** is still the best-known liquor in the state, if not the world (page 232).

✪ **BEST CHANCE FOR SEEING WILDLIFE:** The **Elk and Bison Prairie** is a scenic space where you are likely to see these magnificent beasts at close range (page 237).

✪ **BEST WAY TO EXPLORE UNDERGROUND:** With options to match a wide range of abilities and interests, the **Mammoth Cave Tours** are the best way to explore the miles of caves and centuries of history at Mammoth Cave National Park (page 244).

Mammoth Cave National Park

Day Trips

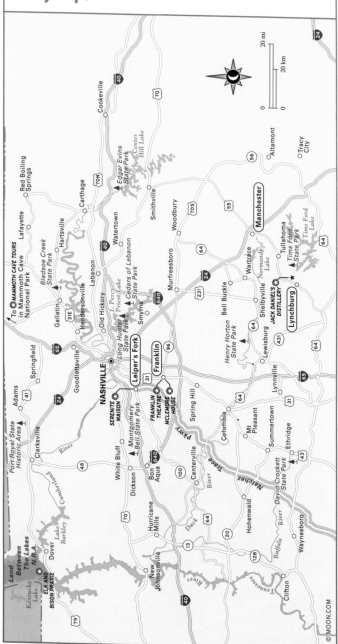

to the south. A two- or three-day weekend is perfect for Land Between the Lakes or Mammoth Cave, with time for exploring, camping, paddling, fishing, and hiking just over the border in Kentucky.

Franklin

The bloody Battle of Franklin that took place in the fields surrounding the town on November 30, 1864, was one of the most important events to take place on this land. Like other towns in the region, it took many years for Franklin to fully recover from the impact of the Civil War. Even now, its Civil War roots are a large part of Franklin's identity.

Just 20 miles (32 km) from Nashville, Franklin is a wealthy bedroom community for Nashville professionals and music industry bigwigs, with centrally located attractions that rival those in Nashville. The city has made efforts to preserve and protect its historical downtown, at least architecturally. The area is quaint and pedestrian-friendly. In recent years, Franklin has done a better job of telling its whole story, adding information about enslavement at historic sites and honoring the Black soldiers that fought in the Civil War.

SIGHTS
HISTORICAL DOWNTOWN

Franklin is one of the most picturesque small towns in Tennessee. Contained within four square blocks, downtown Franklin consists of leafy residential streets with old and carefully restored homes.

For years the center of town was focused around a Confederate monument of a soldier. Like many Confederate monuments in the South, it has been the topic of debate. It hasn't come down, but in 2021, for the celebration of Juneteenth, a bronze statue of a United States Colored Troops soldier went up in Public Square to face it. This newer work, called *March to Freedom,* was designed to tell a more complete story of Franklin's past. Sculptor Joe Howard created the work, which depicts a soldier with one foot on a tree stump resting a rifle across his knee. Signage in the area educates visitors about the more than 180,000 Black men who fought in the Civil War, about 300 of them from Williamson County. There's also information about life for Black people in the area during Reconstruction.

The best way to explore downtown Franklin is on foot. Free parking is available along the streets or in two public garages, one on 2nd Avenue and one on 4th Avenue. Pedestrian concierges (identifiable by their Franklin t-shirts or coats) walk around the area, offering recommendations and directions to visitors. Pick up a walking-tour guide from the Visitor Information Center (400 Main St.).

The walking tour takes you past 39 different buildings, including the Hiram Masonic Lodge (115 2nd Ave. S.), the oldest Masonic

Franklin

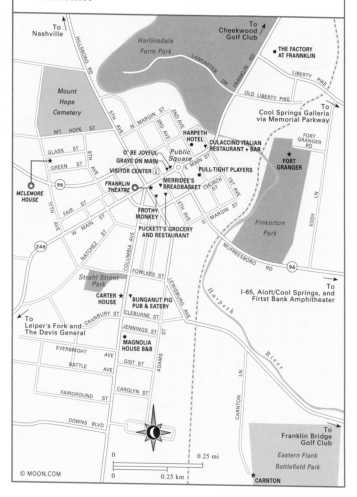

To Nashville

HILLSBORO RD

Harlinsdale Farm Park

LANCASTER DR

To Cheekwood Golf Club

FRANKLIN RD

■ THE FACTORY AT FRANNKLIN

LIBERTY PIKE

OLD LIBERTY PIKE

Mount Hope Cemetery

MT HOPE ST

5TH AVE

N MARGIN ST

3RD AVE

2ND AVE

To Cool Springs Galleria via Memorial Parkway

FORT GRANGER RD

GLASS ST

6TH AVE

GREEN ST

O' BE JOYFUL
GRAYS ON MAIN
VISITOR CENTER ⓘ

HARPETH HOTEL

E MAIN ST

Public Square

CULACCINO ITALIAN RESTAURANT + BAR

PULL-TIGHT PLAYERS

FORT GRANGER

EDDY LN

96

★
MCLEMORE HOUSE

7TH AVE

FRANKLIN THEATRE ✪

MERRIDEE'S ★
BREADBASKET

CHURCH ST

1ST AVE

FAIR ST

4TH AVE

S MARGIN ST

Pinkerton Park

FROTHY MONKEY

W MAIN ST

246

NATCHEZ ST

PUCKETT'S GROCERY AND RESTAURANT

COLUMBIA AVE

S

MURFREESBORO RD

96

To I-65, Aloft/Cool Springs, and Firtst Bank Amphitheater

FOWLKES ST

Strahl Street Park

CARTER ★
HOUSE

GRANBURY ST

▼ BUNGANUT PIG PUB & EATERY

LEWISBURG AVE

CLEBURNE ST

Harpeth

To Leiper's Fork and The Davis General

JENNINGS ST

ADAMS ST

● MAGNOLIA HOUSE B&B

EVERBRIGHT AVE

GIST ST

River

BATTLE AVE

CARNTON LN

FAIRGROUND ST

CAROLYN ST

DOWNS BLVD

To Franklin Bridge Golf Club

Eastern Flank Battlefield Park

0   0.25 mi

© MOON.COM

0   0.25 km

★ CARNTON

lodge in Tennessee and where, in 1830, Andrew Jackson signed the treaty that led to the forced removal of thousands of Native Americans from Tennessee, Georgia, and other Southern states. You will also see the old city cemetery and the old **Franklin Post Office** (510 Columbia Ave.), as well as lots of beautiful old houses and churches,

all of which remain in use today. The walking tour is a good way to become familiar with the town and to appreciate the different types of architecture. It takes 1-2 hours to complete.

Guided walking tours of Franklin are offered by **Franklin on Foot** (615/400-3808, http://franklinonfoot.com). The Classic

Franklin tour provides an overview of the history of the town and its buildings. Other tours include a children's tour, a Southern food tour, and the Haunted Franklin tour. Tours cost $20-49 per person.

✪ FRANKLIN THEATRE

One gem of historical downtown Franklin is the Franklin Theatre (419 Main St., 615/538-2076, www.franklintheatre.com, box office 11am-5pm Tues.-Sat.), a 1937 movie theater that had seen better days until it closed in 2007. In 2011 it reopened after an $8 million restoration funded primarily by donations from locals. The renovation is spot on, bringing the theater, including its striking outdoor marquee, back to its former glory. Lush carpeting, detailed wallpaper, comfortable seats—everything about the theater evokes moviegoing in a different era.

But the Franklin Theatre isn't stuck in the past. It has many modern amenities that make it a great place to have a night out, complete with a concession stand that serves beer, wine, and spirits. Its menu delineates Jack Daniel's from bourbon and other whiskey, as a nod to the locally made favorite spirit. The Franklin Theatre hosts live concerts (many by local residents of acclaim) as well as films.

✪ MCLEMORE HOUSE

Five generations of the McLemore family lived in the white clapboard home at the corner of Glass Street and 11th Avenue in downtown Franklin in a Black neighborhood called Hard Bargain. McLemore House (11th Ave. N. and Glass St., 615/224-3140, www.mclemorehouse.com, 10am-2pm Thurs.-Sat. and by appointment, $10 adults, $5 children) was built in 1880 by Harvey McLemore, a former enslaved man and farmer. This was the first home owned by a formerly enslaved person in Williamson County; the home helped establish Hard Bargain as a middle-class neighborhood.

Alma McLemore, who married into the family, helped oversee a renovation and expansion of the home. Her work has helped cement this small museum as an essential place in understanding the Black experience in Williamson County after the Civil War. On a visit to the home, which features a porch complete with porch swing and two brick fireplaces, you can stop at exhibits that detail the experience of Black people and their path from enslavement to freedom. Artifacts on display include a Tuskegee Airmen's uniform and a number of photographs of the people who built and lived in Hard Bargain. Free porch talks take place at 10am the first Friday of every month.

CARNTON

When Robert Hicks's novel *The Widow of the South* became a best seller in 2005, the staff at Carnton (1345 Eastern Flank Cir., 615/794-0903, https://boft.org, 9am-5pm Mon.-Sat., noon-5pm Sun., adults $18, children 6-15 $8, children under 6 free) noticed an uptick in the number of visitors. The novel is a fictionalized account of Carrie McGavock and how her home, the Carnton Plantation, became a Confederate hospital during the

Fought on November 30, 1864, the Battle of Franklin was one of the biggest hits the Confederate army took during the U.S. Civil War. By the time the fighting ended, more than 10,000 soldiers had lost their lives, been wounded, or gotten captured, all in about a five-hour period.

For those who want to deepen their knowledge about the "War Between the States," suburban Franklin is a good place to learn about this bloody battle that changed the direction of the war. The history of this conflict comes alive, not only through occasional reenactments, but through cemeteries, former war hospitals, and other landmarks that help you understand the rigors of war. Until recently, this history wasn't told through a critical lens; often, the experiences of enslaved people were skimmed over or ignored.

A few of Franklin's Civil War landmarks include Carnton, which served as a Confederate hospital; Fort Granger, which was a Union base; the Carter House, where skirmishes during the battle were fought; and McLemore House, the first home in the county owned by a formerly enslaved person.

Battle of Franklin in the Civil War (how fictionalized is subject for discussion on the tours).

The Carnton mansion, owned by Randal McGavock, a former Nashville mayor and prominent lawyer and businessman, was built in 1826 by enslaved people. Randal had died by the time of the Civil War, and it was his son, John, and John's wife, Carrie, who witnessed the bloody Battle of Franklin on November 30, 1864. Located behind the Confederate line, the Carnton Plantation became a hospital for injured and dying Confederate soldiers. As late as six months after the battle, the McGavock home remained a refuge for recovering veterans. Its operations were largely dependent on the enslaved people forced to work there.

Visitors to Carnton can take a guided tour of the mansion and self-guided tour of the grounds, including a smokehouse, slave house, and garden. You can also take the self-guided tour of the grounds, which includes some exhibits in the gift shop building. The Classic Tour covers some of the experiences of the enslaved people who lived and worked at Carnton, but the 90-minute Slavery and Enslavement Tour goes more in-depth, with details on the lives of the people who were forced into labor here. The Slavery and Enslavement Tours are only available Monday-Friday.

It's a good choice for hard-core history buffs but perhaps too much Civil War lore for the average visitor. Note that the Eastern Flank Circle address may not appear in older GPS systems. Try 1345 Carton Lane as an alternative.

FORT GRANGER

A lesser-visited attraction, Fort Granger is a lovely and interesting place to spend an hour or so. Built between 1862 and 1863 by Union forces, the earthen fort is set on a bluff overlooking the Harpeth River just south of downtown Franklin. The fort was the largest fortification in the area built by Capt. W. E. Merrill during the Federal occupation of Franklin. It saw action twice in 1863 and also in 1864 during the Battle of Franklin.

Fort Granger

Many features of the fort remain intact for today's visitors. You can walk around portions of the breastworks. The interior of the fort is now a grassy field, perfect for a summer picnic or game of catch. An overlook at one end of the fort provides an unmatched view of the surrounding countryside.

You can reach Fort Granger two ways. One is along a short but steep trail departing Pinkerton Park on Murfreesboro Road east of town. Or you can drive straight to the fort by heading out of town on East Main Street. Turn right onto Liberty Pike, right onto Eddy Lane, and finally, right again onto Fort Granger Drive.

The fort, which is maintained by the city of Franklin, is open during daylight hours only. Although there is no office or visitors center at the fort, you may contact Franklin's parks department (615/794-2103) for more information.

CARTER HOUSE

Some of the fiercest fighting in the Battle of Franklin took place around the farm and house belonging to the Carter family, on the outskirts of town. The family took refuge in the basement while Union and Confederate soldiers fought right above them. Today **Carter House** (1140 Columbia Ave., 615/791-1861, www.boft.org, 9am-5pm Mon.-Sat., 11am-5pm Sun., $18 adults, $8 children 6-15) is the best place to come for a detailed examination of the battle and the profound human toll that it exacted on both sides.

You will see hundreds of bullet holes, which help to illustrate the ferocity of the fight. Guides describe some of the worst moments of the battle and bring to life a few of the people who fought it. The house also holds a museum of Civil War uniforms and memorabilia, including photographs and short biographies of many of the men who were killed in Franklin. A video about the battle shows scenes from a reenactment.

RESTAURANTS

A solid choice for baked goods, coffee, and light fare, is **Merridee's Breadbasket** (110 4th Ave., 615/790-3755, www.merridees. com, 7am-5pm Mon.-Wed., 7am-9pm Thurs.-Sat., $3-11). Merridee grew up in Minnesota and learned baking from her Swedish mother. She moved to Middle Tennessee and opened Merridee's Breadbasket in Franklin. Merridee McCray died in 1994, but her restaurant remains one of Franklin's most popular. Come in for omelets, scrambled eggs, or sweet bread in the morning. At lunch choose from the daily soup, casserole, or quiche, or order a sandwich. Merridee's also bakes fresh bread daily; take home a loaf of the always-popular Viking bread. The creaky wood floors and comfortable seating make it a pleasant and relaxing place to refuel.

Housed in a former 1876 pharmacy, **GRAY'S on Main** (332 Main St., 615/435-3603, https:// graysonmain.com, 11am-9pm Sun.-Thurs., 11am-11pm Fri.-Sat., $21-50) is a restaurant, bar, and music venue. The craft cocktails are based on pre-Prohibition recipes, using homemade tinctures and bitters. The same owners have another bar next door, **O' Be Joyful** (328 Main St.), which stocks more than 250 bourbons. If you're interested in the architecture, ask your server if you can take a building tour.

Culaccino Italian Restaurant + Bar (104 E. Main St., 615/435-3539, https://culaccinotn.com, 11am-10pm Mon.-Wed., 11am-1am Thurs.-Fri., 9:30am-1am Sat., 9:30am-9pm Sun., $11-28) is named after the Italian word for the mark a cold glass leaves on a wooden table. Try the soups, pasta, and wood-fired pizza. Culaccino is downtown Franklin's only outdoor bar. It stays open later than many spots in town, great for a post-concert bite or cocktail.

Puckett's Grocery & Restaurant (120 4th Ave. S., 625/794-5527, http://puckettsgro. com, 7am-9pm Sun.-Thurs., 7am-10pm Fri.-Sat., $7-15) offers traditional breakfasts with eggs, bacon, country ham, and biscuits, and plate lunches during the day. In the evening, order up a handmade burger (the locals swear that they're the best in town), fried catfish, or a traditional steak, chicken, or seafood entrée. For vegetarians, they offer a veggie burger or a vegetable plate, as well as salads. Do not skip the fried green beans. The food is well prepared and the service friendly, and there's almost always a crowd, regardless of whether or not there's live music playing. There are other locations in Leiper's Fork and downtown Nashville.

Need a cup of joe before you hit the road? **Frothy Monkey** (125 5th Ave. S., 615/465-6279, www. frothymonkey.com, 7am-9pm daily, $6-17) is a locally beloved coffee shop chain with solid sandwiches (made on house-baked bread) and salads, plus beer and wine.

NIGHTLIFE

Venues that sometimes offer live music include restaurants like **Puckett's Grocery & Restaurant** (120 4th Ave. S., 625/794-5527, http://puckettsgro.com) and **The Bunganut Pig Pub & Eatery** (1143 Columbia Ave., 615/794-4777, www.bunganutpigfranklin.com, 11am-10pm Mon.-Thurs., 11am-1am Fri.-Sat., 11am-9pm Sun.). The **Franklin Theatre** (419 Main St., 615/538-2076, www.franklintheatre.com) has an impressive concert schedule, typically with affordable ticket prices.

Opened in 2021, **FirstBank Amphitheater** (4525 Graystone Quarry Ln., 615/763-3367, http://firstbankamphitheater.com) is a high-end music venue built on the site of a former limestone quarry. The zero-waste facility boasts luxury seats and a park-like atmosphere. It attracts major acts like the Jonas Brothers and Nathaniel Rateliff & the Night Sweats. Getting in and out of the venue can be slow; carpool, bike, or use a ride-hailing app if you can.

ARTS AND CULTURE

Franklin's community theater is the **Pull-Tight Players** (112 2nd Ave. S., 615/791-5007, www.pull-tight.com, tickets $20 adults, $18 seniors, $15 children and students). Performing in an intimate theater in downtown Franklin, Pull-Tight Players puts on about six productions each season, which runs September-June. Productions include many classic stage favorites.

In just a few years the **Pilgrimage Music & Cultural Festival** (The Park at Harlinsdale Farm, 239 Franklin Rd., http://pilgrimagefestival.com, Sept.) has become a major player on the concert festival circuit, which is really saying something in the land of Bonnaroo. The fest, which takes place in September, attracts acts including The Avett Brothers, Grace Potter, Hall & Oates, and Kacey Musgraves. Tennessee native Justin Timberlake is one of the partners in the festival.

For more than 30 years people in Franklin have been donning period Christmas attire each December for **Dickens of a Christmas** (downtown Franklin, http://historicfranklin.com, Dec.). This free street festival recreates the time of Charles Dickens, thanks, in part, to downtown Franklin's Victorian architecture. Festivities include caroling, Victorian-style entertainment, and chestnuts roasting on an open fire.

RECREATION

Pinkerton Park (405 Murfreesboro Rd., 615/794-2103), just southeast of town off Murfreesboro Road, is a pleasant city park. Walking trails, playgrounds, and picnic tables draw dozens of town residents, who come to exercise or simply relax. A short hiking trail takes you to Fort Granger, overlooking the city. You can also take the Sue Douglas Berry Memorial pedestrian bridge over the Harpeth River and walk the six blocks to the town square.

To add a little height (and adrenaline) to your time in Franklin, head to **SOAR Adventure Tower** (3794 Carothers Pkwy., 615/721-5103, www.soaradventure.com, 10am-9pm Mon.-Thurs., 10am-10pm Fri.-Sat., 10am-8pm Sun. June-July, hours vary seasonally; adults $45, children 8-17 $40, children 3-7 $30), where you can climb obstacles in the sky. Or opt for the easy drift of **Middle Tennessee Hot Air Adventures** (615/584-6236, www.tnballoon.com, shared flight $250 pp, private flight $800 for 2 people).

THE PARK AT HARLINSDALE FARM

One of the most famous Tennessee Walking Horse breeding farms has been a public park since 2007. **The Park at Harlinsdale Farm** (239 Franklin Rd., 615/794-2103) was a Franklin landmark for many years, thanks to a very famous horse. Midnight Sun, a stallion, was a world champion walking horse in 1945 and 1946, and all subsequent champions can trace their ancestry to him. The park is a pleasant place to walk or picnic, with a dog park, a pond for catch-and-release fishing, an equestrian trail, and a 5K turf track for running or walking. The park hosts the mega-popular **Pilgrimage Music & Cultural Festival** (http://pilgrimagefestival.com) each September.

GOLF

A few miles southeast of Franklin, **Franklin Bridge Golf Club** (750 Riverview Dr., 615/794-9400, https://franklinbridgegolf.com, $50-75) is an 18-hole par 72 golf course designed by Gary Roger Baird. Just shy of 7,000 yards, the course rating is 77.8, and the slope is 135.

A few miles north of Franklin, the **Cheekwood Golf Club** (285 Spencer Creek Rd., 615/794-8223, www.cheekwoodgolfclub.com, 7am-8pm daily Mar.-Nov., winter hours vary, $25-50) offers 9- and 18-hole options. The course rating is 64.6, and the slope is 105.

SHOPS

For some, shopping is Franklin's greatest attraction. Trendy downtown boutiques, the unique environment of The Factory at Franklin, and proximity to a major mall make this a destination for shoppers. It is also one of Tennessee's most popular antiques shopping destinations.

ANTIQUES

Franklin declares itself "the new antiques capital of Tennessee." Indeed, antiquing is one of the most popular pursuits of Franklin's visitors, and at least two dozen antiques shops serve to quench the thirst for something old. The town's antiques district is huddled around the corner of Margin Street and 2nd Avenue. Other shops are found along Main Street in the downtown shopping district.

The best place to start antiquing is the **Franklin Antique Mall** (251 2nd Ave. S., 615/790-8593, 10am-5pm Mon.-Sat., 1pm-5pm Sun.), inside the town's old icehouse. The mall is a maze of rooms, each with different goods on offer. Possibilities include books, dishware, quilts, furniture, knickknacks, and housewares. Just outside the Franklin Antique Mall are at least five other antiques shops to roam through, including **J. J. Ashley's** (125 S. Margin St., 615/791-0011, 10am-5pm Mon.-Sat.), which specializes in French and English country accessories, as well as European furniture. **Scarlett Scales Antiques** (246 2nd Ave. S., 615/791-4097, 10am-5pm Mon.-Sat., 1pm-5pm Sun.), located in a 1900s shotgun house, has American country furnishings, accessories, and architectural elements arriving daily.

DOWNTOWN

Independent retail is alive and well in Franklin's downtown. West Main Street is the epicenter of the shopping district, though you will find stores scattered around other parts of downtown as well. Home decor, upscale antiques, trendy clothes, and specialty items like candles, tea, and gardening supplies are just a few of the things you'll find in downtown Franklin.

Most shops in downtown Franklin are open by 10am, and many stay open until the evening to catch late-afternoon visitors. You can easily navigate the downtown shopping district on foot, but you may need to stow your parcels in the car trunk if you indulge.

Bink's Outfitters (421 Main St., 615/599-8777, http://binksoutfitters. com, 10am-9pm Mon.-Sat., 11am-7pm Sun.) sells outdoor clothing and equipment, perfect for stocking up for a trip down the nearby Natchez Trace.

Landmark Booksellers (114 E. Main St., 615/791-6400, www. landmarkbooksellers.com, 10am-5pm daily) have a wide selection of both used and new books, including many regional titles and Civil War tomes. For the best in paper and stationery, go to **Rock Paper Scissors** (317 Main St., 615/791-0150, www. rockpaperscissor.com, 10am-6pm Mon.-Fri., 10am-5pm Sat.). **Heart and Hands** (342 Main St., 615/794-2537, www.heartandhandsonline. com, 10am-5pm Mon.-Thurs., 10am-8pm Fri.-Sat., noon-5pm Sun.) is one of several area shops specializing in crafts and home decor.

The Factory at Franklin

THE FACTORY AT FRANKLIN

The most distinctive retail center is **The Factory at Franklin** (230 Franklin Rd., 615/791-1777). A complex of 11 old industrial buildings, The Factory once housed stove factories and a textile mill. Today, The Factory is a vibrant commercial center for the city of Franklin. It houses a collection of local independent retailers, including galleries, **Luna Record Shop** (615/806-9435, http://lunarecordshop.com, 10am-5pm Tues.-Sat.), custom jeweler **Judith Bright** (615/269-5600, https://judithbright.com, 10am-6pm Mon.-Sat., noon-6pm Sun.), and a pet boutique. There are also several studios and learning centers, including **South Gate Studio & Fine Art** (615/599-3360, www. southgatestudio.com), which offers art classes. The Factory also has four restaurants, a fish market, and performance spaces.

Held at The Factory, the **Franklin Farmers Market** (230 Franklin Rd., 615/592-1337, http://

franklinfarmersmarket.com, 8am-1pm Sat.) is one of the finest small-town farmers markets in the state, featuring a wide variety of fruit and vegetable growers; cheese, milk, and meat sellers; and craftspeople and live music.

COOL SPRINGS GALLERIA

Cool Springs Galleria (1800 Galleria Blvd., Cool Springs, 615/771-2050, http://coolspringsgalleria.com, 10am-9pm Mon.-Sat., noon-6pm Sun.) is a mall with more than 165 specialty stores, four major department stores, 15 restaurants, and a 500-seat food court. It is a few miles north of Franklin, convenient to I-65.

Near the mall in Cool Springs Market is **Marti & Liz Shoes** (2000 Mallory Ln., 615/435-8125, www.martiandliz.com, 9am-9pm Mon.-Sat.), a shoe-shopper's bargain dream. **Happy reTales** (101 Creekside Crossing #700, Brentwood, 615/309-1835, https://happyretales.com, 10am-7pm Mon.-Sat., noon-4pm Sun.) is a dog and cat supply store that sends all profits to Happy Tales Rescue, a no-kill dog and cat rescue in Franklin. The store is staffed almost entirely with volunteers. In addition to the healthy food that one might expect at a boutique pet store, they also have a wide selection of pet and people clothing, a variety of dog treats, and pet-inspired artwork.

HOTELS

Franklin generally has two types of accommodations: cozy bed-and-breakfasts and chain motels. The bed-and-breakfasts are in downtown Franklin and the surrounding countryside. The chain motels are clustered around exit 65 off I-65, about 2 miles (3 km) from the city center.

The **Magnolia House Bed and Breakfast** (1317 Columbia Ave., 615/794-8178, http://bbonline.com/tn/magnolia, $175-215) is less than a mile from downtown Franklin, near the Carter House. A large magnolia tree shades the early-20th-century Craftsman home. There are four carpeted guest rooms, each with a private bath. Three have queen-size beds; the fourth has two twin beds. Common areas include a polished sitting room, cozy den, and sunroom, which looks out onto the quiet residential neighborhood. Hosts Jimmy and Robbie Smithson welcome guests and prepare homemade breakfasts according to your preferences.

A hip, urban-feeling hotel option is **Aloft/Cool Springs** (7109 S. Springs Dr., 615/435-8700, http://aloftnashvillecoolsprings.com, $129-184). The hotel boasts a saltwater pool, a better-than-average bar, and a convenient location.

The **Harpeth Hotel** (130 2nd Ave. N., 615/206-7510, www.harpethhotel.com, $212-353) is the first luxury hotel in Franklin. The pet-friendly hotel has 119 guest rooms and a lovely interior courtyard that will make you feel like you're nestled in a European hamlet. Its biggest appeal is its downtown location, walking distance from shopping, eating, and drinking options. Even folks who don't stay overnight like to dine at the hotel's 1799 Kitchen. The menus include brunch and dinner feasts and a full line of cocktails. In fact, the dining room is designed to look like a deconstructed bourbon barrel. There's also a coffee shop on-site.

INFORMATION AND SERVICES

Visit Franklin (615/591-8514, http://visitfranklin.com) publishes guides and maintains a website about Franklin and the surrounding area. They also operate the Visit Franklin Visitor Center (400 Main St., 615/591-8514, 9am-6pm Mon.-Sat., noon-5pm Sun.). The center has a small gift shop.

The Williamson Medical Center (4321 Carothers Pkwy., 615/435-5000) is a full-service medical facility with a 24-hour emergency room.

TRANSPORTATION

Traffic can be heavy in and around Franklin. As it's a thriving bedroom community for commuters working in Nashville, the morning and afternoon rush hours are to be avoided. The city of Franklin offers a trolley bus service around the town and to outlying areas, including Cool Springs Galleria, Williamson Medical Center, Watson Glen Shopping Center, and Independence Square. The trolleys run three different routes 6am-6pm. It can take anywhere from 30 minutes to an hour to get to downtown Franklin from downtown Nashville, depending on traffic. You can pick up a full schedule and route map from the visitors center or download it from http://tmagroup.org. Fares for the Cool Springs Galleria bus are $3 for a one-way trip and $5 for a round-trip.

If you need a cab, call A-1 Brentwood Taxi (615/376-8294), or try a ride-hailing app such as Lyft.

Leiper's Fork

Part bucolic small town, part celebrity enclave, Leiper's Fork is a pleasant place to spend a few hours. It is about a 15-minute drive from

Leiper's Fork

Franklin and near milepost 420 on the Natchez Trace Parkway. The town runs for several miles along Leiper's Fork, a tributary of the West Harpeth River. Beautiful old farmhouses line Old Hillsboro Road, which serves as the main thoroughfare through town.

Some of the earliest settlers of the area were the Benton family, including Thomas Hart Benton, who would go on to become a U.S. senator from Missouri. For many years, Leiper's Fork was called Hillsboro after Hillsborough, North Carolina, where many of its early settlers came

Puckett's Grocery & Restaurant

from. There is another Hillsboro in Coffee County, Tennessee, however, so when this Hillsboro petitioned for a post office in 1818, the U.S. Postal Service insisted that it change its name. Leiper's Fork was born.

Acclaimed furniture maker Dick Poyner was from the Leiper's Fork area. Poyner, a former slave, was famous for his sturdy ladder-back wooden chairs, one of which is on display at the Tennessee State Museum in Nashville.

Leiper's Fork is a pleasant community, with a die-hard group of locals who are proud of their town. Art galleries and antiques shops line the short main drag. Unusually good food can be found at local restaurants, and a laid-back let's-laugh-at-ourselves attitude prevails. Many music mega-powerhouses live here; if you see a celebrity, don't make a fuss. That's why they choose to live in Leiper's Fork.

Bed-and-breakfasts in the area make it a viable destination or a

pleasant pit stop during a tour of the region.

RESTAURANTS

Puckett's Grocery & Restaurant (4142 Old Hillsboro Rd., 615/794-1308, www.puckettsofleipersfork.com, 7am-8pm Tues., 7am-9pm Wed., 7am-10pm Thurs.-Sat., 7am-7pm Sun. summer, reduced hours Dec.-Feb., $6-25) is the heartbeat of Leiper's Fork. An old-time grocery with a small dining room attached, Puckett's serves breakfast, lunch, and dinner. Solid country breakfasts are the order of the day in the mornings, followed by plate lunches. The pulled pork is a favorite, as is the Puckett Burger. Dinner specials include catfish nights, family nights, and a Saturday-night seafood buffet. Friday night the grocery turns upscale with a supper club and live music. Puckett's hours vary by the season, so it's best to call ahead, especially for dinner. This is the location that started it all in the '50s, but there's also a location in Franklin with a more varied menu.

A country store with a laid-back vibe, MoonPies and RC on the shelves, and a bloodhound named Belle on the porch, **The Davis General** (5600 Leipers Creek Rd., 615/830-8503, 9am-4pm Tues.-Sat.) is the epitome of the Leiper's Fork's aesthetic. Grab a sandwich to go for a picnic on the Natchez Trace, or stick around to chat with locals.

NIGHTLIFE

Puckett's Grocery & Restaurant (4142 Old Hillsboro Rd., 615/794-1308, www.puckettsofleipersfork.com) offers live music on Thursday, Friday, and Saturday nights. Thursday is open mic night at 6:30pm, while local bands and singer-songwriters hit the stage at 8pm on Fridays and Saturdays. Cover charge is $10, which is credited to your ticket if you order dinner. Reservations are essential, so call ahead. Check the website to find out who is performing.

ARTS AND CULTURE

Jailhouse Industries operates the Leiper's Fork **Lawn Chair Theatre** (4144 Old Hillsboro Rd., https://leipersforklawnchairtheater.com, May-Sept.), behind Leiper's Creek Gallery. Bring your lawn chair or blanket and enjoy classic movies and kids' favorites on Friday nights, plus concerts. Call 615/477-6799 for more information, or just ask around.

RECREATION

The **Leiper's Fork District** of the **Natchez Trace National Scenic Trail** runs for 24 miles (39 km), starting near milepost 427 and ending at milepost 408, where TN-50 crosses the Natchez Trace Parkway. The trail follows the old Natchez Trace through rural countryside. The best access point is from Garrison Creek Road, which has parking, restrooms, and picnic facilities. You can also access the trail from Davis Hollow Road.

SHOPS

Leiper's Fork's retailers are open 10am-5pm Wednesday-Saturday and 1pm-5pm Sunday. Park the car and set off on foot to explore.

The **Leiper's Creek Gallery** (4144 Old Hillsboro Rd., 615/599-5102, www.leiperscreekgallery.com) focuses on fine arts. It shows a wide selection of paintings by local and regional artists and hosts a variety of arts events year-round. The **Copper Fox Gallery** (4136 Old Hillsboro Rd., 615/569-9191, www.thecopperfoxgallery.com) is stocked with ceramics, jewelry, and paintings. It's a great spot for leisurely browsing.

✪ SERENITE MAISON

The 3,000-square-foot **Serenite Maison** (4149 Old Hillsboro Pike, 615/599-2071, www.serenitemaison.com) houses a well-edited inventory thanks to the smart design sense of Alexandra Cirimelli. A California transplant, Cirimelli has appeared on an episode of *American Pickers* and is known for finding her well-heeled clients (including Holly Williams and several actors and actresses) the perfect farm table or pie safe for their kitchen. Don't overlook the pickin' corner, where locals stop in to play the antique guitars, banjos, and mandolins that hang on the walls.

Lynchburg

A 1.5-hour drive southeast of Nashville, Lynchburg was once a town with a population of 361. It has been transformed by the popularity of Jack Daniel's Tennessee Whiskey, which is made a few blocks from the town square. No other small town in Tennessee sees as many visitors from as many different places as this one.

Critics may object to the tour buses and crowds, but the town has managed to survive its success with relative grace. It has maintained its small-town feel, and it offers its guests a hospitable and heartfelt welcome.

Lynchburg is centered on the Moore County courthouse, a modest redbrick building. Souvenir shops, restaurants, and a few local businesses line the square. Outside of this, Lynchburg is quiet and residential. The Jack Daniel's Distillery is about three blocks away from the town square; a pleasant footpath connects the two.

✪ JACK DANIEL'S DISTILLERY

As you drive into Lynchburg or walk around the town, you might notice some odd-looking gray warehouses peeking out above the treetops. These are barrel houses, where Jack Daniel's Distillery ages its whiskey. Around Moore County there are 74 of these warehouses, and each one holds about one million barrels of whiskey.

Thousands of whiskey drinkers make the pilgrimage every year to Jack Daniel's Distillery (visitors center 133 Lynchburg Hwy./TN-55, 931/759-6357, www.jackdaniels. com, 9am-4:30pm daily) to see how Jack Daniel's is made. And what they find is that, aside from the use of electricity, computers, and the sheer scale of the operation, things have not changed too much since 1866, when Jack Daniel registered his whiskey still at the mouth of Cave Spring near Lynchburg.

Jack Daniel was introduced to the whiskey business by a Lutheran lay preacher named Dan Call, who sold the distillery to Daniel shortly after the Civil War. In 1866, Daniel had the foresight to register his distillery with the federal government, making his the oldest registered distillery in the United States. He never married and had no known children. After Daniel died in 1911, the distillery passed to his nephew, Lem Motlow. The distillery remained

oak barrel at Jack Daniel's Distillery

in the Motlow family until it was sold in 1957 to the Brown-Forman Corporation of Louisville, Kentucky.

Tours offered include the all-ages **Dry County Tour** (9am-4:30pm daily, $15 adults, $7 ages 10-17, free for children under 10), a 70-minute whiskey-free tour that will teach you about the distillery and its history. For those who want a taste, the **Flight of Jack Daniel's Tour** (9am-4:30pm Mon.-Sat., 11am-4:30pm Sun., ages 18-20 tour only, ages 21 and up tour and tasting, $20) lasts 90 minutes and includes tastings of five of the distillery's whiskeys. All tours are offered first-come, first-served, and they sell out, so get there early.

The tour of the distillery begins with a video about the master distillers—Jack Daniel's has had seven in its lifetime—who are the final authority on all facets of the product. You then board a bus that takes you up to the far side of the distillery, and from here you'll walk back to the visitors center, stopping frequently to be told about the key steps in the process. The highlight of the tour for some is seeing Cave Spring, where the distillery gets its iron-free springwater. Others enjoy taking a potent whiff of the sour mash and the mellowing whiskey.

Moore County, where Lynchburg is located, is a dry county, and for 86 years the irony was that Jack Daniel's could not sell any of its whiskey at the distillery. In 1995, however, the county approved a special exemption that allows the distillery to sell souvenir bottles of whiskey at its visitors center. That is all they sell, however; you have to buy other Jack Daniel's merchandise at one of the other gift shops in town.

OTHER SIGHTS

A stately two-story brick building on the southwest corner of the square is the **Moore County Old Jail Museum** (231 Main St., 931/759-4111, 11am-3pm Tues.-Sat., suggested donation $1 adults), which served as the sheriff's residence and the county jail until 1990. The building is now a museum operated by the local historical society. You can see law enforcement memorabilia, old newspaper clippings, and vintage clothes. Go upstairs to see the prisoners' cells.

RESTAURANTS

The most popular place to eat in Lynchburg is **Miss Mary Bobo's Boarding House** (295 Main St., 931/759-7394, seating 11am and 1pm Mon.-Sat., $25). Miss Mary's started life as the home of Thomas Roundtree, the founder of Lynchburg. In 1908, Lacy Jackson Bobo and his wife, Mary Evans Bobo, bought the house and operated it as a boardinghouse until the 1980s. Over the years, word of Mary Bobo's legendary home-cooked meals spread, and this boardinghouse became one of the region's best-known eating houses. Today, Miss Mary's is no longer a boardinghouse, and the restaurant is operated by Miss Lynne Tolley, who has worked hard to keep up the traditions established by Miss Mary. The restaurant is owned by the Jack Daniel's Distillery, and servers are hired from the local community college.

A meal at Miss Mary's will easily be the most distinctive of your trip. Arrive at least 15 minutes early to check in, pay, and be assigned to a dining room. You will be taken to your dining room by a hostess, who stays with you throughout the meal. Everyone sits family-style around a big table. The meal is a traditional Southern dinner, with no less than six side dishes and two meats, plus iced tea (unsweetened), dessert, coffee, and bread. Almost every meal features fried chicken. Side dishes may include green beans, mashed potatoes, fried okra, carrot slaw, and corn bread. Your hostess will answer questions about the food and tell you some stories about the restaurant—if you ask. Call well ahead to make reservations. Meals are fully booked weeks and even months in advance, especially during the busy summer months and on Saturdays.

For a more low-key meal, go to the **Bar-B-Que Caboose Cafe** (217 Main St., 931/759-5180, http://bbqcaboose.com, 11am-4:30pm Mon.-Thurs., 11am-7pm Fri.-Sat., 11:30am-4:30pm Sun., $4-22). The menu offers pulled pork or smoked chicken sandwiches, jambalaya, red beans and rice, and hot dogs.

There are a handful of other restaurants in Lynchburg, all on the town square. **Southern Perks** (10 Short St., 931/759-5552, 7am-3pm Mon.-Sat., $5-13) serves breakfast sandwiches, hand-tossed pizza, salads, wraps, and panini.

HOTELS

The **Belle Fleur Cottage** (Mulberry Creek, 931/580-0671, www.cottagebellefleur.com, $115-125) is a quick walk from the town square and Jack Daniel's Distillery. The three rooms in the B&B are set up for you to relax back to an earlier time but still have some modern-day comforts. Families can enjoy board games or lounge on private patios and porches.

The closest thing to a motel in Lynchburg is the **Lynchburg Country Inn** (423 Majors Blvd., 931/759-5995, www.lynchburgcountryinn.com, $75). Its 25 rooms are each furnished with a microwave, refrigerator, free Wi-Fi, and cable TV. There's a pool out back and rocking chairs on the front and back porches. The motel-style building is modern (constructed in 2003), but the decor is pure country.

Land Between the Lakes

The narrow finger of land that lies between the Cumberland and Tennessee Rivers is a natural wonderland. Comprising 170,000 acres of land and wrapped by 300 miles (485 km) of undeveloped river shoreline, the **Land Between the Lakes National Recreation Area** (100 Van Morgan Dr., Golden Pond, 800/525-7077, www.landbetweenthelakes.us) has become one of the most popular natural areas in this region of the country. Split between Tennessee and Kentucky, the area provides unrivaled opportunities to camp, hike, boat, play, or simply drive through quiet wilderness.

BONNAROO: TENNESSEE'S OFFBEAT MUSIC FESTIVAL

Bonnaroo Music and Arts Festival (www.bonnaroo.com) started out in 2002 as a jam band music festival, but it has evolved into a summertime mega-event for all types of music fans. Bonnaroo takes place over four days in June on a 700-acre rural farm in Manchester, often hosting more than 90,000 attendees. You might think it's the music that really draws the crowds, but the community vibe is what keeps people coming back year after year.

Bonnaroo Music and Arts Festival

Here are some fast facts about the event:

- **Genres of music:** reggae, rock, Americana, jam bands, world, hip-hop, jazz, electronic, folk, gospel, and country
- **Notable past performers:** Lorde, Pearl Jam, The Weeknd, Cardi B, the Red Hot Chili Peppers, and countless others
- **Number of stages:** 10. The music tents have Seussian names, like What Stage, Which Stage, This Tent, That Tent, and The Other Tent.
- **Non-musical activities:** yoga, a 5K run, comedy performances
- **Ticket options:** Four-day general admission passes start at $379; a limited number of reduced-price early-bird tickets go on sale in January each year. Regular tickets go on sale in the spring, after the lineup has been announced, typically in February.
- **What to pack:** A good camping tent, folding chairs, refillable water bottles, and hand sanitizer. Even if you plan to buy most of your food at the festival, pack some emergency snacks. Also bring garbage bags, sunscreen, backup phone chargers, and comfortable clothes for hot weather.
- **Transportation:** A shuttle service between the Nashville airport (available with certain ticket packages) and Bonnaroo helps minimize traffic.

Land Between the Lakes is about a 1.5-hour drive northwest from Nashville. The area lies between what is now called Kentucky Lake (the Tennessee River) and Lake Barkley (the Cumberland River). At its narrowest point, the distance between these two bodies of water is only 1 (0.6 km) mile. The drive from north to south is 43 miles (69 km). About one-third of the park is in Tennessee; the rest is in Kentucky. It is managed by the U.S. Forest Service, an agency of the U.S. Department of Agriculture.

PLANNING YOUR TIME

Some of the best attractions at Land Between the Lakes charge admission. If you are planning to visit all or most of them, consider one of the packages offered by the U.S. Forest Service. A discount package allows you to visit three attractions once over a seven-day period for $15 ($10 for kids ages 5-17). Another option is the $35 LBL Fun

Card: 10 admissions to any of three attractions. It does not expire. You can buy packages at either the north (Kentucky) or south (Tennessee) welcome station or the Golden Pond Visitor Center.

During certain summer weekends there are free two-hour tours of **Lake Barkley's Power Plant and Navigation Lock** (270/362-4236). You must call in advance to reserve a spot and complete a registration form.

There are no restaurants in Land Between the Lakes. Vending machines with snacks and sodas can be found at The Homeplace, Golden Pond Visitor Center, and the Woodlands Nature Station. Picnic facilities abound. A McDonald's sits near the southern entrance to the park. Dover, 5 miles (8 km) east, has other fast-food and local eateries. Twenty miles (32 km) to the southwest, Paris has dozens of restaurants.

SIGHTS
GREAT WESTERN IRON FURNACE

About 11 miles (18 km) inside the park is the **Great Western Iron Furnace**, built by Brian, Newell, and Company in 1854. If you have traveled around this part of Tennessee much, you will have come to recognize the distinctive shape of the old iron furnaces that dot the landscape in the counties between Nashville and the Tennessee River. Like the Great Western Furnace, these plants were used to create high-quality iron from iron ore deposits in the earth.

The Great Western Furnace operated for less than two years. By 1856 panic over reported slave uprisings

elk at Land Between the Lakes

and the coming of the Civil War caused the plant to shut down. It would never make iron again.

THE HOMEPLACE

Just beyond the furnace is The Homeplace (4512 The Trace Rd., Dover, 931/232-6457, 10am-5pm daily Apr.-Oct., 10am-5pm Wed.-Sun. Mar. and Nov., $5 ages 13 and up, $3 children 5-12, free for children under 5, last tickets sold at 4pm), a living-history museum that depicts life in Between the Rivers circa 1850. In the mid-19th century, Between the Rivers was home to an iron ore industry and hundreds of farmers. These farmers raised crops and livestock for their own use, as well as to sell where they could.

The Homeplace recreates an 1850 farmstead. Staff dress in period clothes and perform the labors that settlers would have done: They sow seeds in the spring, harvest in the summer and fall, and prepare the fields for the next year in the winter. The farm includes a dogtrot cabin, where you can see how settlers would have lived, cooked, and slept. Out back there is a small garden, a plot of tobacco, pigs, sheep, oxen, and a barn. You may see farmers splitting shingles, working oxen, sewing quilts, making candles, or another of the dozens of tasks that settlers performed on a regular basis.

The Homeplace publishes a schedule that announces when certain activities will take place, such as canning, shearing of sheep, or harvesting tobacco. Even if you come when there is no special program, you will be able to see staff taking on everyday tasks, and you can ask them about any facet of life on the frontier.

✪ ELK AND BISON PRAIRIE

Archaeological evidence shows that elk and bison once grazed in Tennessee and Kentucky, including the area between the rivers. Settlers quickly destroyed these herds, however. Both bison and elk were easy to hunt, and they were desirable for their meat and skins. By 1800, bison had been killed off, and about 50 years later elk were gone, too.

When Land Between the Lakes was created, elk and bison were reintroduced to the area. The South Bison Range across the road from The Homeplace is one of the places where bison now live. The bison herd that roams on about 160 acres here can sometimes be seen from the main road or from side roads bordering the range.

You can see both bison and elk at the Elk and Bison Prairie (dawn-dusk daily, $5 per vehicle), a 700-acre restoration project located near the midpoint of the Land Between the Lakes. In 1996, 39 bison were relocated here from the south prairie, and 29 elk were transported from Canada. Since then, the populations of both animals have grown.

Visitors may drive through the range along a 3.5-mile (5.6-km) loop (The Trace Rd./TN-453), the entrance to which is directly across The Trace Road from the Jenny Ridge Picnic Area. Take your time, roll down your windows, and keep your eyes peeled for signs of the animals. The best times to view elk and bison are in the early morning or approaching sunset. At other times of day, you may just enjoy the sights and sounds of the grassland. Pay attention to the road as well as the animals, as the car in front of you may slow to take photos of one of these magnificent creatures. You may also see some bison from the Natchez Trace en route.

The loop drive is about 1 mile (1.6 km) north of the Golden Pond Visitor Center. You'll pay your entry fee (cash or credit card) at a machine at an unattended gate. Pets must stay in your vehicle, and your car must be enclosed (no motorcycles or open-top vehicles).

GOLDEN POND VISITOR CENTER AND PLANETARIUM

For the best overview of the history, nature, and significance of the Land Between the Lakes, stop at the **Golden Pond Visitor Center and Planetarium** (239 Visitor Center Dr., 270/924-2233, 10am-5pm daily, visitors center free). The visitors center is home to a small museum about the park, where you can also watch a video about the elk that have been restored on the Elk and Bison Prairie. You'll also find a gift shop, restrooms, and picnic area.

The **planetarium** (10am-5pm daily, adults $6, children 5-12 $3.50, children under 4 free; evening shows $8 for all ages) screens at least four programs daily about astronomy and nature, with more during the holidays. On Saturdays and Sundays at 1pm, you can get a sneak peek at the night sky above.

Golden Pond was the name of Land Between the Lakes' largest town before the park was created. Golden Pond, also called Fungo, was a vibrant town that, at its peak, had a hotel, bank, restaurants, and other

retail outlets. During Prohibition, farmers made moonshine in the woods and sold it in Golden Pond. Golden Pond whiskey was sought after in back-alley saloons as far away as Chicago. When Land Between the Lakes was created in 1963, Golden Pond had a population of about 200 people. Families moved their homes and relocated to communities outside the park. In 1970, when the historical society unveiled a marker at the site of Golden Pond, the strains of "Taps" rang out over the hills.

You can visit the site of Golden Pond by driving a few miles east of the visitors center on KY-80. There is a picnic area.

WOODLANDS NATURE STATION

The final major attraction in Land Between the Lakes is the **Woodlands Nature Station** (north of the visitors center on the Trace, 3146 Silver Trail Rd., Cadiz, KY, 270/924-2020, 10am-5pm daily Apr.-Oct., 10am-5pm Wed.-Sun. Nov. and Mar., $5 ages 13 and up, $3 children 5-12, free for children under 5). Geared toward children, the nature station introduces visitors to animals including bald eagles, coyotes, opossum, and deer. There are also opportunities for staff-led hiking trips. Special events and activities take place nearly every weekend, and during the week in summertime.

CENTER FURNACE

You can see the ruins of **Center Furnace,** once the largest iron furnace in the Land Between the Lakes, along the **Center Furnace Trail.** On the short walk you will see signs that describe the process of making iron and explain why it was practiced in Between the Rivers. The trailhead is just south of Silver Trail Road, near the Woodlands Nature Station. It's about 12 miles (19 km) northeast of the Golden Pond Visitor Center.

Center Furnace was built around 1852. It continued to operate until 1912, much longer than any other furnace in the area.

RECREATION

Promoting outdoor recreation is one of the objectives of Land Between the Lakes. Visitors can enjoy hiking, biking, paddling, horseback riding, hunting, fishing, and camping. An area is even specially designated for all-terrain vehicles.

TRAILS

Land Between the Lakes has 200 miles (320 km) of scenic roads and 500 miles (800 km) of hiking trails. Some of these are also open for mountain biking and horseback riding.

The **Fort Henry Trails** are a network of 26 miles (42 km) of trails near the southern entrance to the park, some of which follow the shoreline of Kentucky Lake. The intricate network of six trails allows hikers to choose anywhere from a 3-mile (4.8-km) loop to much longer hike, and they follow General Grant's troop routes from Fort Henry over to Fort Donelson during the Civil War.

Driving south to north along the scenic main road, or trace, that runs along the middle of the park, you will find the major attractions within Land Between the Lakes.

Access the trails from the south welcome station, or from the Fort Henry Trails parking area, at the end of Fort Henry Road. These trails crisscross the grounds once occupied by the Confederate Fort Henry. They are for bikers and hikers only.

The **North-South Trail** treks the entire length of the Land Between the Lakes. From start to finish, it is 58.6 miles (94.3 km). Three backcountry camping shelters are available along the way for backpackers. The trail crosses the main road in several locations. Portions of the trail are open to horseback riders, and the portion from the Golden Pond Visitor Center to the northern end is also open to mountain bikers.

The 4.5-mile (7.2-km) **Honker Lake Loop Trail** begins at the Woodlands Nature Station. This trail is open to hikers only. Sightings of fallow deer and giant Canada geese are common along this trail. The banks of nearby Hematite Lake are littered with bits of blue stone, remnants of slag from the Center Furnace.

Finally, at the northern end of the park are the **Canal Loop Trails**, a network of hike/bike trails that depart from the north welcome station. These trails meander along the shores of both Kentucky Lake and Lake Barkley. The entire loop is 11 miles (18 km), but connector trails enable you to fashion a shorter hike or ride (1.5 miles/2.4 km and up) if you want.

A detailed map showing all hiking, biking, and horseback trails can be picked up at any of the park visitors centers. You can rent bikes at Hillman Ferry and Piney Campgrounds.

DISTILLERY TOURS

This region of Tennessee has a history of distilling spirits (both legal and illegal). Rather than roam the hills on your own to find some moonshine, take a tour of one of these distilleries.

- **George Dickel** (1950 Cascade Hollow Rd., Tullahoma, 931/408-2410, www.georgedickel.com, 9am-4:30pm Mon. and Wed.-Sat., 11am-4:30pm Sun., $14) makes Tennessee whisky (spelled without the "e") and rye. The distillery is on the National Register of Historic Places.
- **Jack Daniel's Distillery** (280 Lynchburg Hwy./TN-55, 931/759-6357, http://jackdaniels.com, 9am-4:30pm daily) is the best-known still in the Volunteer State.
- **Leiper's Fork Distillery** (3381 Southhall Rd., Franklin, 615/465-6456, http://leipersforkdistillery.com, 9:30am-5pm Tues.-Sat., tours offered on the hour 10am-4pm, extended hours 9:30am-6:30pm Fri.-Sat., 11:30pm-4pm Sun. May-Oct.) is focused on small-batch whiskey. Arrive 15 minutes prior to your tour start time.

OFF-HIGHWAY VEHICLES

There are more than 100 miles (160 km) of trail for off-highway vehicles (OHVs). OHV permits are available for $20 for three days or $75 for an annual pass. Note: The number of annual passes available is limited, and they often sell out early in the year. The nontransferable passes may be purchased at any Land Between the Lakes visitors center. Call 270/924-2233 to find out if any of the trails are closed due to bad weather or poor conditions.

FISHING AND BOATING

Land Between the Lakes offers excellent fishing. The best season for fishing is spring, April-June, when fish move to shallow waters to spawn. Crappie, largemouth bass, and a variety of sunfish may be caught at this time.

Summer and fall offer good fishing, but winter is fair. A fishing license from the state in which you will be fishing is required; these may be purchased from businesses outside the park. Specific size requirements and open dates may be found at any of the visitors centers.

There are 19 different lake access points where you can put in a boat. Canoe and kayak rentals are available at the Energy Lake Campground, which is in Kentucky. Energy Lake is a no-wake lake and perfect for paddling and fishing.

HUNTING

Controlled hunting is one of the tools that the Forest Service uses to manage populations of wild animals in Land Between the Lakes. Hunting also draws thousands of visitors each year. The annual spring turkey hunt and fall deer hunts are the most popular.

Specific rules govern each hunt, and in many cases hunters must apply in advance for a permit. Hunters must also have a $25 LBL Hunter Use Permit, as well as the applicable state licenses. For details on hunting regulations, call the park at 270/924-2065.

CAMPING

There are nine campgrounds at Land Between the Lakes. All campgrounds have facilities for tent and trailer camping.

Most campgrounds are open March-October, but some are open year-round. There's a complicated formula for figuring out the price of campsites, based on which campground it is, the day of the week, and the month of the year. In general, camping costs $10 per night; RV sites range $6-32, depending on whether there is access to electricity, water, and sewer services.

Reservations (270/924-2000, http://lbl.org) are accepted for select campsites at Piney, Energy Lake, Hillman Ferry, and Wrangler Campgrounds up to six months in advance. Cravens Bay, Gatlin Point, Fenton, and Turkey Bay are all self-service.

Piney Campground

Located on the southern tip of Land Between the Lakes, Piney Campground (621 Fort Henry Rd., Dover, 931/232-5331) is convenient to visitors arriving from the Tennessee side of the park and, as a result, can be one of the most crowded campgrounds in LBL. Piney has more than 300 campsites; 283 have electricity; 44 have electricity, water, and sewer; and 57 are primitive tent sites.

Nine rustic one-bedroom camping shelters each have a ceiling fan, table and chairs, electrical outlets, and a large porch. Sleeping accommodations are one double bed and a bunk bed. Outside there is a picnic table and fire ring. There are no bathrooms; shelter guests use the same bathhouses as other campers. Camp shelters cost $50 per night and sleep up to four people.

Piney's amenities include a camp store, bike rental, archery range, playground, swimming beach, boat ramp, and fishing pier.

Energy Lake Campground

Near the midpoint of Land Between the Lakes, Energy Lake Campground (5501 Energy Lake Dr., Golden Pond, KY, 270/924-2270) has tent and trailer campsites, electric sites, and group camp facilities. It tends to be less crowded than some of the other campgrounds and has nice lakeside sites, with a swimming area, volleyball, and other kid-friendly activities. The assembly house has a washer and dryer and offers canoe rentals.

Hillman Ferry Campground

Located near the northern end of Land Between the Lakes, Hillman Ferry Campground (820 Hillman Ferry Rd., Grand Rivers, KY, 270/924-2181) has 374 tent and RV campsites. It is nestled on the shores of Kentucky Lake, between Moss Creek and Pisgah Bay.

Electrical and nonelectrical sites are available. Amenities include a dumping station, bathhouses with showers and flush toilets, drinking water, a camp store, swimming area, a disc golf practice basket, coin-operated laundry, and bike rentals.

BOAT AND HORSE CAMPING

In addition to the campgrounds already listed, Land Between the Lakes operates five lakeside camping areas that are designed for boaters who want to spend the night. Rushing Creek/Jones Creek is the most developed of these camping areas; it has 40 tent or RV sites and a bathhouse with showers and flush toilets. Other campsites, including Birmingham Ferry/Smith Bay, Cravens Bay, Fenton, and Gatlin Point, have chemical toilets, tent camping sites, and grills.

LBL also oversees **Wrangler's Campground** (5100 Laura Furnace Rd., Golden Pond, KY, 270/924-2201), designed for horseback riders. In addition to tent and RV sites, it has camping shelters and horse stalls. Amenities include a camp store, bathhouses, coin laundry, and playground. Horse day-riding permits are required for all horse trailers entering the area ($7 for 1 day, $75 annual).

BACKCOUNTRY CAMPING

Backcountry camping is allowed year-round in Land Between the Lakes. All you need is a **basic camping permit** ($7 for 3 days, $30 annual) and the right gear to enjoy unlimited choices of campsites along the shoreline or in the woodlands.

INFORMATION

The park headquarters is at the **Golden Pond Visitor Center** (238 Visitor Center Dr., 270/924-2000, 9am-5pm daily) in Kentucky. When you arrive, stop at the nearest welcome or visitors center for up-to-date advisories and activity schedules. All of the welcome centers and the visitors center are open 9am-5pm daily.

Friends of Land Between the Lakes (270/924-2088, http://friendsoflbl.org) organizes volunteer opportunities and publishes a detailed tour guide to the park, which includes historical and natural anecdotes.

camping at Land Between the Lakes

Mammoth Cave

The thing about **Mammoth Cave National Park** (1 Visitor Center Pkwy., Mammoth Cave, KY, 270/758-2180, www.nps.gov/maca) is that no one really knows how big it is. Yes, there are 80 square miles (200 square km) that are managed by the National Park Service above ground. But below the surface, where limestone and water have created the largest cave system in the entire world, no one really knows how far it reaches. More than 400 miles (640 km) have been found so far, but exploration is ongoing; there may be another route available in this underground wonderland the next time you visit. The park's name comes from its size, of both its length and of the Rotunda, the massive room at its entrance.

Although Mammoth Cave is in Kentucky, not Tennessee, more than 2 million people a year make their way to this area less than 90 minutes north of Nashville to experience one of Mother Nature's most jaw-dropping but eerie gifts. While hundreds of miles of caves have been discovered, only about 10 miles (16 km) are open to the public, but there's more than enough beauty to keep a family busy above and below ground for days. The caves are also home to the endangered Kentucky cave shrimp, which is a sightless albino shrimp rangers are sure to point out when you take a guided tour. Above ground there are more than 25 endangered plants in this protected ecosystem.

Since 1941 the National Park Service has managed this natural wonder, protecting the land for future generations. Of course, the cave system is the draw, with more than a dozen different tour options. But above ground, there are more than 70 miles (110 km) of trails for hiking and horseback riding, plus fishing and paddling on the Green River.

It took centuries—as much as 6,000 years—for water to carve away at the limestone rock to create this underground maze. Evidence of ancient life has been found in the caves; park researchers believe the first person stepped foot in the caves 4,000 years ago. The first modern discovery of what is now Mammoth Cave took place in 1797. It was a hotbed for tourism from its earliest days, but it also housed a tuberculosis hospital at one point. The national park was established in 1941.

PLANNING YOUR TIME

Because the temperature in the caves hovers around 54°F (12°C) all year, Mammoth Cave is somewhere you can visit no matter the weather outside. However, summer is high season, with people seeking cool comfort underground and enjoying camping and fishing outside. Because there are fewer crowds, cave tours are offered less frequently in winter.

A long weekend of three days is enough to see the Mammoth Cave highlights and whet your appetite for a return visit. Book cave tours in advance, as there are limits on the number of people who can take a

walkway through the woods in Mammoth Cave National Park

tour at one time. Self-guided tours are an option on select routes, but the rangers know their stuff, and you'll be better off with a professional. Several short, free surface-level ranger-led walks are available from the visitors center. There are some accessible options both above and below ground.

SIGHTS
✪ MAMMOTH CAVE TOURS

The main reason most people come to Mammoth Cave National Park is to take one of the Mammoth Cave Tours, where you go underground and explore the 54°F (12°C) underground paradise with the aid of a trained ranger. Full descriptions of each tour, including the number of steps involved, the duration, areas of focus, difficulty, and prices are available online. Some tours overlap sights and information, but not entirely. It is perfectly reasonable, if not desirable, to take more than one tour on a trip to Mammoth Cave.

Book in advance, as tours have limited availability. Tour options are listed below. The times listed are for May to mid-August; off-season times vary.

- **Frozen Niagara Tour** (9:15am, 11:30am, 4:30pm daily; $14 adults, $10 youth ages 6-12): This is an easy 75-minute tour that covers 0.25 mile (0.4 km), including sections that are on many of the longer tours.

- **Historic Tour** (10am, 12:45pm, 3:15pm, 3:45pm daily; $17 adults, $12 youth ages 6-12): Covering 2 miles (3.2 km) over two hours, this is considered a moderate hike.

- **Extended Historic Tour** (9am daily; $18 adults, $13 youth ages 6-12): An extra 15 minutes on the Historic Tour includes a trip to see some of the areas used to treat tuberculosis in the 1840s.

- **Domes and Dripstones Tour** (10am, 11am, 12:15pm, 12:45pm, 2:15pm, 2:45pm daily; $17 adults, $12 youth ages 6-12): Expect lots of stairs and small areas on this moderate two-hour tour.

- **Mammoth Cave Accessible Tour** (9:30am and 1:30pm daily; $20 adults, $14 youth ages 6-12): This two-hour tour is the best option for those in wheelchairs and with mobility issues, as it uses elevators to access the caves.
- **Gothic Avenue Tour** (8:45am daily; $15 adults, $10 youth ages 6-12): This moderate two-hour tour includes some artifacts of early explorers.
- **Violet City Lantern Tour** (2:15pm daily; $20 adults, $15 youth ages 6-12): This is a one-of-a-kind experience, exploring the caves for three hours only by the light of a lantern.
- **River Styx Tour** (3:30pm daily; $18 adults, $13 youth ages 6-12): This 2.5-hour tour is best for folks with an interest in geology.
- **Trog Tour** (9am Sat.-Sun., $20 youth ages 8-12): This tour only runs on weekends, and it's an easy, kids-only option.
- **Introduction to Caving Tour** (1:30pm Sat.-Sun.; $30 adults, $24 youth ages 6-12): Another weekends-only, easy-hike option, this intensive tour teaches proper caving techniques. It's designed for kids, as well as their parents and guardians. Visitors must not be larger than 42 inches in circumference in order to fit through crawl spaces.
- **Great Onyx Tour** (3:30pm daily; $20 adults, $15 youth ages 6-12): For 2.25 hours you can explore unusual rock formations. Great Onyx Cave is not known to

Frozen Niagara in Mammoth Cave National Park

connect with the larger cave system in the park.

GREEN RIVER PADDLE TRAIL

Once you've seen below the land, check out the scenery on the water from the **Green River Paddle Trail** (270/789-2956, $24-30), which starts at Green River Lake Dam in Taylor County and ends at the Hart County Line. Kayak and canoe rentals are available by appointment. The river is spring-fed, meaning the water stays cool (72-75°F/22-24°C) even in the hottest part of summer. **Cave Country Canoe** (865 Old Mammoth Cave Rd., 270/773-5552, hwww.cavecountrycanoeky.com, 8am-3:30pm daily) leads outings on the Green River.

THE OLD GUIDES' CEMETERY

Inside the national park, **The Old Guides' Cemetery** has more than 20 marked graves dating from the mid-1850s. The cemetery is on the National Register of Historic Places, representing the period of discovery and early uses of Mammoth Cave. It is wheelchair accessible via a paved and then dirt trail from the visitors center.

BIG MIKE'S ROCK SHOP

Taking rocks from the national park is verboten, but if your Mammoth Cave tours have piqued your interest, you can purchase some at nearby **Big Mike's Rock Shop** (566 Old Mammoth Cave Rd., Cave City, 270/773-5144, www. bigmikesrockshop.com, 9am-5pm Tues.-Thurs., 9:30am-5pm Fri.-Mon.).

PLAZA THEATRE

Nearby Glasgow is home to the restored **Plaza Theatre** (115 E. Main St., Glasgow, 270/361-2101, www. historicplaza.com, box office 9am-5pm Mon.-Fri.). Built in 1934, it hosts concerts (with a slant toward country music) and theater performances.

RESTAURANTS

If you're not bringing your own hot dogs to cook over the campfire, you'll want to fortify yourself while in the area. The **Lodge at Mammoth Cave** (171 Hotel Rd., 270/451-2283) has two good options in season: **Green River Grill** (8am-10pm daily spring-fall, $12-22), which emphasizes local ingredients, and the more casual **Spelunkers Café** (10am-5pm daily spring-fall, $2.25-7), which also has an ice cream parlor.

Cave City and Glasgow, both in Kentucky, have casual eateries. Cave City tends to be more family-friendly and casual, while Glasgow is slightly more upscale.

ACCOMMODATIONS

The Lodge at Mammoth Cave (171 Hotel Rd., 844/760-2283, www. mammothcavelodge.com, $70-140) is a bit of a misnomer, as these are a collection of historic cottages and other rooms, rather than a tradition lodge. They've been renovated with air-conditioning and Wi-Fi and are the place to stay if you want to be in the park but don't want to sleep on the ground. There's even a day-use dog kennel (844/760-2283, $3.50 an hour, $1 per hour after the first) so your pup can be safe while you go on a cave tour.

Many people who spend the night in the area do so under a tent. **Mammoth Cave Campgrounds** (2811 Mammoth Cave Pkwy., Mammoth Cave, KY, 270/758-2424, www.recreation.gov, $20 tent sites, $50 RV) offers 111 campsites within walking distance of the visitors center. Campsites have picnic tables and fire rings. Reservations are available May to mid-October and must be made online, although you can ask questions of the rangers before booking. Some sites are set aside for first-come, first-serve, to increase the likelihood that you can get a site at the last minute.

If you're willing to stay outside of the park, you have more options. **The Grand Victorian Inn** (5 Old Dixie Hwy., 270/590-1935, www. grandvictorianinnky.com, $99-149) is a renovated inn with 11 rooms, including one ADA-accessible room, free Wi-Fi, and easy access to the biking and hiking trailheads that lead into the park.

Book a **Green River Paddle Trail cabin** (112 Paddle Trail Ln., 270/932-4298, www.greenriver paddletrailcabins.com, $72) or RV hookups for your post-paddle sleep.

The charming town of Glasgow, Kentucky, is just 25 minutes from Mammoth Cave and is home to a sweet downtown with a concert venue, restaurants, shops, and several bed-and-breakfasts. **Hall Place Bed and Breakfast** (313 S. Green St., Glasgow, 270/651-3176, www. grandvictorianinnky.com, $95-120) is one gem with lots of history

connected to it. It is on the National Registry of Historic Places; it was a stop on the Underground Railroad and was visited by Abraham Lincoln.

INFORMATION

The park headquarters and **visitors center** (1 Mammoth Cave Pkwy., Mammoth Cave, KY, 270/758-2180, 8am-6:30pm daily mid-Mar.-mid-Aug., 8am-6pm daily mid-Aug.-Oct., 8:30am-4:30pm Nov.-mid-Mar.) is your best bet for information on last-minute tours and camping spots, as well as ranger-led hikes, museum-style exhibitions about the park, and a gift shop.

GETTING THERE

From the north on I-65, take exit 53 (Cave City). Turn right onto KY-70. Follow KY-70/255, which will become the Mammoth Cave Parkway, where you'll find the visitors center. From the south on I-65, take exit 48 (Park City). Turn left onto KY-255 and follow KY-255 as it becomes the Park City Road into the park. Follow Park City Road until it joins the Mammoth Cave Parkway; turn left. Follow Mammoth Cave Parkway to the visitors center.

Note that GPS systems can be unreliable for getting to Mammoth Cave National Park, sometimes directing visitors to locations that require getting on a ferry (which is often shuttered) to cross the river. Double-check locations, routes, and time zones before leaving. Mammoth Cave is on central time, but some other parts of Kentucky are on eastern time.

BACKGROUND

The Landscape

the Cumberland River and Nashville skyline

Tennessee is a long, narrow state. Shaped roughly like a parallelogram, it is less than 500 miles (800 km) from east to west and 110 miles (175 km) from north to south. Partly due to its unusual shape, Tennessee, along with Missouri, borders more states than any other in the country. Nashville is in the center of the state.

The Cumberland River winds its way through Nashville, bending and turning through its neighborhoods and skyline. The river and its banks provide Music City with the water for its lush, green open spaces. It's also responsible for some of the traffic congestion, as streets curve along its meanders. Occasionally, heading to the next neighborhood requires finding a bridge.

That said, Nashville's location in the Cumberland River basin is part of its appeal. The river gives even Music City's most urban areas a bucolic quality. The neighborhoods are full of hustle and bustle, but it doesn't take much effort to escape when you need some R&R.

GEOGRAPHY

The state is traditionally divided into three regions, East, Middle, and West. Middle Tennessee is home to Tennessee's capital city, Nashville, and some of its most fertile farmland. Before the Civil War, great plantation mansions dotted the countryside south of Nashville. Today, Tennessee Walking

Horse farms, new industries, and the economic success of Nashville continue to make Middle Tennessee prosperous.

Geographically, Middle Tennessee begins with the Cumberland Plateau, which rises to about 2,000 feet (600 meters) above sea level and lies west of East Tennessee's Great Valley. Despite its name, the plateau is not flat; there are a number of steep valleys in the plateau, the largest being the Sequatchie Valley.

The Highland Rim is a region of hills, valleys, and fertile farmland that lies west of the plateau. The largest physical region of Tennessee, the Highland Rim contains 10,650 square miles (27,600 square kilometers) of land, or almost 25 percent of the state. Almost entirely surrounded by the Highland Rim is the Central Basin, a low, flat, and fertile region in north-central Tennessee. Nashville is located in the Central Basin.

Nashville itself sits at 550 feet (170 meters) above sea level. It is the U.S. city with the second-largest landmass: more than 500 square miles (1,300 square kilometers).

CLIMATE

Nashville enjoys a relatively mild climate, with average temperatures ranging from 38°F to 89°F (3-32°C). Summer days can feel very hot, however, and a run of humid 100°F (38°C) days in August is not unusual. A few flakes of snow may fall in the winter, and the city essentially shuts down when there is any accumulation (average snowfall for the year is 7 inches (18 cm), but the school closures will suggest much more). Often, an evening's snowfall has evaporated by midmorning.

The city receives an average of 52 inches (132 cm) of rain per year. Long springs and falls mean a long season for beautiful flowers, but also a long season for allergy sufferers.

FLOODS AND TORNADOES

A devastating flood in Nashville and Middle Tennessee in May 2010 brought the issue of global climate change, combined with human development and water management, to the forefront. The flood caused more than $1.5 billion of damage to Music City, followed by considerable rebuilding and redevelopment. Flash flooding in August 2021 claimed the lives of 20 people in Waverly, a town to the west of Nashville.

Tornadoes hit the region, too. In March 2020, EF3 and EF4 tornadoes hit the area, killing more than 25 people and causing more than $1.6 billion of damage.

History

THE FIRST TENNESSEANS

The first humans settled in what is now Tennessee 12,000-15,000 years ago. Descended from people who crossed into North America during the last ice age, these Paleo-Indians were nomads who hunted large game animals, including mammoth, mastodon, and caribou. Remains of these extinct mammals have been found in West Tennessee, and arrowheads and spear points have been found all over the state. The ice age hunters camped in caves and under rock shelters but remained predominantly nomadic.

About 10,000 years ago, in what's called the Archaic Period, the climate and vegetation of the region changed. The deciduous forest that still covers large parts of the state replaced the evergreen forest of the fading ice age. Large game animals disappeared, and deer and elk arrived, attracted by the forests of hickory, chestnut, and beech. Descendants of the Paleo-Indians gradually abandoned the nomadic lifestyle of their ancestors and established settlements, often near rivers. They hunted deer, bear, and turkey; gathered nuts and wild fruit; and harvested freshwater fish and mussels. They also took a few tentative steps toward cultivation by growing squash and gourds.

This was replaced by the Woodland Period about 3,000 years ago. The people of this era adopted the bow and arrow for hunting and—at the end of their predominance—began cultivating maize and beans as staple crops. Ceramic pottery appeared, and ritualism took on a greater importance in the society. The Pinson Mounds, burial mounds near Jackson in West Tennessee, date from this period, as does the misnamed Old Stone Fort near Manchester, believed to have been built and used for ceremonies by the Indigenous people of the area.

The development of a more complex culture continued, and at about AD 900 the Woodland cultures gave way to the Mississippian Period, an era marked by population growth, an increase in trade and warfare, the rise of the chieftain, and cultural accomplishments. The Mississippian era is best known for the impressive large pyramid mounds that were left behind in places such as Etowah and Toqua in Tennessee and Moundville in Alabama. People of the Mississippian cultures created beautiful ornaments and symbolic objects including combs, pipes, and jewelry.

EUROPEANS ARRIVE

Having conquered Peru, the Spanish nobleman Hernando de Soto embarked on a search for gold in the American southeast in 1539. De Soto's band wandered through Florida, Georgia, and the Carolinas before crossing into what is now Tennessee, probably in June 1540. His exact route is a source of controversy, but historians believe he made his way through parts of East

THE BATTLE OF NASHVILLE

During most of the Civil War, Nashville was occupied by Federal forces. After Fort Donelson, 90 miles (145 km) northeast of Nashville, fell in mid-February 1862, Nashville was in Union hands. Nashville became an important goods depot for the Northern cause, and the Federalists set strict rules for city residents during the occupation.

As the war drew to a close in late 1864, Nashville was the site of what war historians now say was the last major battle of the Western Theater.

The Battle of Nashville came after a string of defeats for the Confederate army of Tennessee, commanded by John Bell Hood. After his bloody and humiliating losses at Spring Hill and Franklin a few miles south, Hood moved north and set up headquarters at Travellers Rest, the home of John Overton. His plan was to set up his troops in an arc around the southern side of the city. Union Maj. Gen. George H. Thomas did not plan to wait for Hood's attack, however. He devised a plan to attack first and drive the Confederates away from Nashville.

A winter storm and frigid temperatures delayed the battle. For two weeks, from December 2 to 14, 1864, the two armies peered at one another across the no-man's-land between the two lines. Then at dawn on December 15, 1864, the Union attack began. Union troops on foot and horse, including at least four U.S. Colored Infantry brigades, attacked various Confederate posts around the city. By the close of the first day of fighting, Hood had withdrawn his troops 2 miles (3.2 km) farther south from the city. Today, signage at the corner of Fiber Glass Road and Polk Avenue tells the story of the formerly enslaved men who fought in the battles, many seeing the first combat of their lives.

The dawn of the second day of battle augured more losses for the Confederates. Unable to hold their line against the Union assault, they fell back again. As darkness fell, General Thomas wired Washington to announce his victory. Pursued by a Union cavalry commanded by Maj. Gen. James Wilson, what remained of the Confederate army of Tennessee marched south and, on the day after Christmas, crossed the Tennessee River into Alabama. Four months later, the war was over.

The **Battle of Nashville Preservation Society, Inc.** (www.bonps.org) offers tours of area battlefield sites. However, many of these tours do not tell the full story of enslaved people. Visitors are encouraged to make decisions on what is appropriate for them.

Tennessee before heading back into Georgia.

It was more than 100 years until another European was reported in the Tennessee wilderness, though life for the Indigenous people was already changing. De Soto and his men brought firearms and disease, and there was news of other Caucasians living to the east. Disease and warfare led to a decline in population for Tennessee's Native Americans during the presettlement period. As a result, Native American communities formed new tribes with each other: The Creek Confederacy and Choctaws were two such groups. In Tennessee, the Shawnee moved south into the Cumberland River country—land previously claimed as hunting ground by the Chickasaw Nation. Also at this time, a new tribe came over the Smoky Mountains from North Carolina, possibly to escape the encroachment of European settlers, to form what would become the most important Native American group in modern Tennessee: the Overhill Cherokees.

In 1673 European scouts entered Tennessee at its eastern and western ends. Englishmen James Needham and Gabriel Arthur and eight hired Native American guides were the first party to enter East Tennessee. Needham did not last long; he was killed by his Native American guides early in the outing. Arthur won over his traveling companions and joined them on war trips and hunts before returning to Virginia in 1674. Meanwhile, on the western end of the state, French explorers Father Jacques Marquette and Louis Joliet came down the Mississippi River and claimed the surrounding valley for the French.

THE LONG HUNTERS

The first Europeans to carve out a foothold in the unknown frontier of Tennessee were traders who made journeys into Native American territory to hunt and trade. These men disappeared for months at a time into the wilderness and were therefore known as long hunters. They left with European-made goods and returned with animal skins. They led pack trains of horses and donkeys over narrow, steep, and crooked mountain trails and through sometimes hostile territory. It was a lonely, hard life, full of uncertainty. Some of the long hunters were no better than crooks; others were respected by both the Native Americans and Europeans.

The long hunters included men like Elisha Walden, Kasper Mansker, and Abraham Bledsoe. Daniel Boone, born in North Carolina, was in present-day Washington County in northeastern Tennessee when, in 1760, he carved on a beech tree that he had "cilled" a "bar" nearby. Thomas

Sharp Spencer became known as Big Foot and is said to have spent the winter in a hollowed-out sycamore tree. Another trader, a Scotch-Irish man named James Adair, traded with the Native Americans for years and eventually wrote *A History of the American Indian* (published in London in 1775), one of the first such accounts.

The animal skins and furs that were the aim of these men's exploits were eventually sold in Charleston and exported to Europe. In 1748 alone, South Carolina merchants exported more than 160,000 skins worth $250,000. The trade was profitable for merchants and, to a lesser extent, the traders themselves. But it was rarely profitable for the Native Americans, and it helped to wipe out much of Tennessee's native animal life.

THE FRENCH AND INDIAN WAR

In 1754 the contest between the French and the British for control of the New World boiled over into war. Native American alliances were seen as critical to success, and so the British set out to win the support of the Cherokee. They did this by agreeing to build a fort in the land over the mountain from North Carolina—territory that came to be known as the Overhill country. The Cherokee wanted the fort to protect their women and children from French or hostile Native American attack while the men were away. The fort was begun in 1756 near the fork of the Little Tennessee and Tellico Rivers, and it was named Fort Loudoun after the commander of British forces in North America.

Twelve cannons were transported over the rough mountain terrain by horse to defend the fort from enemy attack.

The construction of Fort Loudoun did not prove to be the glue to hold the Cherokee and British together. In fact, it was not long before relations deteriorated to the point where the Cherokee chief Standing Turkey directed an attack on the fort. A siege ensued. Reinforcements were called for and dispatched, but the British colonel and 1,300 men turned back before reaching the fort. The English inside the fort were weakened by lack of food and surrendered. On August 9, 1760, 180 men, 60 women, and a few children marched out of Fort Loudoun, on a journey to the nearest British fort. The group had been promised to be allowed to retreat peacefully. But on the first night it was ambushed, and some two dozen people were killed. The rest were taken prisoner. The British had failed to surrender all of their firepower as promised, and so the Cherokee felt their only recourse was to attack. A year later, Col. James Grant led a party bent on revenge into the Lower Cherokee territory, where they destroyed villages, burned homes, and cut down fields of corn.

The French and Indian War ended in 1763, and in the Treaty of Paris the French withdrew any claims to lands east of the Mississippi. This result emboldened European settlers and land speculators who were drawn to the land of the Overhill country. The fact that the land still belonged to the Native Americans did not stop the movement west.

EARLY EUROPEAN SETTLERS

With the issue of French possession resolved, settlers began to filter into the Overhill country. Early white settlers included William Bean, on the Holston River; Evan Shelby, at Sapling Grove (later Bristol); John Carter, in the Carter Valley; and Jacob Brown, on the Nolichucky River. By 1771 the settlers at Watauga and Nolichucky won a lease from the Cherokee, and the next year they formed the Watauga Association, a quasi-government and the first such in Tennessee territory.

The settlers' success in obtaining land concessions from the Native Americans was eclipsed in 1775 when the Transylvania Company, led by Richard Henderson of North Carolina, traded £10,000 of goods for 20 million acres of land in Kentucky and Tennessee. The agreement, negotiated at a treaty conference at Sycamore Shoals, was opposed by the Cherokee chief Dragging Canoe, who warned that the Cherokee were paving the way for their own extinction. Despite his warning, the treaty was signed.

Dragging Canoe remained the leader of the Cherokee resistance to European settlement. In 1776 he orchestrated assaults on the settlements of Watauga, Nolichucky, Long Island, and Carter's Valley. The offensive, called by some the Cherokee War, had limited success at first, but it ended in defeat for the natives. In 1777 the Cherokee signed a peace treaty with the settlers that ceded more land to the Europeans.

Dragging Canoe and others did not accept the treaty and left the Cherokee as a result. He and his followers moved south, near Chickamauga Creek, where they became known as the Chickamauga tribe. Over time, this tribe attracted other Native Americans whose common purpose was opposition to new settlements.

The Native Americans could not, however, overpower the increasing tide of settlers, who brought superior firepower and greater numbers. Pressure on political leaders to free up more and more land for settlement made relations with the Native Americans and land agreements with them one of the most important features of political life on the frontier.

In the end, these leaders delivered on their aims, which had devastating consequences for Indigenous populations for generations. Europeans obtained Native American land in Tennessee through a series of treaties and purchases, beginning with the Sycamore Shoals purchase in 1775 and continuing until 1818 when the Chickasaw ceded all control to their land west of the Mississippi. Negotiating on behalf of the settlers were leaders including William Blount, the territorial governor, and Andrew Jackson, the first U.S. president from Tennessee.

Nashville itself was settled on Christmas Day in 1796.

FORCED REMOVAL OF NATIVE AMERICANS

Contact with Europeans had a significant impact on the Cherokee way of life. Christian missionaries introduced education, and in the 1820s Sequoyah developed a Cherokee alphabet, allowing people to read and write in their own language. The Cherokee adopted some of the Europeans' farming practices, as well as some of their social practices, including slavery. Adoption of the European lifestyle was most common among the significant number of mixed-race Cherokee. In 1827 the Cherokee Nation was established, complete with a constitutional system of government and a capital in New Echota, Georgia. From 1828 until 1832, its newspaper, the *Cherokee Phoenix*, was published in both English and Cherokee.

The census of 1828 counted 15,000 Cherokee remaining in Tennessee. They enslaved 1,000 people and owned 22,400 head of cattle, 7,600 horses, 1,800 spinning wheels, 700 looms, 12 sawmills, 55 blacksmith shops, and six cotton gins.

Despite these beginnings of assimilation, or perhaps because of them, the Cherokee were not welcome to remain in the new territory. White settlers pushed for a strong policy that would lead to the Cherokees' removal, and they looked over the border to Georgia to see that it could be done. There, in 1832, authorities stole land owned by Cherokee and disposed of them by lottery. Laws were passed to prohibit Native American assemblies and bar Native Americans from bringing suit in the state. The majority of Tennessee settlers pushed for similar measures to be adopted.

The Cherokee were divided in their response: Some felt that moving west represented the best future for their people, while others wanted to stay and fight for their land and the Cherokee Nation. In the end, the Cherokee leaders lost hope of remaining, and on December 29, 1835, they signed the removal treaty. Under the agreement, the Cherokee were paid $5 million for all their lands east of the Mississippi, and they were required to move west within two years. When that time expired in 1838 and only a small number of the Cherokee had moved, the U.S. Army evicted the rest by force by what is referred to as The Trail of Tears. Also called Nunna-da-ul-tsun-yi (meaning "the place where they cried" in Cherokee), the Trail of Tears was a brutal policy that forced Indigenous families from the only homes they had known. Most of the forced removals in southeastern Tennessee took place between May 1838 and March 1839.

STATEHOOD

Almost as soon as settlers began living on the Tennessee frontier there were movements to form government. Dissatisfied with the protection offered by North Carolina's distant government, settlers drew up their own governments as early as the 1780s. The Watauga Association and Cumberland Compact were early forms of government. In 1785, settlers in northeastern Tennessee seceded from North Carolina and established the State of Franklin. The experiment was short-lived but foretold that in the future the lands west of the Smoky Mountains would be their own state.

Before Tennessee could become a state, however, it was a territory of the United States. In 1789 North Carolina ratified its own constitution and in doing so ceded its western lands, the Tennessee country, to the U.S. government. These lands eventually became known as the Southwest Territory, and in 1790 President George Washington appointed William Blount its territorial governor.

Blount was a 41-year-old land speculator and businessman who had campaigned actively for the position. A veteran of the War for Independence, Blount knew Washington and was one of the signers of the U.S. Constitution in 1787.

At the time of its establishment, the Southwest Territory was 43,000 square miles (111,400 square kilometers) in area. The population of 35,000 was centered in two main areas: the northeastern corner and the Cumberland settlements near present-day Nashville.

Tennessee's request to become a state was debated in Washington, DC, where finally, on June 1, 1796, President Washington signed the statehood bill and Tennessee became the 16th state in the Union.

FRONTIER LIFE

The new state of Tennessee attracted settlers who were drawn by cheap land and the opportunity it represented. Between 1790 and 1800 the state's population tripled, and by 1810 Tennessee's population had grown to 250,000. The expansion caused a shift in power as the middle and western parts of the state became more populated. The capital moved from Knoxville to Nashville in 1812. It was made the permanent capital of the state in 1843.

Life during the early 19th century in Tennessee was largely rural. For the subsistence farmers who made up the majority of the state's population, life was a relentless cycle of hard work. Many families lived in one- or two-room cabins and spent their days growing food and the fibers needed to make their own clothes; raising animals that supplied farm power, meat, and hides; building or repairing buildings and tools; and cutting firewood in prodigious quantities. Small-hold farmers did not often have enslaved people. Children provided valuable labor on the Tennessee farm. Boys often plowed their first furrow at age nine, and girls of that age were expected to mind younger children, help cook, and learn the skills of midwifery, sewing, and gardening. While women's time was often consumed with child rearing, cooking, and sewing, the housewife also worked in the field alongside her husband when she was needed.

EDUCATION AND RELIGION

There were no public schools on the frontier, and the few private schools that existed were not accessible to the farming class. Religious missionaries were often the only people who could read and write in a community, and the first schools were established by churches. Presbyterian, Methodist, and Baptist ministers were the first to reach many settlements in Tennessee.

Settlements were spread out, and few had established churches. As a result, the camp meeting became entrenched in Tennessee culture. The homegrown spirituality of the camp meeting appealed to Tennesseans' independent spirit, which looked suspiciously at official religion and embraced the informal and deeply personal religion of the camp meeting.

The meetings were major events drawing between a few hundred and thousands of people. Camp services were passionate and emotional, reaching a feverish pitch as men and women were overtaken by the spirit. Many camp meetings attracted both Black and white participants.

THE WAR OF 1812

Tennesseans were among the "War Hawks" in Congress who advocated for war with Great Britain in 1812. The conflict was seen by many as an opportunity to rid their borders once and for all of Native Americans. The government asked for 2,800 volunteers, and 30,000 Tennesseans offered to enlist. This is when Tennessee's nickname as the Volunteer State was born.

Nashville lawyer, politician, and businessman Andrew Jackson was chosen as the leader of the Tennessee volunteers. Despite their shortage of supplies and lack of support from the War Department, Jackson's militia prevailed in a series of lopsided victories. Given command of the southern military district, Jackson led U.S. forces at the Battle of New Orleans on January 8, 1815. The ragtag group inflicted a crushing defeat on the British, and despite its having occurred after the signing of the peace treaty with Great Britain, the battle was the victory that launched Jackson onto the road to the presidency.

Black soldiers fought in the War of 1812 on both sides. Some formerly enslaved Black people hoped that by enlisting they would help gain more freedoms for Black Americans, although that did not come to pass. Some enslaved soldiers hoped they could exchange their combat service for their freedom.

GROWTH OF SLAVERY

The state's first white settlers planted the seed of slavery in Tennessee, and the state's westward expansion cemented the cruel institution. In 1791 there were 3,400 Black people in Tennessee—about 10 percent of the general population. By 1810, Black people constituted more than 20 percent of Tennessee's population. About 1,300 were free; more than 44,000 were enslaved. The invention of the cotton gin and subsequent rise of King Cotton after the turn of the 19th century also caused a rapid expansion of slavery.

Slavery was most important in West Tennessee; eastern Tennessee, with its mountainous landscape and small farms, had the fewest enslaved people. In Middle Tennessee enslaved people were concentrated in the Central Basin, in the counties of Davidson, Maury, Rutherford, and Williamson. By 1860, 40 percent of the state's enslaved people were in West Tennessee, with the greatest concentration in Shelby, Fayette, and Haywood Counties, where cotton was grown on plantations somewhat similar to those of the Deep South.

As slavery grew, markets to sell enslaved people were established in Nashville and Memphis. The ban on the interstate sale of enslaved people was virtually ignored.

From 1790, when the territory was established, until 1831, Tennessee's laws regarding enslaved people were relatively lenient. The law categorized an enslaved person as both chattel and a person, and enslaved people were entitled to expect protection against the elements and other people. Enslavers could free enslaved people for any reason, and many did, causing growth in Tennessee's free Black population in the first half of the 1800s. These free Black people were concentrated in eastern and Middle Tennessee, and particularly the cities of Nashville, Memphis, and Knoxville, where they worked as laborers and artisans.

There were vocal opponents to slavery in Tennessee, particularly in the eastern part of the state. The first newspaper in the United States devoted to emancipation was established in 1819 in Jonesborough by Elihu Embree. Charles Osborne, a Quaker minister, preached against slavery shortly after the turn of the 19th century in Tennessee. Emancipationists formed societies in counties including Washington, Sullivan, Blount, Grainger, and Cocke. Many of these early abolitionists opposed slavery on religious grounds, arguing that it was incompatible with the spirit of Christianity.

These abolitionists often argued for the gradual end of slavery and sometimes advocated for the removal of formerly enslaved people to Africa.

EXPERIENCES OF ENSLAVED PEOPLE

There was no single experience for Tennessee's enslaved people. On the farm, an enslaved person's experience depended on the size of the property, the type of crops that were grown, and the number of other enslaved people on the farm.

Most enslaved people in Tennessee lived on small- or medium-sized farms. The 1860 census showed that only one person in the state enslaved more than 300 people, and 47 enslaved more than 100. More than 75 percent of all enslavers had fewer than 10 enslaved people. Work assignments varied, but almost all enslaved people were expected to contribute to their own subsistence by keeping a vegetable garden. Enslaved people with special skills in areas like carpentry, masonry, blacksmithing, or weaving were hired out.

In cities, enslaved people were domestic workers, coachmen, house painters, launderers, and midwives. Many families owned one or two enslaved people, and it was common for them to be hired out to others in order to provide a source of income for the enslaver. It became customary in some cities for a market day to be held on New Year's Day, referred to as many as "Heartbreak Day," when enslavers purchased enslaved people for the coming year, often breaking up families in the process.

Enslaved people sought to overcome their circumstances by building close-knit communities. These communities acted as surrogate families for people whose own spouse, parents, siblings, and children were often sold, causing lifelong separation.

Religion also served as a survival mechanism for Tennessee's enslaved people. Methodist and Baptist churches opened their doors, providing a space where enslaved people could be together. The musical tradition that resulted is today's gospel music. Religion also provided a vehicle for some enslaved people to learn how to read and write.

THE CIVIL WAR

In the 1830s, Tennessee's position on slavery hardened. The uprising of enslaved people led by Nat Turner in Virginia frightened owners, who instituted patrols to search for escaped enslaved people. In 1834, the state constitution was amended to bar free Black people from voting.

The division between East and West Tennessee widened as many in the east were sympathetic with the antislavery forces that were growing in Northern states. In the west, the support for slavery was unrelenting.

Despite several strident secessionists, including Tennessee governor Isham Harris, Tennessee remained uncertain about separating from the United States. In February 1861, the state voted against a convention on secession. But with the attack on Fort Sumter two months later, followed by President Abraham Lincoln's call for volunteers to apply force to bring the seceded states back to the Union, public opinion shifted. On June 8, 1861, Tennesseans voted 105,000 to 47,000 to secede.

A BORDER STATE

Tennessee was of great strategic importance during the Civil War. It sent an estimated 186,000 men to fight for the Confederacy, more than any other state. Another 31,000 are credited with having joined the Union army.

Tennessee had resources that both the Union and Confederacy deemed important for victory, including agricultural and manufacturing industries, railroads, and rivers. And its geographic position as a long-border state made it nearly unavoidable.

TENNESSEE BATTLES

Some 454 battles and skirmishes were fought in Tennessee during the war. Most were small, but several key battles took place on Tennessee soil.

The first of these was the Union victory at Forts Henry and Donelson in January 1862. Gen. Ulysses S. Grant and 15,000 Union troops steamed up the Tennessee River and quickly captured Fort Henry. They then marched overland to Fort Donelson, and 10 days later, this Confederate fort fell as well. The battle of Fort Donelson is where "U. S. Grant" (or "Unconditional Surrender" Grant) earned this sobriquet: He was asked by the Confederate general the terms of capitulation, and he replied, "unconditional surrender."

The Battle of Shiloh was the bloodiest and largest to take place in Tennessee. The battle happened near Pittsburgh Landing (the Federal name for the struggle), on the Mississippi River about 20 miles (32 km) north of the Mississippi state line. More than 100,000 men took part in this battle, and there were more than 24,000 casualties.

The battle began with a surprise Confederate attack at dawn on April 6, 1862, a Sunday. For several hours, victory seemed within reach for the Southern troops, but the Union rallied and held. They built a strong defensive line covering Pittsburgh Landing, and on April 7 they took the offensive and swept the Confederates from the field. The Confederates' loss was devastating, and Shiloh represented a harbinger of the future bloodletting between Blue and Gray.

Another important Tennessee battle was at Stones River, near Murfreesboro, on December 31, 1862. Like at Shiloh, the early momentum here was with the Confederates, but victory belonged to the Union. The Battle of Chickamauga Creek, fought a few miles over the state line in Georgia, was a rare Confederate victory. It did not come cheaply, however, with 21,000 members of the Army of Tennessee killed.

Federal forces retreated and dug in near Chattanooga, while Confederates occupied the heights above the town. Union reinforcements led by General Grant drove the Confederates back into Georgia at the Battle of Lookout Mountain, also known as the "Battle Above the Clouds," on November 25, 1863.

WARTIME OCCUPATION

Battles were only part of the wartime experience in Tennessee. The Civil War caused hardship for ordinary residents on a scale that many had never before seen. There was famine and poverty. Schools and churches were closed. Harassment and recrimination plagued the state, and fear was widespread.

In February 1863, one observer described the population of Memphis as "11,000 original whites, 5,000 [enslaved people], and 19,000 newcomers of all kinds, including traders, fugitives, hangers-on, and negroes."

Memphis fell to the Union on June 6, 1862, and it was occupied for the remainder of the war. The city's experience during this wartime occupation reversed decades of growth and left it struggling for years.

Those who could fled the city. Many of those who remained stopped doing business (some of these because they refused to pledge allegiance to the Union and were not permitted). Northern traders entered the city and took over many industries; at the same time, formerly enslaved people flooded into the city as they escaped nearby plantations.

As the military focused on punishing Confederate sympathizers, conditions in Memphis deteriorated. Crime and disorder abounded, and guerrilla bands developed to fight the Union occupation. The Federal commander responsible for the city was Maj. Gen. William T. Sherman, and he adopted a policy of collective responsibility, which held civilians responsible for guerrilla attacks in their neighborhoods. Sherman destroyed hundreds of homes, farms, and towns in the exercise of this policy.

The war was equally damaging in other parts of Tennessee. In Middle Tennessee, retreating Confederate soldiers after the fall of Fort Donelson demolished railroads and burned bridges so as not to leave them for the Union. Union troops also destroyed and appropriated the region's resources. Federals took horses, pigs, cows, corn, hay, cotton, fence rails, firearms, and tools. Sometimes this was carried out through official requisitions, but at other times it amounted to little more than pillaging.

Criminals took advantage of the loss of public order, and bands of thieves and bandits began roaming the countryside.

The experience in East Tennessee was different. Because of the region's widespread Union sympathies, it was the Confederacy that first occupied the eastern territory. During this time hundreds of alleged Unionists were charged with treason and jailed. When the Confederates began conscripting men into military service in 1862, tensions in East Tennessee grew. Many East Tennesseans fled to Kentucky, and distrust, bitterness, and violence escalated. In September 1863 the tables turned, however, and the Confederates were replaced by the Federals, whose victories elsewhere enabled them to focus then on occupying friendly East Tennessee.

THE EFFECTS OF THE WAR

Tennessee lost most of a generation of young men to the Civil War. Infrastructure was destroyed, and thousands of farms, homes, and other properties were razed. The state's reputation on the national stage had been tarnished, and it would be decades until Tennessee had the political power that it had enjoyed during the Age of Jackson. But while the war caused tremendous hardships for the state, it also led to the freeing of 275,000 Black Tennesseans from slavery.

RECONSTRUCTION

Tennessee was no less divided during the years following the Civil War than it was during the conflict. The end to the war ushered in a period where former Unionists—now allied with the Radical Republicans in Congress—disenfranchised and otherwise marginalized former Confederates and others who had been sympathetic with the Southern cause.

They also pushed through laws that extended voting and other rights to Black people, changes that led to a powerful backlash and the establishment of such white supremacist groups as the Ku Klux Klan.

The greatest legacy of the Civil War was the emancipation of Tennessee's enslaved people. Following the war, many formerly enslaved people left the countryside and moved to cities, including Memphis, Nashville, Chattanooga, and Knoxville, where they worked as skilled laborers, domestic laborers, and more. Others remained in the countryside, working as wage laborers on farms or sharecropping in exchange for occupancy on part of a former large-scale plantation.

The Freedmen's Bureau worked in Tennessee for a short period after the end of the war, and it succeeded in establishing schools for Black people. During this period the state's first Black colleges were established: Fisk, Tennessee Central, LeMoyne, Roger Williams, Lane, and Knoxville.

As in other states, Black people in Tennessee enjoyed short-lived political power during Reconstruction. The right to vote and the concentration of Black communities in certain urban areas paved the way for Black people to be elected to the Tennessee House of Representatives, beginning with Sampson Keeble of Nashville in 1872. In all, 13 Black men were elected as representatives between 1872 and 1887, including James C. Napier, Edward Shaw, and William Yardley, who also ran for governor.

Initially, these pioneers met mild acceptance from white Tennesseans, but as time progressed white people became uncomfortable sharing power with Black people. By the 1890s, racist Jim Crow policies of segregation, poll taxes, secret ballots, literacy tests, and intimidation prevented Black people from holding elected office—and in many cases, voting—in Tennessee again until after the Civil Rights Movement of the 1960s.

The Republican Party saw the end of its influence with the end of the Brownlow governorship. Democrats rejected the divisive policies of the Radical Republicans, who sought to protect the racial order that set Black people at a disadvantage, and were less concerned about the state's mounting debt than the Republicans.

ECONOMIC RECOVERY

The social and political upheaval caused by the Civil War was matched or exceeded by the economic catastrophe that it represented for the state. Farms and industry were damaged or destroyed, public infrastructure was razed, schools were closed, and the system of slavery that underpinned most of the state's economy was gone. During this period Nashville flourished, as the city grew to become an essential business hub. The Nashville population skyrocketed from less than 17,000 in 1860 to more than 80,000 just 40 years later. In Nashville, new distilleries, sawmills, paper mills, stove factories, and an oil refinery led the way to industrialization.

The economic setback was seen as an opportunity by proponents of the "New South," who advocated for an industrial and economic revival that would catapult the South to prosperity impossible under the agrarian and slavery-based economy of the pre-Civil War era. The New South movement was personified by carpetbagging Northern capitalists who moved to Tennessee and set up industries that would benefit from cheap labor and abundant natural resources. Many Tennesseans welcomed these newcomers and advocated for their fellow Tennesseans to put aside regional differences and also welcome the Northern investors. Mines were opened in Cleveland, flour mills in Jackson, and textile factories in Tullahoma and other parts of the state.

WORLD WAR I

True to its nickname, Tennessee sent a large number of volunteer troops to fight in World War I. Most became part of the 30th "Old Hickory" Division, which entered the war on August 17, 1918. The most famous Tennessee veteran of World War I was Alvin C. York, a farm boy from the Cumberland Mountains who staged a one-man offensive against the German army after becoming separated from his own detachment. Reports say that York killed 20 German soldiers and persuaded 131 more to surrender.

WOMEN'S SUFFRAGE

The movement for women's suffrage had been established in Tennessee prior to the turn of the

20th century, and it gained influence as the century progressed. The Southern Woman Suffrage Conference was held in Memphis in 1906, and a statewide suffrage organization was established. State bills to give women the right to vote failed in 1913 and 1917, but support was gradually growing. In the summer of 1920, the 19th Amendment had been ratified by 35 states, and one more ratification was needed to make it law. Tennessee was one of five states yet to vote on the measure, and on August 9, Governor Roberts called a special sitting of the legislature to consider the amendment.

Furious campaigning and public debate led up to the special sitting. The Senate easily ratified the amendment 25 to 4, but in the House of Representatives the vote was much closer: 49 to 47. Governor Roberts certified the result and notified the secretary of state: Tennessee had cast the deciding vote for women's suffrage.

A sculpture of four of the women who worked hardest to make this power a reality stands in the center of Centennial Park, erected in 2016 and designed by local artist Alan LeQuire.

As progressive as it was, the women's suffrage movement in the United States was largely for and about white women getting the right to vote. Even after the ratification of the 19th Amendment, many states kept laws in place that prevented Black women from voting for several more decades.

THE DEPRESSION

The progress and hope of the 1920s were soon forgotten with the Great

Depression. Tennessee's economic hard times started before the 1929 stock market crash. Farming in the state was hobbled by low prices and low returns during the 1920s. Farmers and laborers displaced by this trend sought work in new industries like the DuPont plant in Old Hickory, Eastman-Kodak in Kingsport, or the Aluminum Company of America in Blount County. But others, including many Black people, left Tennessee for northern cities such as Chicago.

The Depression made bad things worse. Farmers tried to survive, turning to subsistence farming. In cities, unemployed workers lined up for relief. Major bank failures in 1930 brought most financial business in the state to a halt.

President Roosevelt's New Deal provided some relief for Tennesseans. The Civilian Conservation Corps (CCC), Public Works Administration (PWA), and Civil Works Administration (CWA) were established in Tennessee. Through the CCC, more than 7,000 Tennesseans planted millions of pine seedlings, developed parks, and built fire towers. Through the PWA, more than 500 projects were undertaken, including bridges, housing, water systems, and roads. Hundreds of Tennesseans were employed by the CWA to clean public buildings, landscape roads, and do other work.

But no New Deal institution had more impact on Tennessee than the Tennessee Valley Authority (TVA). Architects of TVA saw it as a way to improve agriculture along the Tennessee River, alleviate poverty, and produce electrical power. The dam system would also improve navigation along what was then an often-dangerous river. The law establishing TVA was introduced by Sen. George W. Norris of Nebraska and passed in 1933. Soon after, dams were under construction, and trade on the river increased because of improved navigability. Even more importantly, electric power was now so cheap that even Tennesseans in remote parts of the state could afford it. By 1945, TVA was the largest electrical utility in the nation, and new industries were attracted by cheap energy and improved transportation. Tourists also came to enjoy the so-called Great Lakes of the South.

WORLD WAR II

Tennessee, like the rest of the country, was changed by World War II. The war effort transformed the state's economy and led to a migration to the cities unprecedented in Tennessee's history. The tiny mountain town of Oak Ridge became the state's fifth-largest city almost overnight when it became a production site for the Manhattan Project. The city, nicknamed "Atomic City," became nearly synonymous with the atomic bomb that was dropped on Hiroshima at the final stage of the war.

More than 300,000 Tennesseans served in World War II, and just under 6,000 died. During the war, Camps Forrest, Campbell, and Tyson served as prisoner of war camps. Several hundred war refugees settled in Tennessee, many in the Nashville area.

POSTWAR TENNESSEE

Tennessee's industrialization continued after the war. By 1960 there were more city dwellers than rural dwellers in the state, and Tennessee was ranked the 16th most industrialized state in the United States. Industry that had developed during the war transformed to peacetime operation.

Ex-servicemen were not content with the political machines that had controlled Tennessee politics for decades. In 1948 Congressman Estes Kefauver won a U.S. Senate seat, defeating the candidate chosen by Memphis mayor Ed Crump. The defeat signaled an end to Crump's substantial influence in statewide elections. In 1953 Tennessee repealed the state poll tax, again limiting politicians' ability to manipulate the vote. The tide of change also swept in Sen. Albert Gore Sr. and Gov. Frank Clement in 1952. Kefauver, Gore, and Clement were moderate Democrats of the New South.

CIVIL RIGHTS IN TENNESSEE

The Nashville lunch counter sit-ins of 1960 were an important milestone in both the local and national civil rights movements. Led by students from the city's Black universities, the sit-ins eventually forced an end to racial segregation of the city's public services. Over two months, hundreds of Black students were arrested for sitting at downtown lunch counters. Black consumers' boycott of downtown stores put additional pressure on the business community. On April 19, thousands of protesters marched in silence to the courthouse to confront city officials, and the next day Rev. Martin Luther King Jr. addressed Fisk University. On May 10, 1960, several downtown stores integrated their lunch counters, and Nashville became the first major city in the South to begin desegregating its public facilities.

MODERN TENNESSEE

The industrialization that began during World War II has continued in modern-day Tennessee. In 1980 Nissan built what was then the largest truck assembly plant in the world at Smyrna, Tennessee. In 1987 Saturn Corporation chose Spring Hill as the site for its $2.1 billion automobile plant.

At the same time, however, the state's older industries—including textiles and manufacturing—have suffered losses over the past three decades, in part because of the movement of industry outside of the United States.

During the 1950s and beyond, Tennessee developed a reputation as a hotbed of musical talent. The Grand Ole Opry in Nashville was representative of a second musical genre that came to call Tennessee home—country music. Country legend Roy Acuff helped put the city and its music scene on the map. He founded one of the city's first music publishing companies and later ran for governor of the state.

Nashville is still home to North America's largest-volume vinyl pressing plant. This, literally, is where the music is made.

Greensboro, North Carolina, is often considered the site of the first sit-ins of the American Civil Rights Movement. But in truth, activists in Nashville carried out the first "test" sit-ins in late 1959. In these test cases, protesters left the facilities after being refused service and talking to management about the injustice of segregation. In between these test sit-ins and the moment when Nashville activists would launch a full-scale sit-in campaign, students in Greensboro took that famous first step.

The Nashville sit-ins began on February 13, 1960, when a group of Black students from local colleges and universities sat at a downtown lunch counter and refused to move until they were served. While some refer to these actions as "nonviolent," that only applies to the protesting students. They endured verbal and physical abuse from enraged white segregationists, including having cigarettes extinguished on their arms, and many were arrested for protesting.

Community members raised money for the students' bail, and Black residents of the city began an economic boycott of downtown stores that practiced segregation. On April 19, the home of Z. Alexander Looby, a Black lawyer who was representing the students, was bombed. Later the same day, students led a spontaneous, peaceful, and silent march through the streets of downtown Nashville to the courthouse. Diane Nash, a student leader, asked Nashville mayor Ben West if he thought it was morally right for a restaurant to refuse to serve someone based on the color of his or her skin. Mayor West said, "No."

The march was an important turning point for the city. The combined effect of the sit-ins, the boycott, and the march caused, in 1960, Nashville to be the first major Southern city to experience widespread desegregation of its public facilities. The events also demonstrated to activists in other parts of the South that nonviolence was an effective tool of protest.

The story of the young people who led the Nashville sit-ins is told in the book *The Children* by David Halberstam. In 2001, Nashville resident Bill King was so moved by the story of the protests that he established an endowment to raise funds for a permanent civil rights collection at the Nashville Public Library. In 2003, the Civil Rights Room at the Nashville Public Library was opened. It houses books, oral histories, audiovisual records, microfilm, dissertations, and stunning photographs of the events of 1960 and is one of the must-visit city sights. The words of one then-student organizer, John Lewis, who went on to become a congressman for Georgia and a national leader, are displayed over the entryway: "If not us, then who; if not now, then when?"

Government and Economy

GOVERNMENT

Tennessee is governed by its constitution, unchanged since 1870 when it was revised in light of emancipation, the Civil War, and Reconstruction.

Tennessee has a governor who is elected to four-year terms, a legislature, and a court system. The governor is subject to term limits. The lieutenant governor is chosen by the Senate and also serves as its speaker.

The legislature, or General Assembly, is made up of the 99-member House of Representatives and the 33-member Senate. The Tennessee State Supreme Court is made up of five justices, with no two from the same Grand Division. The Supreme Court chooses the state's attorney general.

Tennessee has 95 counties; the largest is Shelby County, which includes Memphis, although Davidson is a close second. The smallest county by size is Trousdale, with 114 square miles (295 square kilometers); the smallest population is in Pickett County.

The state has 11 electoral college votes in U.S. presidential elections.

MODERN POLITICS

Like other Southern states, Tennessee has seen a gradual shift to the political right since the 1960s. The shift began in 1966 with Howard Baker's election to the U.S. Senate, and it continued with Tennessee's support for Republican presidential candidate Richard Nixon in 1968 and 1972. Despite a few exceptions, the shift has continued into the 21st century, although Nashville, Memphis, and other parts of Middle and West Tennessee remain Democratic territory.

East Tennessee holds distinction as one of a handful of Southern territories that have consistently supported the Republican Party since the Civil War. Today, Republicans outpoll Democrats in this region by as much as three to one.

The statewide trend toward the Republican Party continued in 2008, with Tennessee being one of only a handful of states where Democrat Barack Obama received a lesser proportion of votes than did Senator John Kerry four years earlier. State Republicans also succeeded in gaining control of both houses of the

state legislature. The general shift to the right has continued in the governor's office. Former governor Phil Bredesen is a Democrat (and a U.S. Senate candidate in 2018), but he was succeeded by Republican Bill Haslam. Republican businessman Bill Lee was elected in 2018 when Haslam's second term ended, marking the first time since 1967 that a party has been able to keep the governor's seat for more than two terms. Term limits prevent incumbents from staying in office for more than two terms.

Andrew Jackson may still be the most prominent Tennessean in American political history, but Tennessee politicians continue to play a role on the national stage. Albert Gore Jr., elected to the U.S. House of Representatives in 1976, served as vice president under President Bill Clinton from 1992 until 2000, and he lost the highly contested 2000 presidential contest to George W. Bush. Gore famously lost his home state to Bush. Gore went on to champion global climate change and win the Nobel Peace Prize, and he is often seen around Nashville.

Lamar Alexander, a former governor of Tennessee, was appointed secretary of education by the first President Bush in 1990. Alexander—famous for his flannel shirts—ran unsuccessfully for president and was later elected senator from Tennessee. Bill Frist, a doctor, was also elected senator and rose to be the Republican majority leader during the presidency of George W. Bush, before quitting politics for medical philanthropy. In 2018 Marsha Blackburn, a conservative and supporter of the Tea Party, became the first woman elected to the U.S. Senate from Tennessee.

One of the most persistent political issues for Tennesseans in modern times has been the state's tax structure. The state first established a 2 percent sales tax in 1947, and it was increased incrementally over the years, eventually reaching 7 percent in 2013. With local/city taxes on top of that, it is one of the highest sales tax rates in the country, ringing in at 9.25 percent in Nashville. (The state sales tax on food is 4 percent.) At the same time, the state has failed on more than one occasion—most recently with a state constitutional amendment in 2014—to establish an income tax that would provide greater stability to the state's revenues.

Nashville and Davidson County have a consolidated government, and half a century ago they were the first municipalities to choose this government structure. The system, which celebrated its 50th anniversary in 2013, is often thought of as being more efficient and reducing redundancy.

ECONOMY

Tennessee has the 18th-largest economy in the United States. Important industries include health care, education, farming, electrical power, and tourism. In the past few years, most job growth has been recorded in the areas of leisure, hospitality, education, and health care. Manufacturing, mining, and construction jobs have declined, but auto- and auto-park manufacturing have increased in recent years. Companies including Amazon, Oracle, and AllianceBernstein have opened headquarters and large facilities in Nashville. In 2021 Ford Motor Co. received a $900 million incentive from the state to build an electric vehicle and battery plant in West Tennessee.

According to the state tourism department, the industry generated $23 billion in economic activity in 2019. More than 192,000 Tennessee jobs are linked to tourism. In 2019 Davidson County had $7.5 billion in tourism expenditures.

People typically assume that music is job number one in Nashville. It is true that the music industry is important to the city, but health care, real estate, and education are bigger industries in Music City.

FAMOUS NASHVILLIANS

Since its earliest days, Nashville's siren song has attracted those who wanted to see (or more likely, hear) their name in lights. The wannabe famous come here to get their break, and they stay here because, for the most part, it is an easy place to be famous. Über-stars like Keith Urban and Nicole Kidman can shop at Whole Foods and take their kids to the library without being harassed by paparazzi.

Tons of the music industry's elite call Nashville (or more often than not, suburban Leiper's Fork and Franklin) home. In addition to Keith Urban, Taylor Swift, Brad Paisley, Robert Plant, Ben Folds, members of The Black Keys and the Kings of Leon, Jack White, and Peter Frampton live here at least part of the year.

But it isn't just the musicians who can be seen around town. Travis Stork, of *The Bachelor* and *The Doctors* fame, is often sighted in the 12 South neighborhood. Actor and entrepreneur Kristin Cavallari and her ex-husband, former NFL player Jay Cutler, both live in town.

Al Gore Jr., though born in Washington DC and raised in Carthage, Tennessee, is closely associated with Nashville. After the Vietnam War he attended Vanderbilt University for one year and then spent five years as a reporter for *The Tennessean*. The former U.S. vice president has had a home in Nashville for many decades and is frequently seen around town.

Remember that celebrities like to live in Nashville because they get a chance to be "normal." Use discretion when asking for autographs or taking photos. Most importantly, don't overlook seeing the next soon-to-be-star by searching only for the big-name celebs.

People and Culture

DEMOGRAPHICS

Nashville's population as of 2019 was 669,053 people, according to the U.S. Census. When you look at the entire 13-county metropolitan area, the population is more than 1.8 million. An oft-cited statistic is that more than 80 people per day move to the area. Approximately 78 percent of Tennesseans are white, 17 percent are Black, and 5 percent are Latino or Hispanic. Nashville's foreign-born population tripled during the decade between 1990 and 2000, and 11 percent of the city's population was born outside of the United States. This includes large populations from Mexico, Vietnam, Laos, and Somalia. Nashville is also home to more than 11,000 Kurdish people. The city also welcomed Afghan refugees in 2021. Nashville surpassed Memphis in population to become the state's largest city in 2016.

RELIGION

Nashville is part of the U.S. Bible Belt; conservative Christian faith is both prevalent and prominent all over the state. Of Nashvillians, 59 percent call themselves Christians, and 27 percent identify as Baptist. Nashville is the headquarters of the Southern Baptist Convention, the National Baptist Convention, and the United Methodist Church. The city has growing populations that practice Judaism and Islam.

LANGUAGE

Nashvillians speak English, with a twist. Many have a Tennessee drawl, though with so many transplants from across the world, there's not really a Music City accent. Speech patterns have been documented throughout the state, outlined by Michael Montgomery of the University of South Carolina in the *Tennessee Encyclopedia of History and Culture*. Montgomery writes that Tennesseans tend to pronounce vowels in the words *pen* and *hem* as *pin* and *him;* they shift the accent to the beginning of words, so *Tennessee* becomes *TIN-isee;* they clip or reduce the vowel in words like *ride* so it sounds more like *rad;* and vowels in other words are stretched, so that a single-syllable word like *bed* becomes *bay-ud.*

Local speech patterns are not limited to word pronunciation. Native Tennesseans also tend to speak with folksy and down-home language. Speakers often use colorful metaphors, and greater value is placed on the quality of expression rather than the perfection of grammar. A long, slowly told story is valued more than a brief synopsis.

ESSENTIALS

Getting There

downtown Nashville

Thanks to an accessible, expansive airport, easy access to several interstates, reliable bus services, and many rental car companies, getting to Music City shouldn't be a hassle (although no guarantees about the traffic once you arrive).

Many visitors to Nashville drive their own cars. The highways are good, distances are manageable, and many destinations in the city and surrounding area are not accessible by public transportation.

AIR

The **Nashville International Airport** (BNA, http://flynashville.com) brings back some of the pleasure to air travel. Despite shuttling more than 17 million passengers annually, it is easy to navigate, affordable to park at, and only overwhelmingly crowded during big events. BNA offers email updates that tell travelers when to expect congestion, so they can plan accordingly. BNA is about nine miles east of downtown, a 20-minute drive in average traffic.

The four-runway airport is filled with local art and live music and comfortable waiting areas for those picking up inbound passengers. There's even a health clinic for routine medical care. Exchange currency at the **Business Service Center** (Wright Travel, 615/275-2660) near C/D concourse.

BNA was the first airport in the United States to include "transportation network companies" such as Lyft and Uber in their plans. There's a designated pickup area on Level 1 of the Ground Transportation Center, which is in Terminal Garage 2. Look for signage when you land. Your ride will pick you up in Ride Zones A-C, depending on which service you use.

Many of the major hotels offer shuttles from the airport; a kiosk on the lower level of the terminal can help you find the right one. Taxis are also a feasible option for ground transport from BNA. Rates start at $7 plus $2.10 per mile, plus $1 for each additional passenger. To downtown or Opryland, the flat rate is $25.

BUS

Greyhound (709 5th Ave. S., 615/255-3556, www.greyhound. com) fully serves Music City, with daily routes that crisscross the state in nearly every direction. The environmentally friendly depot has parking for those awaiting passengers, a restaurant, a vending machine area, and ample space for buses coming and going. Service goes to major cities in most directions, including Atlanta, Chattanooga, Memphis, and Louisville.

CAR
ROAD RULES

Tennessee recognizes other states' driver's licenses and learner's permits. New residents are required to obtain a Tennessee license within 30 days of establishing residency, however.

Speed limits vary. On interstates limits range 55-75 miles per hour (90-120 kph). Limits on primary and secondary routes vary based on local conditions. Many neighborhood streets have limits of 25 mph (40 kph). Travelers should pay special attention to slow zones around schools; speeding tickets in these areas often include high penalties.

It is required by law that all drivers and passengers in a moving vehicle wear their seatbelts. Infants less than one year old must be restrained in a rear-facing car seat; children 1-3 years must be restrained in a front-facing car seat. A child of 4-8 years who is less than 4 feet, 9 inches (145 cm) tall must have a booster seat.

Drunk driving is dangerous and against the law. It is illegal to drive in Tennessee with a blood alcohol concentration of 0.08 percent or more.

Because Nissan's U.S. headquarters is in Franklin, Tennessee, and because Nissan is a leader in electric cars, there are more places to pull over and charge an electric car than you might expect. Locally headquartered restaurant chain Cracker Barrel has a lot of charging stations in its parking lots, as do many public lots in the major cities, Loews hotels, and more.

CAR RENTALS

If you don't bring your own car, a dozen different major rental agencies have a fleet of cars, trucks, and SUVs at the airport. Agencies include **Alamo** (844/370-2402, www.alamo.com), **Avis** (615/361-1212, www.avis.com), and **Hertz** (615/275-2600, www.hertz.com). For the best rates, use an online travel search tool, such as **Expedia** (www.expedia.com), **Kayak** (www.kayak.com), or **Travelocity** (www.

CORONAVIRUS IN NASHVILLE

At the time of writing in 2022, Nashville was moderately impacted from the effects of the coronavirus, but the situation is constantly evolving. Statewide legislation generally prevented mask mandates and vaccine requirements. Tennessee has some of the country's lowest vaccination rates. Rates in Nashville are higher than the rest of the state, but lower compared to other major cities. Most of the city's tourist-centric attractions, such as the honky-tonks, have not set capacity limits or enacted other safety measures. Some smaller venues, especially in East Nashville and 12 South, had recommendations on vaccine and mask compliance, as well as limits on party size.

Nashville is considered one of the "healthcare capitals" of the country, as many healthcare businesses have their headquarters here. As a result, hospital capacity may not be as limited as in some other major cities. Note that Nashville's hospitals also serve the surrounding rural counties, so if coronavirus spikes in these areas, the city's hospitals may experience overcrowding.

Now more than ever, Moon encourages its readers to be courteous and ethical in their travel. Be respectful to local residents and mindful of the situation in your chosen destination when planning a trip.

BEFORE YOU GO

- Check websites (listed below) for local restrictions and the overall health status of the destination (and your point of origin). Both Nashville and Tennessee more widely were considered COVID-19 hot spots in 2021. If you're traveling to or from an area that is currently a hot spot, you may want to reconsider your trip.

- Moon encourages readers to get vaccinated if their health status allows and to take a coronavirus test with enough time to receive the results before departure. In Nashville, some venues may require proof of vaccination or a negative COVID test result before arrival, along with a self-quarantine period after arrival. The Metro Public Health Department has offered regular free testing at sites throughout the city, including at farmers' markets and sporting events. Tests may also be available at select Walgreens and CVS locations. It's wise to have a copy of your vaccination card with you when you travel.

travelocity.com), and book the car early, along with your airline tickets.

RECREATIONAL VEHICLES

Recreational vehicles are an increasingly popular way to see Tennessee due to the prevalence of good campgrounds and the beautiful landscape of the state.

All state park campgrounds welcome RVs and provide utilities such as water, electricity, and a dump station. For people who enjoy the outdoors but do not want to forgo the basic comforts of home, RVs provide some real advantages. RVs range from little trailers that pop up to provide space for sleeping to giant homes on wheels. Gas mileage ranges 7-13 miles (11-21 km) per gallon (3.8 liters), depending on the size and age of the RV.

RV RENTALS

You can rent an RV for a one-way or local trip from Cruise America (www.cruiseamerica.com), which has a location in Nashville (201 Donelson Pike, 615/885-4281). Renters should be 25 years or older. Rental rates vary depending on the size of the vehicle and other factors. They also charge for mileage, and you can buy kits that include sheets, towels, dishes, and other basic necessities.

- If you plan to fly, check with your airline and the local health authorities for updated travel requirements. Some airlines may be taking more steps to help you travel safely, such as limiting occupancy; check their websites before buying your ticket. Flights may be less frequent, with increased cancellations.
- Pack hand sanitizer, a thermometer, a pulse oximeter, at-home rapid tests, and plenty of face masks.
- Assess the risk of entering crowded spaces, joining tours, and taking public transit.
- Expect general disruptions. Be prepared for possible closures and reduced services over the course of your travels. Events may be postponed or cancelled. Some restaurants and bars may have capacity limitations. Some tours and venues may require reservations or operate during different hours than the ones listed. Other venues may be closed entirely.
- Live music has been radically affected by coronavirus shutdowns. Concerts may be cancelled, lineups changed, and venues changed as a result of performer illnesses or staffing shortages.

RESOURCES

- Mayo Clinic COVID-19 Hot Spot Tracker (www.mayoclinic.org/coronavirus-covid-19/map): Updated data by county available for Tennessee. Davidson, Williamson, and Wilson Counties are the most relevant for Nashville visitors.
- Metro Public Health Department (www.nashville.gov/departments/health): This site has information on current requirements for vaccinations, negative tests, masks, social distancing, and more. In addition, Metro Public Health often hosts pop-up testing and vaccination events at farmers' markets, sporting events, and in parking lots.
- A Safe Nashville (www.asafenashville.org): This one-stop site provides citywide updates on coronavirus tracking, with numbers and trends on the pandemic. Any citywide restrictions will be listed here, as well as links to vaccination and testing sites.

Getting Around

If you're coming to Nashville for a weekend getaway or a conference and staying downtown or in Music Valley, you may be able to manage without a car. Many of the major attractions are within walking distance of downtown, and a majority of Music Valley hotels have shuttles. But the lack of wheels will limit your ability to visit attractions outside the main tourist areas. If you will have significant time outside your conference room, consider bringing or renting a car, or budget for your taxi tab or a ride-hailing app like Uber or Lyft. Or, if you like traveling on two wheels, rent a B-Cycle bike.

DRIVING

A reliable road map or GPS is essential for exploring Nashville by car. The city is only vaguely laid out on a grid, and even then, the numeric grid is a suggestion, rather than the rule. Roads frequently change names and merge into other roads (even numbered streets that seem like they ought to be parallel do this). Locals know this and are more than willing to give directions, but they often do so using landmarks ("Turn left where the Shoney's used to be") rather than street names. Many numbered streets on the grid have been replaced with names that honor people significant to Nashville's history. For example, Rep. John Lewis Way is what used to be 5th Avenue and Rosa L. Parks Boulevard is the northern part of 8th Avenue.

The interstates are a little easier to navigate than side streets. I-65 and I-24 create a tight inner beltway that encircles the heart of the city. I-440 is an outer beltway that circles the southern half of the city, while I-40 runs horizontally, from east to west. Briley Parkway, shown on some maps as TN-155, is a highway that circles the north and east perimeters of the city.

City residents use the interstates not just for long journeys but for short crosstown jaunts as well. Most businesses give directions according to the closest interstate exit.

Non-interstate thoroughfares emanate out from Nashville like spokes in a wheel. Many are named for the communities that they eventually run into. Murfreesboro Pike runs southeast from the city; Hillsboro Pike (US-431) starts out as 21st Avenue South and takes you to Hillsboro Village and Green Hills and eventually to Leiper's Fork. Broadway becomes West End Avenue, then Harding Pike, and eventually takes you to The Loveless Cafe. It does not take long to realize

that roads in Nashville have a bad habit of changing names all of a sudden, so be prepared, and check the map to avoid getting too confused.

For real-time traffic advisories and road construction closures, dial 511 or go to www.tn511.com.

PARKING

Metered parking is available on most downtown streets, but some have prohibited-parking signs effective during morning and afternoon rush hours. Always read the fine print carefully. Some residential neighborhoods have limited residential-only parking. This may be an issue if you are staying in a vacation rental or headed to a neighborhood restaurant, but otherwise is not cumbersome.

There is plenty of off-street parking in lots and garages. Expect to pay about $34 a day for garage parking. **Park It! Downtown** (www. parkitdowntown.com) is a great resource for finding downtown parking deals, plus information about the **Music City Circuit,** a free downtown shuttle operated by the MTA. The Metro Courthouse Garage and the Public Library Garage typically have discounted rates at night and on weekends.

TRAFFIC REPORTS

Nashville traffic is among the worst in the nation, and the city's growing population has only made it more challenging. For current traffic and road reports, including weather-related closures, construction closures, and traffic jams, dial 511 from any mobile or landline. You can also check online at www.tn511.com.

TAXIS

Licensed taxicabs will have an orange driver permit, usually displayed on the visor or dashboard.

Several reliable cab companies are Allied Cab/Nashville Cab (615/333-3333, www.nashvillecab.com), Checker Cab (615/256-7000, www.nashvilletaxicab.com), and American Music City Taxi Inc. (615/865-4100, www.musiccitycab.com). Taxi rates are $2 per mile.

Ride-hailing companies, including Lyft and Uber, are popular in Nashville. Download their apps to find a local to drive you to your destination. Earth Rides (www.earthrideshare.com) offers similar ride hailing and advance scheduling using electric and hybrid automobiles. Joyride Nashville (615/285-9835, http://joyrideus.com/nashville) offers licensed rides around downtown in a golf cart for a pay-what-you-wish model. Many of the drivers are happy to provide recommendations and tours as well as transportation.

PUBLIC TRANSPORTATION

Nashville's Metropolitan Transit Authority (www.nashvillemta.org) operates the purple WeGo city buses. Pick up a map and schedule from either of the two downtown visitors centers or online. Google maps and other apps also include Nashville transit info. Ticket prices start at $2.

Improvements to the city's public transport system have made it easier to use, but few visitors ride the buses because they can be difficult to understand if you're new to the city. One favorite is the Music City Circuit, a free bus that runs between downtown and The Gulch. These Blue and Green Circuit buses stop at 75 different spots on two different routes. Routes 3 and 5 are good options for getting from downtown to Midtown.

COMMUTER RAIL

In 2006 Nashville debuted the Music City Star Rail (615/862-8833, www.rtarelaxandride.com), a commuter rail system designed to ease congestion around the city. With service Monday-Friday, several times a day, trains connect Donelson, The Hermitage, Mount Juliet, and Lebanon to downtown Nashville. Service is often bumped up during special events, such as the 4th of July celebration downtown.

One-way tickets can be purchased for $2-5.25 each from vending machines at any of the stations. You can prepurchase single-trip tickets, 10-trip packs, and monthly passes at a discount online.

BICYCLING

Riding a bike as transportation, rather than exercise, is still a growing pursuit in Nashville, with more activity in some neighborhoods than others.

Many roadways lack dedicated bike lanes, and while some businesses have bike racks out front, many do not. That said, both those who want to ride their own bikes and those who want to rent will discover that two wheels are a good way to see Music City. Check out Nashville GreenBikes (www.nashville.gov) or B-Cycle (http://nashville.bcycle.com) for options if you aren't bringing your own set of wheels.

The **Music City Bikeway** website (www.nashville.gov/bikeways) offers a downloadable route map of the 26-mile (42-km) bike-friendly route in Nashville. Another good set of downloadable maps is available from **Walk/Bike Nashville** (www.walkbikenashville.org).

The **Harpeth Bike Club** (www.harpethbikeclub.com) is Nashville's largest bike club. It organizes weekend and weekday group rides April-October, plus races and social events where you can meet other bike enthusiasts. Its website is also a good resource for traffic laws for bicyclists and other helpful info.

Bike repair shops can help you get back on the road when needed. If you need assistance, try **Cumberland Transit** (2807 West End Ave., 615/321-4069, http://cumberlandtransit.com), **Shelby Avenue Bicycle Co.** (1629 Shelby Ave., 615/925-3274, https://shelbybicycle.com), **Trace Bikes** (8080B TN-100, 615/646-2485, http://tracebikes.com), or **Halcyon Bike Shop** (2802 12th Ave. S., 615/730-9344, http://halcyonbike.com).

Travel Tips

TRAVELING WITH CHILDREN

While some of Nashville's reputation is as a hard-drinking late-night town, in reality it is hard to imagine a place better for family vacations than Music City. There are museums and kid-friendly exhibits at most of the major attractions and many music venues permit underage listeners for at least part of the day. And don't forget the zoo and railroad excursions. Nearby state parks provide numerous places to camp, hike, swim, fish, and explore.

Many hotels and inns offer special discounts for families, and casual restaurants almost always have a children's menu with lower-priced, kid-friendly choices.

SENIOR TRAVELERS

Road Scholar (800/454-5768, www.roadscholar.org) organizes educational tours for people over 55 in Memphis and Nashville. For discounts and help with trip planning, try **AARP** (888/687-2277, www.aarp.org), which offers a full-service travel agency, trip insurance, a motor club, and the AARP Passport program, which provides you with senior discounts for hotels, car rentals, and other things.

Persons over 55 should always check for a senior citizen discount. Most attractions and some hotels and restaurants have special pricing for senior citizens.

LGBTQ TRAVELERS

Gay, lesbian, bisexual, and transgender people are presented with a mixed bag when visiting Tennessee. In 2013, Tennessee lawmakers introduced a bill, often referred to as the "Don't Say Gay" bill, that would have banned teachers from even saying the word *gay* in the classroom. (It failed to make it through the legislative process.) Other restrictive legislation has been introduced and defeated. In 2021, legislation requiring businesses to state their policies about allowing trans individuals to use restrooms of their choosing became law. An injunction temporarily halted its implementation.

On the other hand, there has been no better time to be gay in Tennessee. More and more social, civic, and political organizations are engaging the gay community, and many Nashville neighborhoods have vibrant gay scenes, with restaurants, bars, music venues, and more that are safe spaces. In general, Nashville's cosmopolitan population tends to be welcoming.

In 2021, the city renamed Carney Street to Bianca Paige Way. Bianca Page was the stage name of Mark Middleton, a local performer who passed away in 2010. As Paige, Middleton raised more than a million dollars for local AIDS and HIV prevention and research efforts.

A number of different publications and websites cover the LGBTQ community in Nashville. Two of the best known are *Out and About* (outandaboutnashville.com), a free monthly newsmagazine, and *Pride Journeys* (www.pridejourneys.com).

Several specific guidebooks and websites give helpful listings of gay-friendly hotels, restaurants, and bars. The **Damron guides** (www.damron.com) offer Tennessee listings; the **International Gay and Lesbian Travel Association** (IGLTA, www.iglta.org) is a trade organization with listings of gay-friendly hotels, tour operators, and much more. California-based **Now, Voyager** (www.nowvoyager.com) is a gay-owned and gay-operated travel agency that specializes in gay tours, vacation packages, and cruises.

TRAVELERS OF COLOR

Many parts of the South have a history of poor and violent treatment of people of color, and Nashville is no exception. It's understandable that may be a concern for some travelers coming to these areas. However, as Music City relies on tourism, it is unlikely that travelers of color will experience unsafe conditions. Thanks to its reputation as a city that attracts thinkers and dreamers, Nashville is home to an increasingly diverse population.

LOCAL CULTURE

According to the U.S. Census Bureau, less than 55 percent of the population is white. Black Nashvillians account for more than one-quarter of the population. More people of Kurdish descent live in Nashville than anywhere else in the United States. The city's Asian American, Pacific Islander, and Latinx populations are smaller.

In neighborhoods in the core of the city, particularly East Nashville, Germantown, Salemtown, Midtown, and along Nolensville Pike, residents and business owners are from diverse communities. Suburban areas, including Franklin, are more homogeneous.

SAFETY ISSUES

Like many other cities, in 2020 Nashville saw civil unrest following the murder of George Floyd. The protests brought racial inequities to light, and local cases of police brutality are now being discussed more openly. In 2021 the Metro Police Force adopted a new use-of-force policy that emphasized de-escalation.

In areas where there are late-night drinking establishments, such as along Lower Broadway and in Midtown, there are higher incidents of fights, hate crimes, and racially motivated crimes.

TOUR OPERATORS AND TRAVEL PROGRAMS

There are several tour operators with programs geared to travelers of color in the Nashville area.

United Street Tours (https://unitedstreettours.com) offers remote and in-person tours of Nashville, with an emphasis on Black history and Black-owned businesses.

While based in Atlanta, Unexpected Atlanta Tours (https://unexpectedatlanta.com) offers virtual music-themed tours that include a guide in Nashville teaching you about the city's music history from afar.

RESOURCES

The following websites and organizations may be of interest to travelers of color.

- Black & Abroad (www.weare blackandabroad.com) is primarily focused on international travel, but this website, geared toward Black travelers, includes updated travel advisories.
- Black Southern Belle (https://blacksouthernbelle.com/nashville-tn-travelogue-how-to-explore-nashvilles-black-

heritage) is a digital magazine focused on Black women in the South. It offers a compelling travelogue to Nashville's Black heritage sites.

- EatOkra (www.eatokra.com) is an app that provides a directory of Black-owned restaurants and other food businesses in various cities.
- National Association for the Advancement of Colored People (NAACP, www.naacp.org) offers rare travel advisories and keeps on top of incidents of racial violence and unrest.
- Nomadness (www.nomadnesstv.com) represents a group of more than 25,000 Black and brown travelers.
- Passports and Grub (https://passportsandgrub.com) is an online luxury food and travel website that partners with the Black Travel Alliance, an organization that works to increase Black representation in the travel industry.
- Soul of America (www.soulof america.com) offers guides to U.S. cities, including Nashville, from a Black perspective.
- Travel Noire (https://travelnoire.com) offers travel guides to various cities, with an emphasis on Black-owned businesses.
- Urbaanite (https://urbaanite.com/) is a resource for Black-owned businesses and events in Nashville.
- We Go, Too (http://wegotoo world.com) is a membership organization that works with Black travel bloggers and other experts to provide tourism tips that go beyond local hot spots.

TRAVELERS WITH DISABILITIES

More people with disabilities are traveling than ever before. The Americans with Disabilities Act requires most public buildings to make provisions for disabled people, although in practice accessibility may be spotty, particularly in neighborhoods with older homes retrofitted as businesses, such as Berry Hill and Printers Alley.

When you make your hotel reservations, always check that the hotel is prepared to accommodate you. Airbnbs and small hotels may have limited accessibility. Airlines will also make special arrangements for you if you request help in advance.

Several national organizations have information and advice about traveling with disabilities. **The Society for Accessible Travel and Hospitality** (www.sath.org) publishes links to major airlines' accessibility policies and publishes travel tips for people with all types of disabilities, including blindness, deafness, mobility disorders, diabetes, kidney disease, and arthritis. The society publishes *Open World,* a magazine about accessible travel.

Wheelchair Getaways (708/536-1842, www.wheelchairgetaways.com) is a national chain specializing in renting vans that are wheelchair accessible or otherwise designed for drivers and travelers with disabilities. Wheelchair Getaways partners with Tennessee companies in Memphis (888/432-9387), Gallatin (877/275-4915), and La Vergne (877/275-4915) to rent wheelchairs; they will deliver to other locations in the state.

Avis offers **Avis Access,** a program for travelers with disabilities. Call the dedicated 24-hour toll-free number (888/879-4273) for help renting a car with features such as transfer boards, hand controls, spinner knobs, and swivel seats.

INTERNATIONAL TRAVELERS

Foreign travelers will find a warm welcome in Nashville. Those in the music and tourist trades are used to working with people from all over the world and will be pleased that you have come from so far away to visit their home. If you are not a native English speaker, it may be difficult to understand the local accent at first. Just smile and ask the person to say it again, a bit slower. Good humor and a positive attitude will help at all times.

Most citizens of a foreign country require a visa to enter the United States. There are many types of visas, issued according to the purpose of your visit. Business and pleasure travelers apply for B-1 and B-2 visas, respectively. When you apply for your visa, you will be required to prove that the purpose of you trip is business, pleasure, or for medical treatment; that you plan to remain in the United States for a limited period; and that you have a place of residence outside the United States. Apply for your visa at the nearest U.S. embassy. For more information, contact the **U.S. Citizenship and Immigration Service** (www.uscis.gov).

The U.S. government's Visa Waiver Program allows tourists from many countries to visit without a visa for up to 90 days. To check if your country is on the list, go to http://travel.state.gov. In recent years the United States has begun to require visa-waiver participants to have upgraded passports with digital photographs and machine-readable information. They have also introduced requirements that visa-waiver citizens register in advance before arriving in the United States.

All foreign travelers are required to participate in U.S. Visit, a program operated by the Department of Homeland Security. Under the program, your fingerprints and photograph are taken—digitally and without ink—as you are being screened by an immigration officer.

Health and Safety

Nashville is a safe city, with the regular concerns of any urban area. Locals, both native and otherwise, are at-the-ready with Southern hospitality and willing to help a visitor who has lost his or her way.

In general, if you stay alert, you should feel free to explore the city's neighborhoods. For the most part, the neighborhoods highlighted in this guide, those that are chock-full of attractions, are safe to venture out in, although crimes that take place in high-tourist areas, like pickpocketing, do happen. Lock your valuables out of sight in your car ("Stow it, don't show it," as they say in Memphis), don't carry large amounts of cash, pay attention to your surroundings, and you'll be fine.

HOSPITALS AND PHARMACIES

Because health care is such a big industry in Nashville, there are a lot of hospitals. Should you need emergency medical care, the majority of the hospitals are clustered in the Midtown neighborhood, near Vanderbilt. **The Monroe Carell Jr. Children's Hospital** at Vanderbilt (2200 Children's Way, 615/936-1000, www.childrenshospital.vanderbilt.org) is among the best in the country. **TriStar Skyline Medical Center** (3441 Dickerson Pike, 615/769-2000, https://tristarskyline.com) is the closest hospital to Music Valley and parts of East Nashville. Others include **Saint Thomas West Hospital** (4220 Harding Pike, 615/222-2111, www.sthealth.com) and **Centennial Medical Center** (2300 Patterson St., 615/342-1000, https://tristarcentennial.com).

Rite Aid, CVS, Walgreens, and the major grocery store chains have drugstores all over Nashville. There's a **CVS** (426 21st Ave. S., 615/321-2590, www.cvs.com) close to Midtown, the Vanderbilt and Belmont campuses, and Music Row.

EMERGENCY SERVICES

Dial **911** for police, fire, or ambulance in an emergency. The local number for "urgency without emergency" is 615/862-8600. For help with a traffic accident, call the **Tennessee Highway Patrol** at 615/741-3181. The concierge at major hotels can also help direct you in the event of an emergency.

Nashville Veterinary Specialists (2971 Sidco Dr., 615/386-0107, www.nashvillevetspecialists.com) has an emergency staff ready and waiting for anything that happens to your pet while you are traveling. The Wi-Fi and snacks help keep worried humans occupied while waiting.

Information and Services

BANKS

Dozens of local, regional, and national banks operate in Nashville. Most banks will cash travelers checks, exchange currency, and send wire transfers. Banks are generally open weekdays 9am-5pm, although some are open later and on Saturday. Automatic teller machines (ATMs) are ubiquitous at grocery stores, live music venues, and elsewhere. Expect to pay $3-5 in fees to get cash from an ATM that does not belong to your own bank.

SALES TAX

Sales tax is charged on all goods, including food and groceries.

The sales tax you pay is split between the state and local governments. Tennessee's sales tax is 4 percent on food and groceries and 7 percent on all other goods. Cities and towns add an additional "local use tax" of 1.5-2.75 percent. In Nashville it all adds up to 9.25 percent on the goods you buy.

TIPPING

You should tip waitstaff 15-20 percent in a sit-down restaurant. You can tip 5-10 percent in a cafeteria or restaurant where you collect your own food from the counter.

Tip a bellhop or bag handler at least $1 per bag, more if they went out of their way to help you. Hotel housekeeping staff should receive $5-10 per night. Musicians who play requests and have tip jars (or hats) should be tipped based on the amount of time you listen to them.

INTERNET SERVICES

You can go online free at the **Nashville Public Library** (615 Church St., 615/862-5800, https://library.nashville.org). There is free wireless access at the **5th and Broadway visitors center** (501 Broadway, 615/259-4747, www.visitmusiccity.com). Many local restaurants, coffee shops, and hotels also offer free wireless internet.

MAIL SERVICES

The **United States Postal Service** maintains a branch in almost every Nashville neighborhood. Search for specific locations at www.usps.gov. If you need to mail a letter or buy stamps while downtown, you have a few options. The post office at 901 Broadway (615/255-3613) is found on the basement level of the **Frist Art Museum**, which itself used to be a post office before it was renovated for the museum space. There is also a post office in the downtown Arcade and at 1718 Church Street in Midtown.

Both **FedEx** (800/463-3339, www.fedex.com) and **UPS** (800/742-5877, www.ups.com) have several locations downtown and drop boxes in local hotels and businesses.

CELL PHONES

Cell phone signals are powerful and reliable in the greater Nashville area and along the interstates. In rural parts of the state you may not be able to count on having service.

Many hotels, restaurants, and valet services use texting services to provide information about availability and reservations. Many restaurants are now using QR codes for menus. Using ride-hailing services and renting scooters and bicycles require the use of apps, so it is wise to have your phone fully charged before you head out for the day.

AREA CODES

Tennessee has seven different area codes. Nashville and vicinity use 615 and 629; 931 covers Clarksville and Cookeville.

TIME ZONES

All of Middle Tennessee, including Nashville and its environs, is in the central time zone. The time zone line runs a slanted course from Signal Mountain (near Chattanooga) in the south to the Big South Fork National River and Recreation Area in the north. The time zone line falls at mile marker 340 along I-40, just west of Rockwood and a few miles east of Crossville. Chattanooga, Dayton, Rockwood, Crossville, Rugby, Fall Creek Falls State Park, the Catoosa Wildlife Management Area, and Big South Fork lie close to or on the time zone line, and visitors to these areas to the east of Nashville should take special care to ensure they are on the right clock.

RESOURCES

Suggested Reading

PHOTOGRAPHY AND ART

Escott, Colin. *The Grand Ole Opry: The Making of an American Icon.* Nashville, TN: Center Street, 2006. An authorized (and somewhat sanitized) look at the Grand Ole Opry, this makes for an attractive coffee-table book with lots of pictures, reminiscences, and short sidebars.

McDaniel, Karina. *Nashville Then and Now.* London: Pavilion Books, 2014. This is an illustrated guide of what makes Music City tick, written by an archivist for the Tennessee State Library and Archives.

McGuire, Jim. *Nashville Portraits: Legends of Country Music.* Guilford, CT: The Lyons Press, 2007. Sixty stunning photographs of country music legends, including Johnny Cash, Waylon Jennings, Doc Watson, and Dolly Parton, are found in this companion book to an eponymous exhibit that debuted in 2007.

Sherraden, Jim, Paul Kingsbury, and Elek Horvath. *Hatch Show Print: The History of a Great American Poster Shop.* San Francisco: Chronicle Books, 2001. This fully illustrated, beautiful book explores Hatch Show Print, the Nashville advertising and letter press founded in 1897.

TRAVEL GUIDES

Brandt, Robert. *Touring the Middle Tennessee Backroads.* Winston-Salem, NC: John F. Blair Publisher, 1995. Robert Brandt is a Nashville judge and self-professed "zealot" for Middle Tennessee. His guidebook details 15 driving tours through backroads in the heartland of Tennessee. Brandt's knowledge of local history and architecture cannot be surpassed, and his enthusiasm for his subject shines through the prose. While some of the entries are now dated, the guide remains an invaluable source of information about small towns in the region.

Littman, Margaret. *Moon Nashville to New Orleans Road Trip.* Avalon Travel Publishing, 2020. An in-depth guide to all 444 miles of the scenic Natchez Trace Parkway, as well as the Mississippi Blues Trail and other sights, this book is a handy resource for those who want to get outside major cities and explore the region's history.

Van West, Carroll. *Tennessee's Historical Landscapes: A Traveler's Guide.* Knoxville: University of Tennessee Press, 1995. The editor of the *Tennessee Historical Quarterly* and a professor of history at Middle Tennessee State University, Carroll Van West guides readers along highways and byways, pointing out historical structures and other signs of history along the way. A good traveling companion, especially for students of architecture and landscape.

The WPA Guide to Tennessee. Knoxville: University of Tennessee Press, 1986. The Works Progress Administration guide to Tennessee, written in 1939 and originally published by Viking Press, is a fascinating portrait of Depression-era Tennessee. Published as part of a New Deal project to employ writers and document the culture and character of the nation, the guide contains visitor information, historical sketches, and profiles of the state's literature, culture, agriculture, industry, and more. The guide, republished as part of Tennessee's "Homecoming '86," is a delightful traveling companion.

HISTORY

Bergeron, Paul H. *Paths of the Past: Tennessee, 1770-1970.* Knoxville: University of Tennessee Press, 1979. This is a concise, straight-up history of Tennessee, with a few illustrations and maps.

Corlew, Robert E. *Tennessee: A Short History.* Knoxville: University of Tennessee Press, 1990. The definitive survey of Tennessee history, this text was first written in 1969 and has been updated several times by writers including Stanley J. Folmsbee and Enoch Mitchell. This is a useful reference guide for a serious reader.

Dykeman, Wilma. *Tennessee.* New York: W. W. Norton & Company and the American Association for State and Local History, 1984. Novelist

and essayist Wilma Dykeman says more about the people of Tennessee and the events that shaped the modern state in this slim and highly readable volume than you would find in the most detailed and plodding historical account. It becomes a companion, and a means through which to understand the Tennessee spirit and character.

Egerton, John. *Speak Now Against the Day: The Generation Before the Civil Rights Movement in the South.* Chapel Hill: University of North Carolina Press, 1995. Nashville native John Egerton tells the relatively unacknowledged story of Southerners, African American and Caucasian, who stood up against segregation and racial hatred during the years before the civil rights movement.

Egerton, John. *Visions of Utopia.* Knoxville: University of Tennessee Press, 1977. An accessible and fascinating portrait of three intentional Tennessee communities—Ruskin in Middle Tennessee, Nashoba in West Tennessee, and Rugby in East Tennessee. Egerton's usual sterling prose and sensitive observations make this volume well worth reading.

Sword, Wiley. *The Confederacy's Last Hurrah: Spring Hill, Franklin and Nashville.* Lawrence: University Press of Kansas, 2004. This is a well-written and devastating account of John Bell Hood's disastrous campaign through Middle Tennessee during the waning months of the Confederacy. It was a campaign that cost the South more than 23,000 men. With unflinching honesty, Sword describes the opportunities lost and poor decisions made by General Hood.

Thurber, Amie and Learotha Williams. *I'll Take You There: Exploring Nashville's Social Justice Sites.* Nashville: Vanderbilt University Press, 2021. This engaging book tells the tales of Nashville's social justice and civil rights' fights in a format that is part guidebook, part essay collection.

MUSIC

Carlin, Richard. *Country Music.* New York: Black Dog and Leventhal Publishers, 2006. This is a highly illustrated, well-written, and useful reference for fans of country music. It profiles the people, places, and events that contributed to country's evolution. With lots of graphic elements and photographs, it is a good book to dip into.

Chapman, Marshall. *They Came to Nashville.* Nashville, TN: Vanderbilt University Press, 2010. Singer-songwriter Chapman tells her tales, as well as those of many others, as they came to Music City and set about hitting the big time.

Escott, Colin. *Hank Williams The Biography.* Back Bay Books, 2004. No country star had a bigger impact on Nashville's evolution to Music City than Hank Williams. This detailed history shares his failings, downfall, and remarkable legacy.

Havighurst, Craig. *Air Castle of the South: WSM and the Making of Music City (Music in American Life).* Urbana and Chicago: University of Illinois Press, 2007. Havighurst is known as the preeminent Nashville music historian, and this tome delves deep into an important piece in Nashville's musical hierarchy.

Kingsbury, Paul, ed. *Will the Circle Be Unbroken: Country Music in America.* London: DK Adult, 2006. An illustrated collection of articles by 43 writers, including several performing artists, this book is a useful reference on the genre's development from 1920 until the present.

Kossner, Michael. *How Nashville Became Music City: 50 Years of Music Row.* Milwaukee, WI: Hal Leonard, 2006. Forget about the stars and the singers; this profile of country music focuses on the people you've never heard of: the executives, songwriters, and behind-the-scenes technicians who really make the music happen. It's an interesting read for fans who don't mind seeing how the sausage is made and a good introduction for people aspiring to be a part of the scene.

Parton, Dolly and Robert K. Oermann. *Dolly Parton, Songteller: My Life in Lyrics.* San Francisco: Chronicle Books, 2020. Dolly's songs are the soundtrack to the region. This book lets you focus on the words of her famous tunes.

REFERENCE

Van West, Carroll, ed. *The Tennessee Encyclopedia of History and Culture.* Nashville: Tennessee Historical Society and Rutledge Hill Press, 1998. Perhaps the most valuable tome on Tennessee, this 1,200-page encyclopedia covers the people, places, events, and movements that defined

Tennessee history and the culture of its people. Dip in frequently and you will be all the wiser.

FICTION

Burton, Linda, ed. *Stories from Tennessee.* Knoxville: University of Tennessee Press, 1983. An anthology of Tennessee literature, the volume begins with a story by David Crockett on hunting in Tennessee and concludes with works by 20th-century authors such as Shelby Foote, Cormac McCarthy, and Robert Drake.

Hicks, Rover. *The Widow of the South.* New York: Warner Books, 2005. Tour guides at Carton Plantation gripe about the poetic license taken with some facts in this fictional tale, but it offers a moving story of the Battle of Franklin and the high emotional costs of the Civil War.

Randall, Alice. *Ada's Rules.* New York: Bloomsbury USA, 2012. Nashvillian and author of the critically acclaimed *Black Bottom Saints,* Randall wrote this fun novel set in Nashville.

Taylor, Peter. *Summons to Memphis.* New York: Knopf Publishing Group, 1986. Celebrated and award-winning Tennessee writer Peter Taylor won the Pulitzer Prize for fiction for this novel in 1986. Phillip Carver returns home to Tennessee at the request of his three older sisters to talk his father out of remarrying. In so doing, he is forced to confront a troubling family history. This is a classic of American literature, set in a South that is fading away.

Wilson, Kevin. *Nothing To See Here.* New York: Harper Collins, 2020. Tennessee native Wilson set this story of children who spontaneously burst into flames in suburban Franklin, and the sense of place is so strong and so believable the kids' affliction becomes believable, too.

FOOD

Donovan, Lisa. *Our Lady of Perpetual Hunger.* New York: Penguin Press, 2020. Donovan is a pastry chef who has worked in many of Nashville's best kitchens. In this memoir she tells the stories of their kitchens alongside her own more personal tales.

Justus, Jennifer. *Nashville Eats: Hot Chicken, Buttermilk Biscuits, and 100 More Southern Recipes from Music City.* New York: Stewart, Tabori & Chang, 2015. Compiled by a former newspaper reporter, this is the guide to making all the local foods you fall in love with on your trip.

Lewis, Edna, and Scott Peacock. *The Gift of Southern Cooking: Recipes and Revelations from Two Great American Cooks.* New York: Knopf Publishing Group, 2003. Grande dame of Southern food Edna Lewis and son-of-the-soil chef Scott Peacock joined forces on this seminal text of Southern cuisine. It demystifies, documents, and inspires. Ideal for those who really care about Southern food ways.

Lundy, Ronnie, ed. *Cornbread Nation 3.* Chapel Hill: University of North Carolina Press, 2006. The third in a series of collections on Southern food and cooking. Published in collaboration with the Southern Foodways Alliance, which is dedicated to preserving and celebrating Southern food traditions, the Cornbread Nation collection is an ode to food traditions large and small. Topics include pawpaws, corn, and pork. *Cornbread Nation 2* focused on barbecue. *Cornbread Nation 1* was edited by restaurateur and Southern food celebrant John Egerton.

Stern, Jane, and Michael Stern. *Southern Country Cooking from The Loveless Cafe: Biscuits, Hams, and Jams from Nashville's Favorite Café.* Nashville, TN: Rutledge Hill Press, 2005. Road-food aficionados wrote the cookbook on Nashville's most famous pit stop: The Loveless Cafe. Located at the northern terminus of the Natchez Trace Parkway, The Loveless is quintessential Southern cooking—delectable biscuits, country ham, and homemade preserves. Now you can take some of that down-home flavor back with you.

Internet and Digital Resources

FOOD AND DRINK

Eater Nashville
www.nashville.eater.com
The local outpost for the national website has up-to-date information on restaurant openings and closings.

HISTORY AND REFERENCE

Tennessee Civil War 150
A free app for iPhone and iPad provides quick-hit history lessons about Civil War battle sites, plus information about visiting them. The battlefield for much of the bloodiest combat of the Civil War took place outside Nashville. While some historic sites tell the whole story of what happened here, readers are encouraged to determine if particular sites are appropriate stops for them based on the information shared.

Tennessee Encyclopedia of History and Culture
www.tennesseeencyclopedia.net
The online edition of an excellent reference book, this website is a great starting point on all topics Tennessee. Articles about people, places, and events are written by hundreds of different experts. Online entries are updated regularly.

NEWSPAPERS AND MAGAZINES

Nashville Lifestyles
www.nashvillelifestyles.com
The website of this monthly magazine has great information about what's going on in the city, whether you want to eat, shop, dance, or all of the above.

The Nashville Scene
www.nashvillescene.com
Nashville's alternative weekly has a great website. The dining guide is

in-depth, the stories interesting and archived, and the entertainment calendar is the best in town. Go to "Our Critics' Picks" for a rundown on the best shows in town. The annual Best of Nashville readers' choice section is a great resource, and other special editions are useful for newcomers and old-timers alike.

The Tennessean
www.tennessean.com
Nashville's major newspaper posts news, entertainment, sports, and business stories online. Sign up for a daily newsletter of headlines from Music City or search the archives.

OUTDOOR RECREATION

NashVitality
Download this free app created by the mayor's office for GPS-specific information on where to get outdoors in Music City. The app includes water launches, bike trails, greenways, and more.

Tennessee State Parks
www.tnstateparks.com
An online directory of all Tennessee state parks, this site provides useful details, including campground descriptions, cabin rental information, and the lowdown on activities. A free downloadable smartphone app is also available.

TVA Lake Info
This free iPad and iPhone app lists recreational dam release schedules for across the state.

TOURIST INFORMATION

Nashville Convention and Visitors Corporation
www.visitmusiccity.com
The official tourism website for Nashville, this site offers concert listings, hotel booking services, and useful visitor information. You can also order a visitors guide and money-saving coupons. Listen to the Highway 65 Nashville-centric music stream as you browse. There's also a free app to help you on the road.

Tennessee Department of Tourism Development
www.tnvacation.com
On Tennessee's official tourism website you can request a visitors guide, search for upcoming events, or look up details about hundreds of attractions, hotels, and restaurants. This is a great resource for suggested scenic drives. A printed guide is also available.

Urbaanite
https://urbaanite.com
This website provides lists of Black-owned businesses and events in Nashville.

Index

Restaurants Index

Nightlife Index

Shops Index

Hotels Index

Photo Credits

All photos © Margaret Littman, except page 1: Nashville Convention & Visitors Corp.; page 2 © Jake Matthews/NCVC; page 4 © (top left) Brenda Kean | Dreamstime.com; (left middle) Brent Hofacker / Shutterstock; page 5 © Nashville Convention & Visitors Corp.; page 6 © Image courtesy of the Grand Ole Opry Archives; page 8 © (top) courtesy of the Nashville Public Library; (bottom) Planet Cowboy; page 9 © courtesy of Nelson's Green Brier Distillery; page 11 © 353Media Group; page 12 © (bottom) Glenn Nagel | Dreamstime. com; page 13 © Gerry Matthews / Shutterstock; page 14 © (bottom) Courtesy of 21c Museum Hotels; page 15 © F11photo | Dreamstime.com; page 18 © Goo Goo Chocolate Co.; page 19 © (bottom) Nashville Convention & Visitors Corp.; page 22 © Elliston Place Soda Shop; page 23 © Redwood8 | Dreamstime.com; page 24 © (bottom) Bill Steber and Pat Casey Daley/Nashville Visitors & Convention Corp.; page 25 © (top) Image courtesy of the Grand Ole Opry Archives; page 26 © (bottom) Kenn Stilger | Dreamstime.com; page 27 © (top) Joe Sohm | Dreamstime.com; page 28 © Jeremy Christensen | Dreamstime.com; page 29 © (bottom) Asakalaskas | Dreamstime.com; page 30 © (top) Walk Eat Nashville; page 31 © Ttempleman | Dreamstime.com; page 33 © Tony Bosse | Dreamstime.com; Nashville Convention & Visitors Corp.; Edgar Hernandez | Dreamstime.com; 353Media Group; page 36 © Wangkun Jia | Dreamstime.com; page 38 © (top) Nashville Convention & Visitors Corp.; page 40 © John Schweikert / Nashville Convention & Visitors Corp.; page 41 © Erik Lattwein | Dreamstime.com; page 48 © (top) Andrew Thomas Lee; page 51 © Erik Lattwein | Dreamstime.com; page 52 © (top) aLive Coverage/NCVC; page 54 © Courtesy of The Listening Room; page 55 © Nashville Convention & Visitors Corp.; page 56 © House of Cards; page 58 © Casa Rosa Nashville; page 60 © James Kirkikis | Dreamstime.com; page 63 © (bottom) Nashville Convention & Visitors Corp.; page 68 © (top) Nashville Convention & Visitors Corp.; page 70 © Goo Goo Chocolate Co.; page 75 © Nashville Visitors & Convention Corp.; Thomas Lohr | Dreamstime.com; Zrfphoto | Dreamstime.com; page 78 © (bottom) Kevin Ruck | Dreamstime.com; page 79 © (top) Nashville Visitors & Convention Corp.; page 80 © Andreykr | Dreamstime.com; (top) Tony Bosse | Dreamstime.com; page 87 © Paul Brady | Dreamstime.com; page 89 © (bottom) Nashville Visitors & Convention Corp.; page 93 © Planet Cowboy; Nashville Convention & Visitors Corp.; Planet Cowboy; page 98 © Jiawangkun | Dreamstime.com; page 99 © Nashville Convention & Visitors Corp.; (top) Sean Pavone | Dreamstime.com; page 103 © (top) Nashville Convention & Visitors Corp.; page 104 © (top) Elliston Place Soda Shop; page 113 © Karen Foley | Dreamstime. com; page 117 © Nashville Convention & Visitors Corp.; page 118 © (bottom) Calvin L. Leake | Dreamstime.com; page 121 © (bottom) Planet Cowboy; page 123 © Nashville Convention & Visitors Corp.; page 134 © Courtesy of The Game Point Café; page 140 © Walter Arce | Dreamstime.com; page 141 © Anthony Aneese Totah Jr | Dreamstime. com; page 147 © Paul Brennan | Dreamstime.com; Kathleen Mays | Dreamstime.com; Joe Hendrickson / Shutterstock; page 149 © (bottom) Crackerclips | Dreamstime.com; page 150 © Erik Lattwein | Dreamstime.com; page 151 © Wendy Clark | Dreamstime. com; page 154 © (top) Joe Hendrickson | Dreamstime.com; page 156 © Calvin L. Leake | Dreamstime.com; page 159 © Andrew Thomas Lee; Andrew Thomas Lee; Alexis Kirkman | Dreamstime.com; page 161 © (bottom) Nashville Convention & Visitors Corp.; page 163 © Brian Conway | Dreamstime.com; page 165 © (bottom) Andrew Thomas Lee; page 175 © Arne Beruldsen | Dreamstime.com; Legacy1995 | Dreamstime.com; page 182 © Bhofack2 | Dreamstime.com; page 190 © Robindoddphoto | Dreamstime.com; page 193 © (bottom) Chet Nowlen | Dreamstime.com; page 195 © Kenn Stilger | Dreamstime.com; page 197 © (bottom) Nashville Paddle Co.; page 199 © (bottom) Courtesy of Haus of Yarn; page 202 © The Joseph, a Luxury Collection Hotel, Nashville; page 203 © Leigh Warner | Dreamstime. com; page 206 © The Hermitage Hotel / Diana Marie Photography; page 218 © Accountrwc | Dreamstime.com; page 219 © Kottapsm | Dreamstime.com; page 232 © (top) Erik Lattwein | Dreamstime.com; page 234 © Karen Foley | Dreamstime.com; page 237 © Nicole Gheorghe of Dope Yogi; page 244 © (bottom) Jesse Kunerth | Dreamstime.com; page 246 © (top) Skpgarts | Dreamstime.com; page 247 © (bottom) Wangkun Jia | Dreamstime.com; page 251 © Joe Sohm | Dreamstime.com; page 273 © Sean Pavone | Dreamstime.com

Acknowledgments

Even under the pressure of looming deadlines, the complications of an extended pandemic, and navigating piles of marked-up maps covering the floor, I'm convinced I have the world's best job. I have legitimate, work-related excuses to strap the paddleboard to my car and explore a brand-new river access point. Or to call a few friends and ask them to help me check out Nashville's honky-tonks. Or taste test the newest vegan hot chicken contender.

I'm grateful to many people who helped me synthesize what I've heard, seen, and experienced into something coherent that others could use. Perhaps the only person who loves Music City as much as I do is Heather Middleton of the Nashville Convention and Visitors Corp. She and Rachel Ricker are always available for brainstorming and, of course, providing photos.

Samantha War, Garrett Fuller, and Tiffany Herron pitched in verifying the alphabet soup of phone numbers and URLs involved in fact-checking, plus tracking down photos and permissions.

I first worked with the crackerjack staff of Avalon Travel on *The Dog Lover's Companion to Chicago,* and decades later I continue to be grateful for their great expertise and better attitudes. Particular thanks, again, this time around to the endlessly patient Leah Gordon and Darren Alessi, Kat Bennett, Nikki Ioakimedes, Erika Lara, and Crystal Turnau. While the city is almost unrecognizable from when they wrote about it, continued thanks to those who worked on previous editions of *Moon Tennessee* and *Moon Nashville,* including Susanna Henighan Potter and Jeff Bradley.

As always, I am grateful for the help and support of my family and friends, who tolerate my working long hours on "vacation" and dragging them to sightsee wherever we are, not to mention my soundtrack of bluegrass and country music, and the ever-expanding wardrobe of cowboy boots.

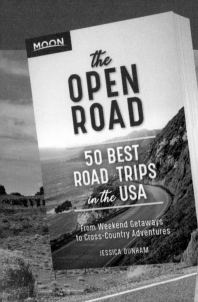

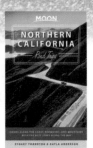

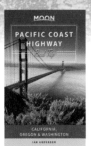

ROAD TRIP GUIDES FROM MOON

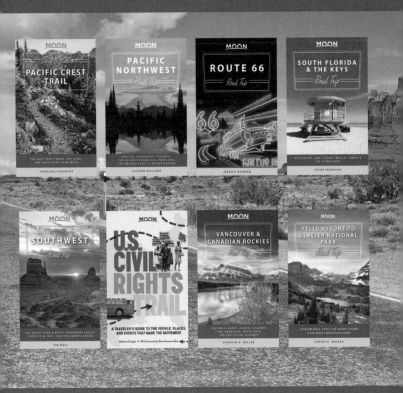

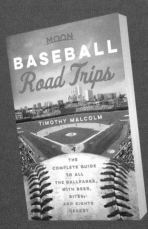

MAP SYMBOLS

═══ Major Hwy	▭ Pedestrian Friendly	------- Trail	·········· Ferry
── Road/Hwy	▭ Tunnel	▭▭▭▭▭ Stairs	----- Railroad

▬ **Sights**	⊛ National Capital	▲ Mountain
▬ **Restaurants**	◉ State Capital	✦ Unique Feature
▬ **Nightlife**	○ City/Town	⎨ Waterfall
▬ Arts and Culture	✪ Highlight	⚑ Park
▬ **Recreation**	★ Point of Interest	⬟ Archaeological Site
▬ Shops	• Accommodation	🅃 Trailhead
▬ Hotels	▼ Restaurant/Bar	🄿 Parking Area
	▪ Other Location	

CONVERSION TABLES

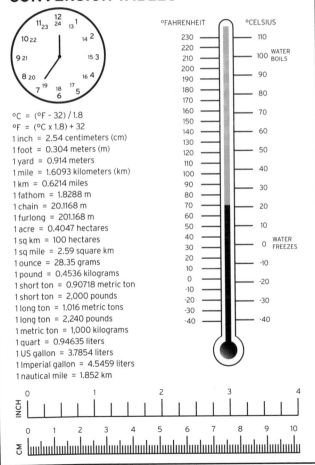

$$°C = (°F - 32) / 1.8$$
$$°F = (°C \times 1.8) + 32$$

1 inch = 2.54 centimeters (cm)
1 foot = 0.304 meters (m)
1 yard = 0.914 meters
1 mile = 1.6093 kilometers (km)
1 km = 0.6214 miles
1 fathom = 1.8288 m
1 chain = 20.1168 m
1 furlong = 201.168 m
1 acre = 0.4047 hectares
1 sq km = 100 hectares
1 sq mile = 2.59 square km
1 ounce = 28.35 grams
1 pound = 0.4536 kilograms
1 short ton = 0.90718 metric ton
1 short ton = 2,000 pounds
1 long ton = 1.016 metric tons
1 long ton = 2,240 pounds
1 metric ton = 1,000 kilograms
1 quart = 0.94635 liters
1 US gallon = 3.7854 liters
1 Imperial gallon = 4.5459 liters
1 nautical mile = 1.852 km

MOON NASHVILLE
Avalon Travel
Hachette Book Group
1700 Fourth Street
Berkeley, CA 94710, USA
www.moon.com

Editor and Series Manager: Leah Gordon
Graphics Coordinator: Darren Alessi
Production Coordinator: Darren Alessi
Cover Design: Toni Tajima
Interior Design: Megan Jones Design
Map Editor: Kat Bennett
Proofreader: Deana Shields
Cartographers: John Culp, Kat Bennett

ISBN-13: 9781640496231

Printing History
1st Edition — 2014
5th Edition — September 2022
5 4 3 2 1

Front cover photo: neon guitar hanging in front of Ernest Tubb Record Shop on Broadway
© Pgiam / Getty Images
Back cover photo: Nashville style hot chicken © Voltan1 | Dreamstime.com

Printed in Malaysia for Imago